Lepgold

Internal Affairs

INTERNAL AFFAIRS

How the Structure of NGOs Transforms Human Rights

WENDY H. WONG

CORNELL UNIVERSITY PRESS
ITHACA AND LONDON

First published 2012 by Cornell University Press
Printed in the United States of America

Library of Congress Cataloging-in-Publication Data

Wong, Wendy H., 1980–
    Internal affairs : how the structure of NGOs transforms human rights /
Wendy H. Wong.
        p. cm.
    Includes bibliographical references and index.
    ISBN 978-0-8014-5079-2 (cloth : alk. paper)
    1. Human rights advocacy.   2. Non-governmental organizations.
    3. Organizational behavior.   I. Title.
    JC571. W876 2012
    323—dc23   2012002420

Cornell University Press strives to use environmentally responsible
suppliers and materials to the fullest extent possible in the publishing of
its books. Such materials include vegetable-based, low-VOC inks and
acid-free papers that are recycled, totally chlorine-free, or partly composed
of nonwood fibers. For further information, visit our website at www.
cornellpress.cornell.edu.

Cloth printing   10 9 8 7 6 5 4 3 2 1

To my family

CONTENTS

ACKNOWLEDGMENTS

This book began in a formative time in my career and has benefitted from years of research, revision, and discussion. The research would not have been possible without generous financial support from the Canadian Institute for Advanced Research; the Connaught Start-up Fund at the University of Toronto; the University of California Institute on Global Conflict and Cooperation; the Institute for International, Comparative, and Area Studies at the University of California, San Diego; and the Rohr Chair for Pacific and International Relations at the University of California, San Diego. Many thanks to the Department of Political Science and the Munk School of Global Affairs at the University of Toronto for funding a book workshop, from which I gained invaluable comments. I also thank Fiona Bolt and Heather Faulkner for granting me access to files at Amnesty International's International Secretariat.

I was very fortunate to have the scholarly support of so many people as my ideas developed on this project, and more important, those who were willing to read chapters, give advice, and bring new perspectives to the research. First among these individuals is my mentor, friend, and colleague David Lake. David has always been willing to read something again, freely offer guidance, and somehow always finds new ways to improve what I have written. For his patience, kindness, and willingness to teach, I will forever be indebted, and I hope that indeed, I will one day be able to pay it forward. To the non–University of Toronto participants of the book workshop that took place during April 2010—Michael Barnett, Miles Kahler, Jim Ron—I am thankful for the candid feedback on the manuscript and the publishing process, and know that this final version is better for it. To Miles I am especially happy that after so many years, the encouragement and snappy exchanges keep coming. I am also grateful to my colleagues, Emanuel Adler, Steven Bernstein, Matt Hoffmann, Lou Pauly, and Joe Wong, who made thoughtful suggestions throughout and taught me how to pitch a book project and write a book. I hope that this iteration has justly incorporated your incisive comments. I also thank David Cameron, for his support as department chair. A special thanks goes to Janice Stein, who has made sure that I have had the tools to finish this project from the first day I arrived in Toronto.

I thank Roger Haydon, my editor, for his support throughout this process. From our very first meeting in New York, he was helpful, thoughtful, and encouraging. His suggestions have helped me transform a narrow PhD project into a much broader research agenda.

Several Toronto colleagues and I formed a writing group during the most fervent stages of writing, and I will always look back fondly at the lively exchanges at Bar Mercurio and L'Espresso with Nancy Bertoldi, Antoinette Handley, Lilach Gilady, and Phil Triadafilopoulos. To Lilach especially, I thank you for helping iron out the awkward parts before general viewing. A special thanks to Andy Paras as well, for her enthusiasm about the project, and her willingness to comment on any and all parts of the book. And, of course, I am indebted to Lindsay Heger and Danielle Jung, who were part of the "original" UCSD writing group, for their friendship and collaboration. I also thank Cliff Bob, Charli Carpenter, Joe Carens, Peter Gourevitch, Todd Hall, Audie Klotz, Catherine Lu, Steve Saideman, Hans Peter Schmitz, Sarah Stroup, David Welch, and Nick Weller for reading earlier and later versions of this argument, and their generous encouragement. Helen Yanacopulos, I cannot thank you enough for making my final research trip to London memorable and productive. Thank you to Saleha Ali, for your incomparable organizing and research skills.

This project would not have been possible without the help of all of the human rights activists with whom I spoke. I am still in awe about the number of people who were willing to spend an hour—often more—talking to me about their organizations and their work, and I am grateful for their time and graciousness. Special thanks go to Avril Benoit for her willingness to network me into Médecins sans Frontières; Joe Saunders at Human Rights Watch for answering all of my questions beyond wildest expectation; and Andrew Blane, Curt Goering, and Margo Picken, all of whom brainstormed with me about who to interview in Amnesty and beyond. I also thank Scott Harrison and Ellen Moore, whose initial support of my research gave me the confidence and materials to proceed, and their hospitality when I visited Ned.

I have also been fortunate to have hugely supportive friends, who bring laughter, warmth, and levity to my life. In no particular order, big thanks to Fonna Forman-Barzilai, Cullen Hendrix, Nancy Gilson, Paul Frymer, Emily Matthews, Lissa Rogers, Idean Salehyan, Jennifer Thai, Oliva Lopez, Sean Hawkins, Shaheen Haji, Andrew Poe, Ron Levi, Lee Ann Fujii, Steph Haggard, Cristina Badescu, Heather Smith, Mary Reid, Ruth Marshall, Matt Light, Christian Breunig, Jennifer Tackett, and Wil Kurth.

Finally, I would like to thank my family. I am grateful for my parents, Boon and Carrie, whose excitement about the book has been the palpable fuel to finish. Thank you for your advice, love, and cheerleading. Eileen, I appreciate your courage to make forays into social science to be able to understand my work better, and for proofing the entire book. I am also touched by the support that Mamá, Maria, and Irene have expressed, demanding updates on the progress of the book in our weekly calls. And finally, to Theo, for reading every last word of this version and others, and making sure that I balanced work and life as I finished. You have taught me, at least in our case, the importance of decentralizing some aspects of agenda setting.

Abbreviations

ACLU	American Civil Liberties Union
AI-Mexico	Amnesty International—Mexico
AI	Amnesty International
AIUSA	Amnesty International—USA
ANC	African National Congress
ARV	Antiretroviral drugs
ASI	Anti-Slavery International
CAT	Convention against Torture
Comecon	Council for Mutual and Economic Assistance
DNDi	Drugs for Neglected Diseases Initiative
ECHR	European Convention on Human Rights
ECOSOC	United Nations Economic and Social Council
FIDH	Fédération Internationale des Droits de L'homme
HRW	Human Rights Watch
IANSA	International Action Network on Small Arms
ICBL	International Campaign to Ban Landmines

ICCPR	International Covenant for Civil and Political Rights
ICESCR	International Covenant for Economic, Social, and Cultural Rights
ICJ	International Commission of Jurists
ICM	International Council of Meetings
ICRC	International Committee of the Red Cross
IEC	International Executive Council
IGO	Intergovernmental organization
ILHR	International League of Human Rights
IO	International organization
IS	International Secretariat
LGBT	Lesbian, gay, bisexual, and transgender
LMT	Leadership and Management Team at HRW
MSF	Médecins sans Frontières
NGO	Nongovernmental organization
OCA	Operational Center—Amsterdam
OCB	Operation Center—Brussels
OC	Operational Center
OCP	Operational Center—Paris
Oxfam GB	Oxfam—Great Britain
POC	Prisoners of conscience
RIOD	Restricted International Operations Directors
TRIPS	Trade-Related Aspects of Intellectual Property Rights
UA	Urgent Action Program
UDHR	Universal Declaration of Human Rights
UNESCO	United Nations Educational, Scientific and Cultural Organization
WHO	World Health Organization
WOOC	Work on Own Country policy
WTO	World Trade Organization

Internal Affairs

INTRODUCTION

Internal Affairs and External Influence

Notwithstanding their ubiquity, human rights remain largely a contested political concept. When the Universal Declaration of Human Rights (UDHR) was signed unanimously in 1948,[1] leaders from the United Nations congratulated themselves for forging an inclusive document that explicitly did not require states to commit to a hard and fast legal apparatus, which had accounted for the many concerns raised during the meetings of the Human Rights Commission that guided its drafting. Not one state, in the end, stood in the way of the approval of the UDHR in the General Assembly.[2] These drafters had ushered in a new world, built around the notion that all states needed to protect basic human rights. But their work also left undecided many of the key questions regarding the subsequent enforcement of human rights. Which of the thirty rights were more important? Which ones should be enforced first, or hold priority if multiple rights are violated simultaneously? States were torn about which rights were fundamental, and thus hesitated to legally elevate some rights over others.

This deliberation surrounding rights can be found at the domestic level as well. Despite being the first of its kind in the Western world,[3] the Canadian Museum for Human Rights has weathered criticisms of the selection criteria it has employed to pick from among various Canadian stories of discrimination. Until January 2010, the museum was actively soliciting individual stories of human rights that would be "subjected to secondary research," with a list that included gender, age, ability, culture and beliefs, as well as language rights.[4] Other rights, however, are not so automatically recognized. The gay and lesbian community in particular has feared exclusion from the official Canadian story about human rights.[5] Beyond groups not wanting to be left out of the rush to be included in the official annals of Canadian human rights, critics of the museum have raised questions about a "hierarchy of suffering," whereby excluded claims become of secondary importance.[6] The question of the content of human rights, even in the Canadian context, is unresolved even as the country is poised to be one of the first to enshrine a national human rights statement to the world.

The lack of consensus of states regarding human rights has allowed nonstate actors to make substantial contributions to human rights politics, in terms of definition, spread, and applicability across different contexts. The most active participants in the debate over human rights have been nongovernmental organizations (NGOs), which create international focal points around certain rights, making some more politically salient than others. Even though various worldviews surround the importance of different types of rights, and even though states have yet to reach a consensus about which rights are "most important" and essential to protect, we would be remiss to claim that we do not know what human rights are. In the sixty-two years that separate the UDHR and the Canadian Museum, states have complicated the list of human rights, as an increasing number of treaties shows. We know that some rights have become part of a shared, albeit contested, international vision that constantly evolves as NGOs seek to move policy closer to their respective advocacy positions. NGOs, not states, are central to shifts in the politics of human rights, diffusing their respective visions through advocacy and generating both local and international support for their agendas.

Increasingly, NGOs, whose numbers have been rising since the end of the Cold War, have become part and parcel of international debates over human rights policy (Gaer 1995) (Smith, Pagnucco, and Romeril 1994;

Keck and Sikkink 1998; Smith, Pagnucco, and Lopez 1998). In the mid-nineteenth century, there were six transnational NGOs; today, there are more than sixty thousand (Davies 2008). I approach NGOs as organizations that are involved in shaping transnational political projects and make no assumptions about their moral or principled nature, as others have (see Sikkink 1993; Clark 2001). My focus here is on organizational differences between NGOs, the effect of structural choices on advocacy outcomes, and whether these organizational choices change over time. Organizational structure has an effect both on the political salience of NGOs themselves and on the degree to which they can influence international norms.

This book is about the political salience of NGOs and ideas in international politics. It is primarily concerned with explaining why some NGOs have developed as focal points in international human rights politics, and similarly, how ideas become politically salient. First, what explains the political salience of certain NGOs, and are all actors equally likely to become salient? Second, given the political and contested stakes involved in defining and implementing human rights, how do prominent NGOs contribute to the recognition of some human rights as "obvious," whereas others remain mired in debate? These two forms of political salience, although linked, do not always occur together, as we will see.

I begin with the proposition that NGOs are integral to creating the political salience of human rights, but they are not all equally influential. We know that NGOs play an important role in framing debates, setting the political agenda, calling attention to gaps in compliance with international law, and pressuring noncompliant states to change their behavior (Carpenter 2003; Joachim 2003; Khagram, Riker, and Sikkink 2002; Price 1998; Risse, Ropp, and Sikkink 1999). All of this work leads to the prominence of certain rights—those that NGOs have selected to pursue and to which states respond—and what we understand as "human rights." Human rights are political constructs, and NGOs, in addition to states, play a key role in setting the agenda on the politics around rights. Before the Cold War ended, NGOs helped establish the political salience of rights that prohibited torture and arbitrary arrest and protected freedom of expression, speech, and religion. Since the 1990s, NGOs working in human rights have widened the agenda to include other types of rights, such as those that mitigate against globalization or prohibit the use of certain weapons, in the international agenda.

What makes some NGOs better than others at influencing the political salience of rights is their organizational structure. We know empirically that only a few NGOs decide which issues become politically salient (Carpenter 2011). What is less well-known about NGOs—the prominent, transnational ones in particular—is that underneath the superficial differences in terms of image, advocacy focus, and branding, they are also remarkably varied in terms of their organizational structure. These organizational differences have important implications for understanding why some NGOs seem poised to "make it," whereas others do not.

Organizational structure affects agenda setting and agenda implementation, and can be either centralized or decentralized. All transnational NGOs must navigate what we can term a transnational dilemma: appealing to broad-based principles while acknowledging local differences. Centralizing agenda-setting powers helps transnational NGOs formulate coherent advocacy positions across national contexts. An opposite dynamic, however, is necessary for the diffusion of these positions and the implementation of the agenda at the domestic and international levels. Decentralizing the implementation of the agenda is a necessary condition for changing the conversation about human rights at the international level. By shifting human rights perceptions at the local level, NGOs build support for their advocacy. Thus, to be influential, NGOs must balance the control over the agenda with the reality that international change comes from domestic—and perhaps substate—sources. Success at international advocacy thus requires adopting the right balance that accounts for both the need for a defined agenda and widespread support.

The NGOs in human rights that have achieved this structural balance have been far and few between. Anti-Slavery International (ASI), or as it was known in its time, the Anti-Slavery Society, was the forerunner to all subsequent organizations that wanted to change state law and practices at both the international and the domestic levels. By the end of the nineteenth century, its exploits, coordinated with other like-minded groups in Europe and the United States, succeeded in ending the transatlantic slave trade. Its efforts to rally local support in the United Kingdom in particular would become a bellwether of methods used by later groups. Amnesty International, one of the earliest NGOs in the modern human rights movement, pioneered the technique of transnational letter-writing campaigns, shining a light on individual cases of abuse while lobbying international organizations and domestic politicians to put an end to odious practices such as torture, the death penalty, and the practice of "disappearing" dissenters. Both of these NGOs effectively centralized agenda setting by maintaining tight control over what the NGO advocated, while capitalizing on the ability of local populations to transform the debate through activism and political pressure.

This book counters the widespread assumptions that NGOs are good and moral political actors by definition and that their authority and power stems from such morality (as summarized in Avant, Finnemore, and Sell 2010, 13). At bottom, despite their good intentions, NGOs are organizations and need to be examined as such (Cooley and Ron 2002; Sell and Prakash 2004). Organizations have goals and make choices, some of which may not be motivated by "doing good." Organizations also have a purpose, whether that means saving children from laboring, making profits for shareholders, or creating a community for the resident Pentecostals in a town. To achieve their respective purposes, organizations have structure and they have strategies. Resources, namely time and money, are finite, and organizations must make the most of those resources to attain their objectives. Human rights NGOs, despite their desire to do good and stop the abuse of people by state and nonstate actors, are subject to the same constraints as other organizations. Similarly, the degree to which an NGO is able to succeed in changing the political salience of human rights lies not in the group's morality or stated values, but in the way it has divided up its resources to meet its goal of preventing human rights abuses and holding states to their international agreements.

Political Salience

In this book, I use the term *political salience* deliberately to mark a departure from the voluminous work on norms and norm change (among others, Adler 1992; Finnemore and Sikkink 1998; Risse 2000a). Political salience identifies focal points in international politics around which coordination might happen, in a way similar to how ideas have come to shape research in the discipline of international relations (IR): "Ideas can serve as focal points, as solutions to problems associated with incomplete contracting, or as the means to counteract problems of collective action" (Goldstein and Keohane 1993, 17–18). Like ideas, political salience serves as a general concept and can explain why in international politics some issues or actors become the focus. From the norms literature, we know quite a bit about how ideas become politically salient, but to date, there has been silence in terms of explaining how the attributes of political actors can make them more salient as organizations and for the issues they promote. Not all actors (states, IGOs, NGOs) necessarily have to agree with the importance of a position (e.g. East Timorese independence), but through public accusation, reporting, and advocacy of their specific policy positions, NGO can engender support for a cause. NGOs are in the business of creating international focal points, and in the doing this, may help create new norms or enforce extant ones. Thus the concept is compatible with current conceptions of norms in IR but expands the ways in which we think about important, dominant ideas, actors, and practices.

Norms do some heavy conceptual lifting in IR, as they are seen as both constitutive and regulative (Katzenstein 1996). In light of this, scholars have gone to great lengths to show how NGOs socialize states to follow human rights law (regulative) and convince them respect for human rights is part of being a "good" state (Risse, Ropp, and Sikkink 1999). Political salience steps back from this dynamic by underscoring the importance of creating focal points in international discourse. Without having to enforce, NGOs can contribute to international understandings and uses of "human rights," enabling other, more positive types of actions—new conventions, creating regulative bodies, or revised standards in statecraft, for example. A further reason is to distance this work from the debates among norms scholars, where a schism has developed between those who think of norms as structuring relationships and those who think of norms as they are used relationally (Wiener 2009). Although work on defining norms largely has been settled as standards of behavior for a given identity (Finnemore and Sikkink 1998), how actors implement norms and use them is an area of both empirical and scholarly contestation (Wiener and Puetter 2009).

Political salience, by contrast, serves to combine these kinds of concerns. In some ways, it relaxes the need to demonstrate that there are defined standards that are necessarily identity driven, and account for the contestation between various norms. International law and norms might be stated in formal and informal ways, but the way that domestic actors implement international concerns varies depending on the domestic context (Risse-Kappen 1994; Cortell and Davis 1996). Thus the way international law is lived (i.e., its legality) is subject to interpretation by a multiplicity of actors (see Brunnée and Toope 2010), often NGOs, that inform and change the political salience of legal edicts.

Political salience does not signify unanimity. Instead, political salience means producing the possibility of coalescing around a new set of ideas at the international level. Political salience gets us closer to understanding what NGOs and other nonstate actors do. In the absence of independent enforceability, NGOs resort to setting the agenda, raising the status of certain issues, and bringing attention to a core advocacy agenda that may or may not generate attention from states and other actors. Political salience in human rights politics can manifest itself in different ways, which I review in the next chapter. One way to think about it, and this has been the way that constructivists have largely thought about norms, is to see how international norms shape state behavior (Checkel 1997, 2001; Risse 2000b) by understanding the conditions under which international norms become domestic law. Perhaps the most systematic way to do so is by evaluating the signing, ratification, and compliance with international treaties. Another method is to consider what topics emerge from NGO networks themselves. Finally, we can scrutinize how human rights appear in other areas of international politics to see to what extent states have absorbed the norms of human rights. While economic sanctions are certainly not as costly as military intervention or the use of force, they do affect both sanctioner and target states, and as such require more political capital than other forms of human rights politics. Analyzing the justifications used by states to levy economic sanctions on one another reveals the growing importance of human rights in statecraft but also demonstrates which rights states deem of sufficient importance to necessitate such actions. These justifications make some rights more politically salient.

The Power of NGOs and Networks

Keck and Sikkink's seminal study opened the door for why some transnational advocacy efforts succeed (Busby 2010; Clark 2001; Clark, Friedman, and Hochstetler 1998; Rutherford 2000) and what it is that transnational advocates do (see Keck and Sikkink 1998, 16–27). In spite of all the works on the topic, many have failed to note the differences between NGOs, or have focused on the differences between North and South (Bandy and Smith 2005; Hertel 2006). An implicit assumption lying at the core of scholarship on nonstate actors is that NGOs in a common field somehow share characteristics that obscure their differences, and that studying one or another prominent NGO helps explain the rest of the field's struggles and successes. In-depth single NGO studies are common (Clark 2001; Ron, Ramos, and Rodgers 2005; Hopgood 2006). Comparative NGO studies tend to focus on prima facie differences between NGOs (Korey 1998; Welch 2001). Others who have studied the nuances of transnational advocacy have focused on aspects related to the state and its receptivity (Busby 2010) rather than characteristics of the NGOs themselves that make their claims more likely to resonate with state leaders and policy gatekeepers. Finally, those who have looked at NGO differences have focused largely on the differences between NGOs within networks without accounting for how the big players among human rights NGOs came to be dominant (Bob 2005; Carpenter 2007a, 2007b).

Digging into the meat of organizational differences reveals answers not accounted for by existing explanations. While ideas clearly matter, and the characteristics of certain issues might on first glance seem to lend themselves to international agreement, this prima facie ease is misleading. This process is often post hoc and, moreover, mediated by the very organizations that promote ideas about human rights. The job of nonstate actors, whether NGOs or social movements or other entities, is to frame issues (Benford and Snow 2000; Gamson and Meyer 1996; McAdam, Tarrow, and Tilly 2001; Snow, Rochford, Worden, and Benford 1986). Sometimes they are first to raise an issue—such the International Committee of the Red Cross's opposition to the use of landmines—and sometimes they raise an issue generated by the state institutions. The reason organizational structure matters is that it tells us about the process by which NGOs and their advocacy issues became politically salient. If NGOs mediate the way ideas are perceived and norms are formed, then the very way those organizations structure themselves as transnational entities ought to have bearing on the political tools NGOs employ. NGOs that centralize agenda setting have a greater capacity to coordinate their campaigns internationally. In turn, those NGOs that can capitalize on their national-level linkages and use them to diffuse a common set of ideas and advocacy goals will be able to make "their" human rights more salient.

Do NGOs Really Matter?

The focus on NGOs' effects, while not entirely new, contributes new insights to the broader conversation about the evolution of human rights. Two alternate explanations, which I review here, fall short because they lack an account of agential change that explains why some rights are politically salient. These arguments can be broadly classified as prioritizing American hegemony (states) and state power, and those that provide a path-dependent argument about world history and the timing of the human rights regime via the analysis of the structures of political opportunity. While alternative explanations can demonstrate that NGOs operated within a political and social context that made human rights much more likely, they cannot explain why some rights were more politically salient than others, and they most certainly do not account for the great variation in NGO structures and advocacy areas that we observe. More to the point, they are both fundamentally sound narratives, but they lack a conception of agency and the variations between agents. Arguments that focus on American hegemony and the structure of political opportunity do a good job clarifying broader structural patterns, but they do not give us a clear sense of the timing and content of possible changes.

American Hegemony

One primary set of arguments privileges state action in creating the political salience of rights, and specifically US hegemony after World War II. While the United States and other Western states played a role in constructing our contemporary normative landscape for human rights, this explanation in itself is insufficient for explaining why some rights are politically salient. American hegemony certainly affected human rights during and after the Cold War, but to argue that it is the sole, or even the most important, influence on international human rights norms ignores the work of both critics of the US (such as the Soviet Union but also smaller states) and also the frequent periods in which human rights took a backseat to other concerns in the era. Furthermore, inconsistencies in US policy regarding human rights at the bilateral and multilateral levels highlight the difficulty of generalizing about the US hegemon's position on human rights.

The foregrounding of state action is not surprising, given IR's emphasis. The dominance of the two major paradigms in international relations, realism and liberalism, demonstrate the favoring of state over nonstate actions in political outcomes. Not only do states matter most significantly for international relations (Bull 1977; Gilpin 1996, 25–26; Legro and Moravcsik 1999; Milner 1998; Moravcsik 1997; Morgenthau 1948), but only the great powers matter (Waltz 1979). Thus powerful states determine the course of human rights politics (Krasner 1993). The standards of realism and liberalism negate the importance of anything but states and their leaders, and not until the classic pieces by Huntington and Nye and Keohane do we get anything that even acknowledges the importance of other-than-state actions on international relations (Huntington 1973; Nye and Keohane 1971a; Nye and Keohane 1971b). States limit the power of nonstate actors in all kinds of ways (Mearsheimer 1994–95), including determining the terms of their participation in international meetings (Raustiala 1997). One could take the lessons from hegemonic stability theory (Snidal 1985), for instance, and explain human rights politics through the creation of the neoliberal order in the twentieth century.

Following this logic, some have claimed that the modern focus on civil and political rights results from the political dominance of the United States since at least the end of World War II (Evans 1996; Kirkup and Evans 2009) and its effort to merge liberal economics with liberal politics (Baxi 1998; Evans 1998; Mutua 2001). There are two significant problems with this perspective. First, the United States as a champion of human rights is an artifact of the Carter administration. Prior to Carter's presidency, and even subsequent to it, human rights have not been a consistent aspect of US foreign policy. The second major problem concerns the content of human rights, and the "US" or "Western" perspective.

While support by the US and other Western states certainly helped the political salience of some rights by the end of the 1970s, the United States was not a consistent mover and shaker in the world of human rights during the Cold War. Human rights took a backseat to US-Soviet concerns over maintaining security and economic hegemonies (Forsythe 2006). Rhetorically and politically, the US conflation of anticommunism with human rights contributed to the focus on fighting socialism through the support of repressive regimes in Latin America and Africa (Donnelly 2006, 115–144), rather than positively enforcing rights. When President Carter prioritized human rights in foreign policy, noted political adviser Arthur Schlesinger commented that "nothing the Carter Administration has done has excited more hope, puzzlement, and confusion than the effort to make human rights a primary theme in the international relations of the United States" (as quoted in Forsythe 2006, 43). The real American enemy during the Cold War was communism (Huntington 1997, 30–31), perhaps explaining the inconsistencies in the human rights policies of different US administrations (Sikkink 2004).

The United States historically (and arguably now) has vacillated in its support of international human rights precisely because of its sense of exceptionalism (Koh 2003; Mertus 2008) and has acted against international human rights agreements to advance its own interests (Donnelly 2007). Much of the institutionalization of human rights happened outside of the United States. With the establishment of the European Court of Human Rights through the European Convention on Human Rights (1950), European states created a forum for their citizens to bring cases of abuse forward. To help with individual cases, European institutions granted the court strong monitoring powers and gave it authority in adjudicating human rights claims (Donnelly 1986). De facto, the court was given the power to set the human rights agenda in the European region because it chose the cases to be heard, privileging the cases it selected as "human rights issues."[7] The Americas have analogous bodies: American Convention on Human Rights (1969), the Inter-American Commission of Human Rights (1959), and the Inter-American Court of Human Rights (1979), but these institutions did not engage in prickly issues until the 1980s.

Furthermore, the assumption that certain civil and political rights comprise the totality of Western conceptions of human rights—and the refusal to accept the existence of alternatives within the Western tradition (Franck 2001; Whelan and Donnelly 2007), or even the American tradition—is an obfuscation of historical remnants of broader debates that have since been settled through the politics of the Cold War. Support of economic and social rights as well as civil and political rights was integral to social democracies that Western governments established after World War II. As Forsythe (2006, 40) notes: "It cannot be stressed too much that in the mid-1940s the US Executive was in favor of socio-economic as well as civil-political rights." Even as early as Franklin Delano Roosevelt's famous 1941 "Four Freedoms" speech,[8] one can see that the American conception of human rights could include economic rights such as the right to a useful job, right to earn enough to provide for basic needs, right for farmers to sell their wares at a decent price, right to trade fairly in business, right to a decent home, right to health care, right to protections from unforeseen actions and old age, and the right to an education (Sunstein 2006). The concern with economic and social rights was echoed by the Carter administration (Bite 1981; Schlesinger 1978).

If the United States tried to dominate the normative human rights conversation during the Cold War and after through its hegemonic role, it only partially succeeded in taking over the debate. American influence has been most trenchant from the 1990s onward with the issue of democratization and free elections, but this was after other human rights, such as the freedom of speech, religion, and political dissent, and freedom from torture had already been established. Clearly, economic and social rights have not received as much attention or as much legitimacy in international politics as other types of rights, and certainly they are not the "obvious" human rights. The international system is tilted toward protecting civil and political rights as a consequence of not just American or Western power, but also NGOs' agenda-setting capabilities to shape how we understand human rights.

Given the inconsistencies and gaps in the enforcement of human rights by the United States, the hegemonic explanation does not elucidate why some rights are more salient than others. The political salience of human rights that ban torture and arbitrary arrest and protect speech and rights of expression rights does not come directly from the hegemonic interests of the United States. The role of NGOs as agents of change forces the political salience of some rights onto the international agenda and helps direct how we understand human rights norms.

Political Opportunity Structures

Another way to understand the changes in the political salience of human rights might be to contextualize human rights developments in the broader political tapestry. As politics change, the ability for actors to gain headway in their advocacy campaigns might increase or decrease. This is the basic intuition behind theories that discuss the political opportunity structure of social movements (Tarrow 1998) and transnational campaigns (Khagram, Riker, and Sikkink 2002, 18–20; Klotz 2002). Change in society can happen as political actors mobilize collective action when "patterns of political opportunities and constraints change...creat[ing] new opportunities, which are used by others in widening cycles of contention" (Tarrow 1998, 19). Rights may not emerge as important, or may not generate the same support they otherwise would, in a hostile political environment. Thus we can explain why the human rights agenda emerged in the post–World War II world: states not only made human rights part of the main pillars of the UN Charter, but they also created the Economic and Social Council (ECOSOC) to allow for civil society interactions.

Such sweeping arguments use happenstance and unexpected opportunity to explain why contentious politics (McAdam, Tarrow, and Tilly 2001; Tilly and Tarrow 2007) sometimes succeed. This tells us very little a priori about when to expect change, and while Tarrow gives us a sense of the need to build ties between elements of social movements—mobilizing resources, forging links, creating repertoires of contention—political opportunity structures do not tell us in a precise way how agents of change can vary in their approaches, nor how agents might be able to create their own political opportunities through setting the agenda for change. Moreover, explanations for good political opportunities (and bad ones) are rarely detectable until after the fact. Thus political opportunity structure explanations tend to err on the side of explaining what won out, rather than explaining the spectrum of possible choices. The bias toward nonstate success misses the point that political opportunities run both ways—a point Tarrow acknowledges but does not sufficiently develop. Opportunities allow for change, but they also allow for actors, such as states, to slyly maintain the status quo through their own actions in response to political shifts.

In the case of human rights, it would seem that political opportunities have given an opening for the creation and settling of international norms. After the UDHR, it became much easier for states and nonstate actors alike to resist abusive behavior by states, creating new constraints and expectations (Simmons 2009). As human rights have become much more acceptable to states, we could expect that rights would become embedded as international norms. Coupled with the growth in democracies as a worldwide trend, one could argue that the latter half of the twentieth century was indeed the time for human rights to shine. Both internationally and domestically, political opportunity created ripe conditions for human rights and their advocates to succeed in making the world a better place.

Following the logic of political opportunities, one might argue that Cold War politics created the possibility of having human rights in the first place. The United States, after all, largely harped on rights that the Soviets did not provide, such as freedom of expression, speech, religion, and political dissent. The 1970s marked a period of détente between the superpowers, and it makes sense why we see the rise of human rights in that decade. This perspective misses two important historical points. First, the Soviets continually pointed out the racial inequality found in the United States and used international fora such as the UN to shame the United States on its attitude toward black Americans (Dudziak 2002, 23–37), so the critique was not unidirectional. Second, human rights took on even more furor after détente ended in the 1980s under President Ronald Reagan. One must acknowledge that the human rights agenda took on much more force, especially after the founding of Americas Watch, which targeted its condemnation toward US inconsistencies in foreign affairs.

It is important to note that political opportunities work both ways. While the analysis of political opportunities highlights the opportunities for human rights advocates, it also creates an environment that allows those that do not support the cause to contest the human rights agenda. While NGOs certainly benefitted from increased international human rights law and state receptivity from the 1970s onward, creating political salience for human rights does not hinge on being in the right place at the right time. Most certainly, the political salience of certain rights is not predetermined by the structure of political opportunities. The human rights institutions that have been created in the past sixty years have opened up many possibilities, but fewer of them have become accepted as prominent human rights.

Moreover, political opportunity structures cannot explain why an issue such as the right to food or health, which is protected in the UDHR and ICESCR, did not ascend to political salience at the international level until the 1990s. International institutions, such as the World Health Organization, which came into force in 1948 with the goal of promoting a right to health (Meier 2010), provided plenty of structures for those wanting to advocate such rights. NGOs such as Oxfam GB (before it helped create Oxfam International) existed, but they were unable to get the right to food or health on the human rights agenda. Concerns about access to food, or healthcare, for that matter, only became human rights issues in the late 1990s, even though Oxfam's founding mission in 1942 was to provide starving Greeks food by breaking the Nazi blockade. If political opportunities were open for human rights NGOs advocating freedom of expression and religion, why not freedom from starvation? Why did the right to health and food not come to the forefront of international politics until after the Cold War?

It is hard to counter an argument as amorphous and encompassing as political opportunity structures, and in many ways the political opportunity argument is correct. But the political opportunity argument is not the only factor to explain why human rights became prominent when they did, why some NGOs seemed to have no trouble seizing the international human rights agenda, and others seem to flounder in spite of prominent supporters or auspicious timing. NGOs' organizational choices—how they distribute internal agenda-setting powers—has important consequences for their ability to shape the international normative framework for human rights.

Both American hegemony and political opportunity structure theories offer thorough structural accounts, but lack a clear conception of agents within that structure. More to the point, they are largely state-centric and do not account for nonstate actors in a coherent way. If we understand the emphasis on human rights as a phenomenon that began in the 1970s with a new vocabulary and ideology to replace the nationalism of decades prior (Moyn 2010), then we must acknowledge that the reasons for this shift cannot just come from states, which were deeply immersed in the nationalist project. NGOs emboldened alternative positions, contributing to the moment of change and the salience of certain types of rights. Hence, the account I present in this book provides a new perspective on the question of where human rights norms come from and why NGOs are important by demonstrating that the characteristics of agents affect how successful they are in dealing with the constraints of international structures. My approach is aligned with recent developments in international law on the interactional nature of law (Brunnée and Toope 2000, 2010), and how actors beyond states can shape, condition, and contribute to international law.

How Organizational Structure Matters

If we think about political salience as a process and an outcome, NGOs shape the way we understand human rights much more than is commonly acknowledged. NGOs act through other means beyond compelling state action, such as issuing press releases, writing country and topical reports, and mobilizing supporters. In reporting and rallying support around their ideas, NGOs contribute to the legality around different international human rights standards. But how do we know that NGOs have an effect if they cannot compel states to change their actions? How do we counter the frequent observation that NGOs condemn states' abuses, only to be greeted with silence by other states? Finally, does the work of some NGOs matter more than others?

One way is to look beyond what states do immediately following NGO action. The US State Department, which is the only government that systematically reports on other governments' human rights performances, uses Amnesty's Background and Yearly Reports in its Country Reports on Human Rights Practices (Cingranelli and Richards 2001). Scholars have compared State Department reports to Amnesty's as a way to evaluate the US bias in reporting (Poe, Carey, and Vazquez 2001), which in a sense, is not a very deep comparison—the findings showed, in fact, that in the period evaluated, the differences between US and Amnesty reports were slight. HRW's topical reporting is aimed at policymakers in the United States, at international and regional organizations, and in regional powers such as Japan and South Africa. Human Rights First (formerly the Lawyer's Committee for Human Rights) also targets governments with their reporting. All NGOs have a particular portrayal of human rights, grounded firmly in international law but nonetheless shaped by their advocacy agendas and strategic choices. The agendas and choices cannot be discerned if we think about NGOs monolithically. Such organizational differences affect the ability of major transnational NGOs to influence the political salience of the rights they advocate.

This book offers a way to think about how to evaluate the effectiveness of transnational human rights NGOs through an analysis of their distribution of internal agenda-setting power. The distribution of that power is what we can call organizational structure. Organizational structure can be observed as a combination of formal rules and informal relationships.

Formal rules are codified and consented to by various members of the NGOs—they are the contracts that have garnered consent, outlining purposes, accountability, and tasks. Informal relationships, by contrast, are not necessarily written down, and come about through the day-to-day operations of an NGO. Informal relationships are no less important than formal ones, but they are informal in the sense that nothing has been written down and agreed to, and things happen de facto rather than de jure (see Moravcsik 1999). That being said, the persistence of informal relationships vis-à-vis formal rules can indicate either a perceived lack of need to codify something that already works, or an inability to agree on either the existing system or an alternative by all of the members of the organization.

Formally, organizations can be more or less centralized along a range of governance options. For many reasons, international NGOs can often be more appropriately conceived as networks of domestic-level groups, and not as cohesive, formally organized groups with clear lines of authority and rule-bound members. Most international NGOs are not the not-for-profit version to hierarchical corporations. International NGOs tend to range from a decentralized model of loosely affiliated national sections that share a common name to more formalized agreements between national sections that have an obligation to follow a certain organizational standard or directive. There are also international NGOs that are highly centralized, able to concentrate all of their advocacy decisions in a single entity, despite their presence in multiple countries. Another factor that affects structure is the role of membership. Human rights NGOs can be run by volunteers (board or grassroots level) or paid staff. This crucial difference creates legitimacy for an NGO's claims in different venues, but it also has implications for internal operations and the degree to which the organization can be efficacious in its advocacy at the state and international levels.

Formal and informal organizational structure specifically influences three mechanisms of agenda-setting power in an NGO: proposal power, enforcement power, and implementation power (also referred to separately as agenda implementation). Though agenda-setting power can be formalized through statutes and bylaws, informal relationships, the nature of which often cannot be anticipated, also affect these three mechanisms, and therefore agenda setting sometimes must be formulated on the spot. These three can each vary in the degree to which they are centralized or decentralized. The more inclusive each of these mechanisms is, the more politicking and struggle there is over the content of the principles of NGO advocacy.

The fewer entities within an NGO who have influence over each of these three mechanisms, the more centralized the NGO. Proposal power is the ability to put things forward for consideration among other parts of the NGO. Proposal power can be held by one actor (CEO, executive director), a body with multiple individuals (ruling council, board), and/or multiple bodies within the organization (leaders of national sections). The more that proposal power is spread around in an NGO, the harder it is for a coherent advocacy agenda to exist, particularly for international NGOs. Competing ideas can be difficult to resolve among different parts of the organization, and politicking between members can result in a lack of coherence, or even a lack of collective advocacy agenda. The fewer actors who have the power of suggestion, the more centralized proposal power is, and thus, the fewer options national sections have to struggle over to get a common agenda. Limiting proposal power can also be thought of as implicitly vetoing ideas by never allowing them to come up for consideration.

Enforcement power is the power to veto and enforce compliance with those vetoes. Veto power allows actors to refuse proposals. Vetoing without enforcement, however, does not actually keep items off of the agenda if a veto can be disregarded by another actor. For instance, vetoing a decision to pick cases in Kenya does not carry weight unless the vetoer can ensure that others do not continue to pursue projects in Kenya. The more enforceable decisions are, the more centralized the NGO, as enforcement corrals the agenda and prevents different parts of the NGO from making decisions that do not agree with, or are even counterproductive toward, the decisions of the whole. Enforcement can range from shaming to more punitive measures, such as pulling resources or ostracization. Using enforcement power too often might result in trouble between various parts of the NGO, or contribute to feelings of unfairness for those who do not have such power. Nonetheless, it is important in maintaining unity across different national contexts.

Finally, we can compare NGOs based on how they distribute the implementation of their agenda. Some NGOs have a very narrow sense of implementation, whereas others are more open to input and can be more ad hoc. Does each national section have its distinct set of tasks (more centralized) or are tasks taken on and decided on by the leadership of each section? Does a central actor delegate tasks to others in the organization, or do sub-parts of the NGO decide on the situations to pursue, and how to pursue them? Since "advocacy" denotes a wide variety of activities, from writing and publishing reports to clogging streets with protests and candlelight vigils to closed-door bargains with diplomats, the degree to which implementation is centralized can have significant implications for the types of advocacy that NGOs pursue. A highly centralized implementation system will not be conducive to marching in Western capitals, but it may allow for targeted negotiations with UN officials. The fewer parts of the organization that control the way tasks are distributed for the broader NGO, the more centralized it is. By extension, the more parts of the NGO required for implementing advocacy, the more decentralized this aspect of agenda setting is.

NGOs that manage to limit proposal power, enforcement power, and implementation power to a few identifiable entities (or even one entity) within the organization are centralized under the definition provided here. Those that allow for input from many parts of the organization on the four mechanisms identified above are decentralized. Of course, the idea of centralization falls along a continuum: breaking up centrality along these mechanisms gives us a sense of variation along several criteria, allowing us to consider cases where NGOs might be centralized in some aspects and not in others. These three mechanisms specify how the book will examine the degree of centralization/decentralization among different international human rights NGOs.

It is important to bear in mind that centralization is not the only important factor for successful advocacy at the international level. In fact, forcing an absolutely centralized advocacy agenda actually decreases the advocacy effectiveness of NGOs because of the perceived bias of information. Effecting norm change requires sway at the international policymaking level, such as the UN and other intergovernmental organizations, and also generating credibility to domestic actors who appeal to their governments to change their own or others' behavior.

Thus all transnational human rights NGOs must wade through the transnational dilemma, making critical choices about centralizing or decentralizing their agenda-setting powers. The challenge is to adopt an organizational structure that balances centralization without stifling local creativity so that what the organization stands for is clear all sections. Centralizing proposal and enforcement powers and decentralizing implementation power gives transnational NGOs tremendous advantages when it comes to making the rights they advocate politically salient.

The Plan of the Book

Methodology

The theoretical development in this book is weighted toward a thorough exposition of the independent variable, organizational structure, through analysis of historical and current NGO cases. I have chosen cases based on their influence in international politics and their public stature, as well as their appeal to broader interests beyond academic and policy circles (Van Evera 1997). I have also tried to avoid "selecting on the dependent variable" by looking for NGOs that did not succeed in advocacy (Mahoney and Collier 1996), a problem which persists in studies of transnational advocacy (Price 1998). The core motivation is thinking about why organizations might look different, and the consequences of those structural differences. NGOs make initial decisions when they are founded, such as where the main office(s) will be, what the tactics and strategies are, what governments or other entities to target, and where their resources will come from. These initial decisions shape the future for NGOs, but NGOs are not necessarily restricted by those first selections. Some NGOs, as we will see in the following chapters, make drastic changes to both their organizational structure and their advocacy focus, whereas some stay remarkably the same. To shape the political salience of rights at the international level, leaders at NGOs eventually turn to the arrangement that balances the tensions between local and global action.

In studying the political salience, one inevitable conundrum we face is selection on success. That is, it is a lot easier to study NGOs or human rights campaigns that have triumphed. After all, failed efforts simply disappear with the passage of time, and moreover, losers may not want to talk as readily as winners. We want to know why things are the way they are, and so the logical thing to do is to study how currently salient ideas beat out alternatives. However, what we need to keep in mind is that all things equal, achieving a ban against slavery is no easier than gaining worldwide acceptance for debt forgiveness or fair trade practices. All human rights norms require that states give up some aspect of sovereignty and a degree of control over their populations. Protecting human rights requires taking on costs, whether political, sovereign, economic, and even at times, humanitarian. What I seek to do here is to provide an account for how NGOs actualized differences in political salience among human rights. That the political salience of torture and the protection of expression, religion, and political belief emerged in the 1970s and 1980s is not an indication of the ease with which these rights could be accepted, but testimony to the focus of human rights NGOs, which continually put violations of those rights on the international agenda or forced domestic leaders to justify or explain their actions.

The theoretical perspective in this book emerged in my initial fieldwork on Amnesty International. Observers have hailed Amnesty as the most influential human rights NGO, whose success has resulted in a "widespread dissemination of a conception of human rights which is partial...a rather distorted list of basic human rights which would reflect the list of core 'mandate' issues pursued by Amnesty and little more" (see Alston 1990, 8–9). Despite this crediting, few scholars have studied how Amnesty's success could be transferred to other NGOs; the extant work on Amnesty implies its success as sui generis. In closely examining its organizational structure, however, it soon became apparent that not only was Amnesty's way of doing things replicable, but the reasons for its success in the twentieth century rested precisely on the centralization of proposal and enforcement powers and the decentralization of agenda implementation. Amnesty gained political salience in the mid-twentieth century because there was no other human rights organization like it, but in other periods, including today, other NGOs have used the same structure to similar success, in both organizational and advocacy terms.

The cases in this book have been selected carefully with these concerns in mind. First, the notion of "human rights" is not limited to the practioner's or analyst's narrow lens. In the NGO industry, "human rights" NGOs are not "humanitarian" NGOs, which are distinct from "development" NGOs and "health" NGOs. Many NGOs have created niches for themselves to better identify themselves to their relevant publics and to funders. Nonetheless, the issues that these different NGOs focus on heavily overlap one another, as some observers have noted (Nelson and Dorsey 2008; Osiatynski 2009; Chong 2010), sometimes on purpose, sometimes unconsciously to adjust to the environment around them. Even humanitarianism NGOs, which had defined themselves as "antipolitical," now face a world where "simply alleviating suffering" means taking a political position (see Barnett 2005). By selecting beyond human rights in the narrow sense—advocacy-only, legalistic NGOs—and expanding the scope of inquiry to organizations that contribute to the spirit of human rights in international politics—service-oriented NGOs that deliver assistance to communities and individuals—this book serves to capture the dynamics of defining the notion of human rights. All of the organizations covered in this book work to preserve human dignity, and increasingly, the modern NGOs use the language of rights and the tools of legalization and broad-based advocacy to achieve their goals.

Defining "human rights" is thus not reserved solely for organizations that identify themselves as such. To understand how different types of rights become politically salient, and identified with the international canon of rights that demand protection and assurance, we need to broaden our scope of concern. We need to look at both salient and unsalient NGOs, just as we need to examine salient and unsalient campaigns to highlight human rights issues. This book includes (as much as possible) NGOs that did not become politically salient, in addition to well-known NGOs struggling for more human rights. I include in the analysis not only NGOs working on human rights in the broad sense but those that use advocacy as a tool for generating transnational support for their cause—global citizen campaigns, use of the international media, lobbying governments and intergovernmental organizations. I also expand the period covered by the analysis to illustrate the utility of using an organizational structure approach. Most human rights studies begin the post–World War II era, or even the post–Cold War era. But transnational human rights NGOs, campaigns, and concerns began as early as the movements in the nineteenth century against chattel slavery and the treatment of military combatants. These two movements form the backbone of the human rights institutions that emerged with the UDHR and beyond. In both cases, organizational structure played a key role in the political salience of the respective organizations and their advocacy campaigns.

Rather than solely pursue a study of the "biggest" human rights NGOs, Amnesty and HRW, I have broadened the discussion to include actors that we would typically label as "humanitarian" NGOs: Médecins sans Frontières (MSF) and Oxfam International. Both MSF and Oxfam have strong traditions of advocacy, even if their other job is to provide services. MSF nonetheless has built its reputation vis-à-vis the International Committee of the Red Cross (ICRC) in speaking out, or *témoignage,* against atrocity and calling on governments to cease their negligent or destructive behaviors. By expanding the scope of relevant organizations we can try to overcome the challenge of studying failed NGOs. These organizations often leave little trace of ever having existed, making the universe of cases small. Studying advocacy organizations that have affected human rights, rather than self-identified human rights NGOs, is not only a way to increase the number of cases but also a more accurate way to understand the political salience of human rights, as more and more actors have developed the language of rights (Chong 2010).

In other chapters, I also include the International Committee of the Red Cross (ICRC), although the ICRC is not technically an NGO. As the enumerated protector of the Geneva Conventions, the ICRC has long conceived itself as having a somewhat different status from NGOs, which have no roles as deemed by international treaty. Nonetheless, the ICRC certainly is not a state, and increasingly has found itself criticizing the actions of states in the conduct of war, which makes it much more advocacy NGO-like than an impartial enforcer of the Geneva Conventions. Finally, I include a discussion of ASI and the International League of Human Rights, both of which have been relatively silent in contemporary human rights debates, but nonetheless persist as organizations, and at times have asserted their agendas.

This project posed challenges for the use of systematic techniques to examine each NGO, as each organization maintains data collections of varying quality and accessibility. Thus I am forced to approach these cases consulting a variety of sources. Secondary sources also vary in terms of quantity and quality. While a growing secondary literature exists on Amnesty, MSF, and Oxfam, HRW receives relatively scant academic coverage. For HRW, I rely on semistructured interviews with past and present staffers. I began with a short list of likely interviewees, and used snowball sampling techniques to supplement my data. I received permission from all of my interview subjects, but only a number wished to be directly attributed for their contribution. For the sake of anonymity, I have identified all interviewees by organization and a generic interview number. I used primary documents when relevant and available, but HRW does not release much about its organizational structure or decision-making processes. I conducted semistructured interviews with past and present staff of Oxfam, Amnesty, and MSF as well for a total of sixty-three interviews. Although the interviews provided a broad basis from which to generalize about the NGOs, I use them in a very limited sense. Many of them were conducted over telephone and not recorded. Thus I use very little direct quoting. I have attempted to limit attribution to facts that could not be gleaned from otherwise researching the organization, or perspectives that were expressed by sources that could not otherwise be known.

In addition, I consulted archives on Amnesty-USA and the International Secretariat. These archives are housed at Columbia University (US section),[9] the International Institute of Social History in Amsterdam, and at the Amnesty's London headquarters, which maintains an impressive number of documents (many of which remain closed to the public). An internal Amnesty oral history project conducted in the early 1980s supplemented other primary documents.

The Plan of the Book

Chapter 1 delves into the question of political salience. If political salience is about creating international focal points, how can we think about it? In IR, we commonly use standards that we devise for studying states to study other actors. This practice is dubious for the study of NGOs, which are quite distinct from states. We should not expect that NGOs invested in creating international norms have the same kinds of results that states do. To this end, I use three different perspectives to think about how to measure political salience, showing the strengths and weaknesses of each method. First, I review the dominant perspective of using international law to determine the normativeness of certain ideas. Second, I take into account the view of looking at the ideas and organizations that emerge from NGO networks. Third, I introduce a new way of thinking about political salience by probing the justifications used by states to levy economic sanctions against one another. Taken together, each of these perspectives reveals a different view of what human rights are politically salient at the international level. They each allow us to think about the different ways that we can think about political salience and the norms of human rights, and the standards by which we evaluate NGO effectiveness and prominence.

In the second chapter, I flesh out the argument summarized above regarding the effects of organizational structure on NGO success in making some rights politically salient. Starting from the insights made by network theory as a critique and an addendum to organization theories from business and sociology, I argue that NGOs that balance the advantages of centralized agenda setting for proposal and enforcement power with decentralized implementation power will be able influence the international debate over human rights. The rights that such NGOs advocate are far more likely to become politically salient, which can mean the creation of conventions, declarations, and other types of policy, or it can lead to other types of state actions, such as diplomatic or economic sanctioning, public condemnations, or the incorporation of those rights into trade agreements. While the pursuit of nonadvocacy goals (service provision) might lead NGOs to adopt different kinds of structures, once they make the turn toward international advocacy, they shift to centralize proposal and enforcement powers and decentralize the implementation of the agenda. To be successful as both transnational organizations and advocates, NGOs adopt this structure.

The propositions formulated from the theory in chapter 2 will then be evaluated in three subsequent chapters. Chapter 3 focuses on the classic case of centralized proposal and enforcement powers and decentralized implementation power: Amnesty. As the most-prominent human rights advocacy NGO to emerge during the Cold War, Amnesty forged a structure and a technique that led to its political salience as an important agenda setter in terms of both ideas and organizational salience. While previous transnational organizations had largely struggled with centralized agenda setting, Amnesty was the first to have a strong central office, the International Secretariat, which had control over the agenda in spite of strong national sections throughout Europe. Even though the Secretariat did not have control over the purse strings of the transnational NGO, it did control proposal and enforcement powers. Amnesty successfully implemented its agenda through decentralized prisoner adoption groups and, later, massive letter-writing campaigns that led to its triumphant advancements against torture and disappearances in Latin America and in securing the Convention Against Torture in 1984 (Huckerby and Rodley 2009). Since the end of the Cold War, it has gone through some changes, which have solidified the Secretariat's agenda-setting powers.

Chapter 4 offers an analysis of historical and contemporary cases and the failure of some NGOs to make their rights politically salient. In this section, I look at the International League of Human Rights, as well as ASI in the modern and historical periods to demonstrate how organizational choices shaped their fortunes in generating political salience for their ideas and for their respective organizations. I then turn to an analysis of the earlier periods of both Oxfam and MSF to show how, particularly in the case of MSF, advocacy failed to work because there were too many agenda setters and no way to centralize proposal power, enforcement power, or implementation power. Early on, their advocacy campaigns floundered. By contrast, because of their work in service provision, both Oxfam and MSF were able to become politically salient as organizations, and in recent years their organizational structures have shifted, resulting in political salience for their human rights ideas (discussed in chapter 5).

The last empirical chapter turns to campaigns as the unit of analysis to demonstrate how changes in NGO structure lead to differential impact in shaping international human rights. Considering NGO campaigns exposes the distinct processes of building political salience for ideas against organizational salience. Similar to the problems with collecting data on failed NGOs, it is also challenging to find data on failed campaigns—NGOs that have moved on often do not want to discuss their policy shortcomings. To account for this, I include one negative (and ongoing) case, the network against small arms and light weapons (IANSA). However, it is easier in the case of campaigns to look at before and after pictures of the organizational structure. Using campaigns that form a "critical juncture" (Collier and Collier 1991) from previous NGO practices, I show how new strategies and/or tactics led to traction in international politics that the NGO had not had with other efforts. In this chapter, I explore three contemporary cases: HRW's landmines and cluster munitions campaigns, Oxfam's fair trade project, and MSF's attempts to make essential medicines affordable. These campaigns show that changes in the approach to advocacy in each of these organizations resulted in making those issues politically salient in a way that changed the debates around what counts as human rights. I then use two historical campaign examples, the ICRC's struggle for humanitarian norms and ASI's campaign against chattel slavery, to show that the efficacy of a centralized proposal and enforcement powers matched with a decentralized implementation power is not a historically delimited advantage in organizational structure.

Finally, in the conclusion, I blend the discussion of the structure of agents and their choices with a discussion of norms and the notion of norm entrepreneurs in international politics. Using examples of the cases, I construct a case for using political salience as the rubric for thinking about what NGOs do, and the importance of the relationship between the salience of organizations and the salience of ideas, and how we can distinguish between the two. I conclude with the applicability of using organizational structure as the lens to analyze politically salient environmental NGOs—Greenpeace International—and the most successful church riding the wave of religious "reverse missions" from the global South to developed countries—Nigeria's Redeemed Christian Church of God. While the details of the policies might vary, the organizational structure of the most prominent and successful organizations will reflect the decision to create mechanisms that centralize the advocacy agenda and decentralize its implementation.

The core insight this book provides is that organizational structure, which is an internal characteristic of NGOs, has vast implications for how well NGOs will do in their external advocacy functions. Their choices of how to distribute proposal, enforcement, and implementation power have consequences for the extent to which NGOs will be able to establish themselves as organizations internationally, and how salient their advocacy agenda will be politically. Influencing human rights requires not just a moral stance and a desire to do good, but the right structure to change the agenda at the international level.

1

SALIENCE IN HUMAN RIGHTS

Part of the difficulty with working on the subject of human rights is the ubiquity with which it appears in the public imagination. As Oestreich neatly summarizes, "The concept of 'rights' is often used in very unspecific ways and often seems designed to justify any agenda with a moral or values-based component.... In other words, the concept of a right gets used quite a lot in world politics, often with little or no precision and little agreement on what counts as a right" (Oestreich 2007, 19–20). Many actors now adopt the language of rights for their own political causes, enlarging the scope of human rights' applicability (Levitt and Merry 2009; Goodale and Merry 2007).

Nonetheless, there are clearly some rights that are more salient than others in international politics. In international relations, we can call these more salient rights norms, and they are most frequently identified with international law. What political salience points to are focal points, whether these are found in organizations or ideas. These salient rights do not require justification to be called human rights: freedom from torture,

freedom of expression and religion, freedom from arbitrary arrest and execution, the so-called physical integrity rights (Cingranelli and Pasquarello
1985; Poe and Tate 1994). As others have shown (Wiener 2009; Wiener and
Puetter 2009), and as we see below, using international law as the yardstick
by which to evaluate the salience of human rights vis-à-vis one another
yields significant mismeasurement. A significant amount of interpretation goes into the enactment of international law, and as such, despite the
plethora of binding and nonbinding statements regarding human rights in
international politics, there are very few rights that are salient, recognized
by states, and thus, close to what we might consider to be *normative* at the
international level. Political salience gets at the heart of understanding the
different levels of acceptability among human rights, and helps us focus on
those rights employed by states rather than those that remain debatable in
spite of international declarations or law (e.g., the right to development,
migrant workers' rights, and the like). As such, the concept is compatible
with, although broader than, existing definitions of norms.

After a review of the strengths and weaknesses of legalization as political salience, I turn to an alternative view of political salience, as proposed
by scholars examining the effect of NGO networks. From this view, the
politics within networks create salience for causes among activists, who in
turn work to make those causes salient at the international level. Finally, I
suggest a new method of evaluating the political salience of human rights
by looking at how states use human rights to justify use of economic sanctions against other states. There are several advantages of using economic
sanctions, rather than international law, or even the work of NGOs, as a
way to measure of political salience. First, it moves away from the use of
international law *specific* to human rights to think about how state inter-
nalize the norms of human rights in other types of activity. This leads to
the second advantage: economic sanctions justifications offer a way to look
at the level of socialization, following the spiral model advanced by Risse,
Ropp, and Sikkink (1999). They tell us to what extent states are willing to
engage in costly political behavior in the name of rights, as promoted by
NGO networks. Third, because human rights are ultimately implemented
and ensured by states, examining how states use human rights in other
aspects of statecraft illustrates the extent to which norms have taken hold.
We can see how rights can become politically salient through other ways in
which states interact. Most important, states may seem inured from NGO

demands by refusing to sign or ratify certain human rights treaties, but they can still be influenced by NGOs and can act in other ways that reflect the effect of human rights advocacy. Economic sanctions are one way states can apply rights to a non–rights specific context. In some ways, doing so speaks far more to the salience of those particular rights than compliance to human rights-specific norms, as states engage in rule-consistent behavior in other facets of statecraft.

Legalization

In this book, I question the common wisdom of using legalization as the proxy for political salience and international norms. If we take into account the work of NGOs in promoting rights and how their work causes some rights to become politically salient, legalization is but one way to be politically salient. NGOs often employ other means that may have a goal of legalization (Amnesty's campaign against torture), but in the process also create a means to name and shame rights violators in such a way as to elevate the salience of certain rights in the absence of law (Chong 2010). NGOs are not just in the business of making law, they are also in the business of creating the definitions of human rights through other means of advocacy.[1]

If we are to understand the role of NGOs in international politics better, we also have to be clear that not all NGOs measure their success on the formation of new international legal instruments. As international relations scholars, we use legalization as a handy measure of international norms, but we need to remember that advocacy NGOs are in the business of making their human rights agendas politically salient more broadly speaking. Thus, in thinking about norms as political salience, we can include legalization as one visible measurement of norms, but the work of NGOs goes beyond that. For instance, fair trade products are ubiquitous, and there are multiple labels to denote "fair trade" standards. No international agreement exists on fair trade, yet markets and individuals have responded to this rights-based claim about fair wage for fair work. NGOs, notably Oxfam, have contributed to making fair trade politically salient, creating *focal points* in international politics. States have been asked to provide domestic protections for coffee farmers on a case basis to hedge the harmful effect of globalization, but as yet, there is not a push to construct an international legal instrument around the notion of fair trade. At the same time, fair trade is a focal point in international politics, spurring states to enact policies to protect producers of export goods such as coffee.

Political salience is a concept that attempts to capture some of the effects that NGOs have in setting the agenda on human rights in international politics. Focal points might involve creating international law, which is an oft-invoked indicator of the existence of international norms. Not all NGO campaigns aim for the formalization and legalization of international norms, however, and some pursue other types of ways to protect rights—domestic change or market institutions. Those kinds of actions also create focal points. NGOs that successfully make their human rights agendas salient can create ways to solve coordination problems: the putative equality of human rights, for example, can be overcome if NGOs bring a limited set of rights into focus for states. Repeated over time in different types of campaigns, NGOs can continually emphasize the rights they believe are most important, generating salience around these issues. Once NGOs achieve some buy-in by some states, encouraging other states to accept the political salience of an NGO's advocacy agenda becomes a question of reaching a certain threshold before a norm can be identified.[2]

Why Political Salience Is Not Simply Law

Scholars of international norms often point to the institutionalization of human rights in law as evidence of their normative validity or strength (Lutz and Sikkink 2000; Simmons 2009). After all, law is a product of consensus, and once codified, provides limits to state actions. States also accede to international law, at least through treaties, voluntarily, and it is this willingness to agree to constraints on their own behavior that signals the normative power of the law (Chayes and Chayes 1993) and the start of domestic institution reform (Goodman and Jinks 2003). Even if domestic practices do not measure up to international legal standards, some have argued in favor of human rights law in spite of these gaps because of the dynamic between international pressure and law (Goodman and Jinks 2008). Law is a good starting place for thinking about political salience, because law creates salience once in place, or it can be an indicator of the issues states choose to formalize because of their importance.

However, legalization falls short on a number of counts. First, it privileges the position of states in human rights politics, as states are the only actors that can accede to and enact international law. NGOs are busily part of the political debate, even if they cannot legalize. The establishment of the United Nations solidified the place of NGOs in international politics. The UN's founders consciously included NGOs into the formal apparatus of the organization, granting consultative status via ECOSOC.[3] NGOs and policy entrepreneurs immediately reacted to this policy, soliciting support and creating organizations for their political projects. Whereas the lineup of NGOs that lobbied the League of Nations and even at the San Francisco conference that led to the founding of the UN were largely offshoots of churches and unions, the NGOs that emerged in the UN era have increasingly dropped their ties to such nonstate stalwarts. In other words, the post–World War II NGO story is one of increasing professionalization and independence from conventional sources of nonstate power as NGOs gained in legitimacy and numbers. NGOs have set the agenda for many of the developments in human rights at the international level; states have responded to NGO demands, and one of the consequences has been a variegated and ever-expanding universe of human rights conventions, declarations, and other international documents that assert the importance of human rights.

Second, law can only tell us some of the things states consider important. The turn to hard (legally binding) law is the exception, and alternatives (i.e., soft law) might range from obligation-free declarations to political agreements (Abbott and Snidal 2000). International law generally does not encompass political deals or ad hoc agreements, thus the widening scope of international human rights law does not mean that all of the rights that are now defined by *legal* language are equally salient *politically*. What I mean by this is that even though we see more and more issues bearing the human rights mantle and witness the expansion of human rights through formalization of international law (via treaties or declarations), not all of these iterations of "human rights" are received similarly. Their universality may be questioned, their support might be limited, or their link as a rights issue could be disputed. Thus, although indigenous groups or migrant workers may have gotten UN-level declarations and conventions, these rights are not politically salient in the same way as rights protecting against torture or ill-treatment, even if there are conventions covering both. Political salience is not just recognition in law, but it is also a way to think about how human rights are used politically, and what rights are cited when states or nonstate actors pursue "human rights" agendas.

This leads to the third shortcoming of legalization: political salience is a political process that involves the creation, and later, the interpretation and enforcement of law. One argument for favoring the politics over the legality of human rights emphasizes the putative equality among different rights that states claimed when creating the pillars of the international human rights regime: the UDHR, the International Covenant on Civil and Political Rights (ICCPR), and the International Covenant on Economic, Social, and Cultural Rights (ICESCR), and more recently, in the Vienna Declaration and Program of Action.[4] Common wisdom tells us that the Soviets and the Eastern bloc characteristically emphasized economic and social rights, and the Anglo-American allies selected mostly civil and political rights. However, such a position also denies the importance of the newly independent states, which emphasized self-determination and cultural rights. Other European and Latin American states took stances in-between the Cold War antagonists (Waltz 2001). This culturally essentialist account also leaves out the politics of creating an international human rights regime. At the time of the UDHR, and later with the ICCPR and ICESCR, states tiptoed around which rights were more important because they wanted universal assent to human rights documents. To properly set up the human rights project, and especially at the time of the UDHR, states wanted consensus so that later on, they could refer to the universality of the claims they advanced (see Glendon 2002). From a formal legal standpoint, therefore, human rights have mostly putative equality vis-à-vis one another because of *political* concerns.

The human rights project needed the support of states caught in the midst of the Cold War. To gain political support, the UDHR, ICCPR, and ICESCR needed to establish a baseline that allowed for wiggle room by states. The application of international law is subject to political concerns, and drafters of the UDHR, ICCPR, and ICESCR recognized a need to allow for politicking to affect the application of (or exception to) law in order to achieve support for the new instruments.

Some might argue that while the nonbinding UDHR did not identify more important rights, the ICCPR did with the establishment of nonderogable rights. Derogation provides an example of how the law was crafted specifically with its political application in mind. Part of the debate over the ICCPR spurred by the British was the question of derogration, that is, could states, when faced with threats, derogate from the human rights obligations they promised to adhere to during normal times? Allowing derogation would provide the wiggle room that states desired, but other states argued that derogation needed constraints so that the human rights instruments would have relevance.[5] States disagreed over the number of appropriate constraints, that is, how many of the rights would be nonderogable in cases of threats to states or in wartime. Nonderogable rights cannot be violated even in times of duress.[6] The nonderogability of certain rights has led some legal scholars to identify a clear hierarchy of rights (Koji 2001). Thus an international lawyer might argue that the political salience of the freedom from torture is a function of its legal standing as a nonderogable right in the ICCPR.

The problem with equating political salience to a legal concept such as nonderogability, however, is that we also know from the practice of politics that international law has not inhibited states from violating human rights when they have deemed it politically necessary (Hafner-Burton and Tsutsui 2005), and we know that states often have other motivations besides a belief in human rights to ratify treaties (Hathaway 2007; Vreeland 2008; Wotipka and Tsutsui 2008). We also know that while states might sign treaties such as the Convention against Torture, they are far more reluctant to sign on to the Optional Protocols that allow for individual petitions and other more stringent enforcement mechanisms (Vreeland 2008). Therefore, the political salience of certain rights does not necessarily only derive from the law surrounding their protection, but also by the way states (and others) understand, apply, and shirk these restrictions. Other domestic factors such as regime type and civil society engagement limit the effects of treaties (Landman 2005; Neumayer 2005) as well.

The difference in the political salience of various human rights demonstrates the influence of human rights NGOs. Making rights salient involves not just raising issues at international fora, but persistent campaigning, monitoring, and reporting to force to states to recognize inconsistencies with their behaviors and acknowledge the validity of existing domestic or international human rights institutions. Since the end of World War II, states have continuously expanded the means by which human rights can be protected through treaty making, bilateral trade agreements (Hafner-Burton 2009), and international institutions such as the European Court of Human Rights and the International Criminal Court. States, however, have not been the only significant players in determining the rules of the game. Human rights have grown, and certain human rights have become salient through the activity of NGOs. NGOs have been at the forefront of creating international treaties—for instance, the role of Amnesty in promoting a convention against torture and the effort of Human Rights Watch (HRW) in the campaign against landmines and cluster munitions—and they have also forced states to answer accusations of human rights abuses through persistent reporting and monitoring.

Table 1 shows an upward trend since the 1970s in the number of reports and press releases that Amnesty has issued, documenting human rights abuses and naming and shaming abusive governments publicly, demanding that states respond to their accusations (Ron, Ramos, and Rodgers

TABLE 1. Amnesty background reports and press releases, 1975–2000

Year	Amnesty background reports	Amnesty press releases
1975	19	21
1976	62	46
1977	104	57
1978	148	51
1979	166	47
1980	195	57
1981	216	31
1982	338	18
1983	403	25
1984	483	17
1985	566	21
1986	603	17
1987	590	37
1988	625	54
1989	595	48
1990	759	69
1991	937	43
1992	857	29
1993	865	17
1994	556	359
1995	560	304
1996	469	353
1997	569	329
1998	604	431
1999	578	471
2000	578	570

Source: Adapted from Ron, Ramos, and Rodgers 2005.

2005). Since 1983, Amnesty has averaged more than one Background Report a day, and increased its statements to the media in the mid-1990s so that by 2000, the number of press releases and reports was nearly the same. While international law on human rights changes incrementally, states can change behavior much more rapidly in response to NGO statements about their abusive actions.

Political salience also means raising issues through advocacy as a way to force states to respond to accusations. Political salience, therefore, is more than just advances in international law, though legalization is an important part of that conception. NGOs have pursued changes in international policy, but some NGOs have also pursued engagement with local populations, domestic governments, and other avenues of influence as ways to set the human rights agenda. These other ways are less measurable and less quantifiable, but they nonetheless contribute to setting the agenda on international human rights by making the rights they pursue politically salient. When Amnesty decides to target violations of political expression rights in Burma, it de facto prioritizes that kind of violation. Similarly, when Oxfam pursues a rights-based approach to development that connects the right to unionize coffee growers in Kenya with economic well-being, it makes a claim about the importance of that right. These actions raise the political salience of a given right, and forces their target states (both third parties and violator states) to respond. Following the logic of influential transnational advocacy models such as the boomerang pattern (Keck and Sikkink 1998) or the spiral model (Risse, Ropp, and Sikkink 1999),[7] NGO advocacy can lead to all sorts of outcomes, including legalization. Political salience, therefore, is an idea that encompasses and goes beyond legalization.

Using NGO Networks to Evaluate Salience

An alternative way to assess salience might be to refer to the work of NGOs themselves. Since the late 1990s, there has been an increasing interest in the power of NGOs and other nonstate actors in effecting political change. At first, the word *network* was employed largely as a descriptive or metaphorical way to consider different types of political actors (Keck and Sikkink 1998), but as scholarship has advanced, the analysis of both nonstate actors and their affiliated networks has become more nuanced, focusing not just on revealing what these actors are vis-à-vis states, but also how power actually emerges from networks to shape international policy. Through their work, networks create political salience for rights, and since NGOs cannot work on all issues all of the time, the issues that garner NGO attention should rise to the top of international politics.

Establishing that NGOs and networks have influence on international politics was the goal of early work in this vein. Empirically, however, theory did not match up well to reality. While early enthusiasm about the effect of NGOs assumed an equality between these actors and the generalized effect of injecting "civil society" into state-dominated politics (Brysk 1993; Lipschutz 1992; Wapner 1995), it soon became evident that not all NGOs are equally influential. Powerful NGOs, such as Amnesty or Greenpeace, can effectively shut out ideas from the global marketplace by choosing to champion a certain cause (e.g. Tibetans in China) over many others (e.g. Uighurs, Zhang, Hui, Yi, and Mongols) (Bob 2005; see also Carpenter 2010). Some of the most innovative work has explored the dynamics of different actors within NGO networks. Scholars such as Bob and Carpenter identify powerful "gatekeeper" NGOs that can filter ideas for "follower" NGOs (Bob 2010; Carpenter 2011). Others have asserted a more positive agenda-setting power for NGO networks, showing that powerful NGOs can promote a subset of ideas that, over time, become part of the overall network agenda (Lake and Wong 2009). For instance, the notion of women and children as "vulnerable populations" in wartime is a gender-based conception that is promulgated by NGOs and IGOs, but one that does not necessarily align with the actual risk of death or injury (Carpenter 2003). The lopsided quality of the international human rights NGO network is also geographical, as resource-rich NGOs tend to congregate in the global North (Bandy and Smith 2005; Smith and Wiest 2005). This can create problems of economic dependence that create incentives for Southern movements to "soften" or alter their claims in order to better fit in with the mainstream political agenda of dominant NGOs (Bob 2005; Murdie, et al. 2009).

Thus evaluating the work of NGO networks requires that we acknowledge that this is primarily examining the strategies and successes of large, Western-based NGOs. To be successful, smaller social movements, domestic NGOs, and even smaller, less-well-known Western NGOs working on human rights must link to more prominent organizations, the gatekeepers. Gatekeepers limit the types of things that can be addressed as human rights at the international level, thus determining at least the admissibility of topics for debate. As Bob argues, "Even if gatekeepers do not communicate concerns directly to other network members, their choices have powerful demonstration effects...gatekeepers are easy to identify" (Bob 2005, 18–19). Time and again, using multiple methods, research has shown that the NGO gatekeepers for the contemporary human rights movement are Amnesty and HRW (Bob 2005; Lake and Wong 2009; Murdie, et al. 2009).

Amnesty and HRW's reluctance to adopt economic, social, and cultural rights following the end of the Cold War, for instance, generated resistance, external and internal criticism, and finally, policy changes in both NGOs in the late 1990s (HRW) and 2001 (Amnesty). This fundamentally reshaped the agenda of the NGO network, which had previously focused on political dissidents, expression and religious rights, and physical integrity rights. Opening up the prospects of casting various causes as human rights related has led to an explicit attempt by development NGOs, such as Oxfam International and Save the Children, to adopt rights-based approaches to their work (Nelson and Dorsey 2008). Similarly, a quick look at Amnesty and HRW's most recent forays into economic, social, and cultural rights reveals a more development-angled approach. The current Secretary General of Amnesty, for instance, Salil Shetty, directed the UN Millennium Campaign, and it has adopted both an international justice and a "demand dignity" campaign.[8] We can therefore use the work of the broader human rights network, and the NGO gatekeepers within them, as a yardstick for gauging the political salience of different rights. NGOs certainly do not control the human rights network, which also includes public intellectuals and various international bodies concerned with human rights, such as the UN High Commissioner for Human Rights, but their work signals acceptance of certain ideas about human rights to both their NGO peers and to movements vying for international support.

In Chapter 5, I focus on NGO efforts to make rights salient through specific campaigns. Not all campaigns succeed in gaining traction at the international level, whether in terms of securing rights or gaining recognition as an international problem needing a solution. Furthermore, although it is important to look at how salience is achieved among NGOs and other nonstate actors, this begs the question of whether there are better ways to evaluate the work of NGOs without referencing NGOs themselves. Given the problematic nature of legalization approaches, a better indicator of political salience would be able to account for politics while also indicating a commitment from states that the rights to which they agree or the ones they choose to implement are the important ones. Hence, we turn to how states justify the use of economic sanctions.

Economic Sanctions as Indicators of Political Salience

Using economic sanctions as an indicator of political salience provides an alternative to current legalized conceptions of international norms. A preliminary appraisal of the descriptive statistics from the twentieth century shows that a very limited swath of human rights get employed for justifying economic sanctions. I argue, based on this evidence, that economic sanctions might offer a new direction in future research for evaluating not just the political salience of ideas but also the norms of human rights. First, the very act of imposing an economic sanction makes the justification for the sanction politically salient. Furthermore, it is a non-human-rights-specific instrument that states can use for nearly anything in order to express their political demands.[9] As such, it is quite telling that the pattern of economic sanctions over the twentieth century reflected a complete lack of human rights-based sanctions until the 1960s, after which human rights-based sanctions became prevalent (see table 2 below). Finally, the content of the human rights justifications, that is, the violation of which human rights were chosen by states to sanction other states, is an important indicator of the priorities of sanctioners and those states being sanctioned. For the sanctioners, this means that they are willing to incur economic and political costs to impose a sanction based on certain human rights in order to compel change in state behavior. For the sanctioned, resistance to sanctions by another state can signal (1) normative resolve or (2) desire to be viewed as resolute on a domestically salient issue. In line with arguments about war as a bargaining failure, the fact that negotiations resulted in economic sanctions signal the failure of diplomatic efforts to resolve disagreement over human rights, and can also be taken as an indication of that a norm is valid and in play. That is, I expect that when states punish one another via economic sanction for bad human rights behavior, the sender states' use of rights as justification reflect those they find most important *and* those that the target state flaunts. The sender wants to change behavior in the target to what it understands to be normative.[10] This section walks through the logic of economic sanctions as norms and presents aggregate data from the twentieth century.

Sanctions are one method by which states try to compel behaviors in other states.[11] They are punishments (Nossal 1989). Sanctions come in many forms—besides economic sanctions, states can employ social sanctioning, in which pariah states are created, or diplomatic sanctioning, when states discontinue relations or deny targeted nationals the right to travel. Unlike some of the other types of sanctions, economic sanctions are more easily measurable, and these measures are readily available.

Economic sanctioning is the attempt for one state, the sender, to change the policies of another state, the target, through alterations of market relationships. There are three main types of economic sanctions: constricting exports, limiting or banning imports, and directly affecting finances in the target country (Hufbauer, Schott, and Elliott 2007). Economic sanctions can be instrumental or symbolic (Galtung 1967). In this case, sanctions sent symbolically or instrumentally do not actually make a difference in terms of thinking about how they signal norms. The very fact that states do send economic sanctions based on human rights signals the importance of human rights to that state; the types of rights those states cite, therefore, can give us insight into the normative importance of those rights. Sanctions do not have to be successful in order to signal the normative reasons for which they are sent.

The use of sanctions data presents its own biases, but they provide a good test for the normative importance of certain human rights over others. First, economic sanctions are costly for states to institute, and implementing them for any reason signals that the state is sufficiently invested in its justification to follow through on its demands politically and economically (Drezner 1999, 2003). Second, economic sanctions are neither overtly nor exclusively about "human rights" in the same way that human rights treaties are: the fact that states choose to send sanctions in the name of human rights signals their importance vis-à-vis other reasons. Following, the specific rights raised in sanctions should signal the importance of those rights (whatever the motivation) versus the other human rights possibilities from which states could have chosen. Third, states (1) have alternatives to sanctioning another state and (2) do not have to choose to accuse another state of violating human rights. As Neta Crawford puts it: "If ethical arguments and normative beliefs have power, we should expect the use of international sanctions…to change the behavior of those who violate the normative prescriptions" (Crawford 2002, 396). Sanctions provide a way for states to act in a costly fashion short of armed conflict and war. It is quite reasonable to assume that states will then employ sanctions in contexts in which they are willing to bear high costs in order to get their way, thus revealing the political salience of the rights. Fourth and finally, if sanctions are indeed punishments, then the reasons that states chose to justify sanctions must comport to some commonly held standard—a norm—that target states, and even nonsanctioning states, states would understand to be correct. If a state indeed sanctioned another state based on reasons that others found ridiculous or unimportant, this would certainly dilute the effect of the economic punishment both in material, but also reputational, ways. To be effective, economic sanctions draw on declarations of right and wrong that rest on widely held standards.

Economically sanctioning another state is a politically costly signal in international relations, even if many of them end up not compelling states to change their behavior.[12] Their costliness is one reason why they are relatively rare, and thus, when they occur, they can be conceived as a breakdown in negotiation. That is, target states guess wrongly about a sender state's resolve, or sender states underestimate the cost of implementing the sanction (Eaton and Engers 1999). Either way, it is a failure of both states to avoid costly consequences. The failure to avoid the consequences while pursuing human rights, then, emphasizes the fact that sender states are invested in whatever rights they pursue through sanctions. Furthermore, economics sanctions are a very public means of publicizing another state's behavior, and thus make the issues over which sanctions are issued politically salient.

This cost can be conceptualized in terms of domestic costs, primarily as the loss of trade and financial flows, which hurt domestic constituencies. Since economic sanctions are not necessarily effective for compelling behavior, the fact that states would pursue such a policy even when they fail to "do anything" while hurting parts of the population is a risky cost to bear. First and foremost, violating another state's sovereignty is costly. Sender states however, may be willing to take on the cost if it convinces other states to come on board as well (Hufbauer, Schott, and Elliott 2007). The higher the political cost, the more committed a state is to a particular issue (Martin 1992). In some cases, economic sanctions may benefit sender states domestically, distracting the public from other problems, or sating a demand for action (Dorussen and Mo 2001; Kaempfer and Lowenberg 1988), as in the movement against apartheid (Crawford 2002, 382; Hufbauer and Schott 1985). Despite the possible benefits at home, we would not expect states to sanction one another for low-priority issues, and we could reasonably expect that a state is committed to a particular outcome when it employs a sanction.

Another way to think about the costs of sending sanctions is reputational. The consequences of economic sanctions can have negative humanitarian consequences (Lopez and Cortright 1997), which can hurt a state's international reputation if pursued in excess. The extent to which sanctions have harmed civilian populations is amply documented in cases of developing countries, such as Haiti and Iraq (Cortright and Lopez 2000; Drezner 1999; Gibbons 1999; Weiss, Cortright, Lopez, and Minear 1997; Werleigh 1995).[13] State reputation may also suffer in the context of prior relations with the target state. Resorting to economic sanctions may sever a previously positive relationship. We expect as a result that states will only economically sanction one another sparingly. Therefore, to sanction in the name of human rights carries with it a deeper commitment than other types of behavior.

Using available studies (Drury 1998; Hufbauer, Schott, and Elliott 1990, 2007),[14] I have compiled the data on economic sanctions between 1910 and 2006, organized by justification for the sanction. Table 2 shows, by decade, the percentage of all sanctions that were enacted for human rights violations. For the purposes of calculating these figures, I include not just cases that are "human rights," as labeled by the original coders, but also cases involving demands for democratization, which became part of the canon of human rights discourse after the Reagan administration and became more powerful after the dissolution of the USSR. Human rights were used to justify sanctions only beginning in the 1960s, increasing dramatically in the 1970s and 1980s to more than one-third of all sanctions episodes.

Table 2 also demonstrates how the political salience of human rights changes over time. Whereas physical integrity and expression rights dominated the sanctions episodes in the 1970s, by the 1980s, elections had

TABLE 2. Economic sanctions episodes by decade, 1910–2006

Decade	Human rights-based sanctions	Total sanctions	Percentage of human rights sanctions	Number of cases that involve physical integrity or expression rights	Number of cases that involve elections or democracy
1910–1919	0	3	0%	0	0
1920–1929	0	2	0%	0	0
1930–1939	0	9	0%	0	0
1940–1949	0	12	0%	0	0
1950–1959	0	15	0%	0	0
1960–1969	2	24	8.3%	1	2
1970–1979	14	43	32.6%	13	1
1980–1989	15	34	44.1%	11	9
1990–1999	28	61	46%	18	25
2000–2006	6	13	46.2%	6	5
Total	65	216	—	49	42

Sources: Hufbauer et al. (1990), Drury (1998), and Hufbauer et al. (2007). Note that some cases involve multiple human rights abuses, and therefore appear in columns for both types of rights.

become important as justifications for economic sanctions. By the 1990s, the number of elections, or democratically driven sanctions, outnumbered those concerned with physical integrity and expression rights. Physical integrity and expression rights, however, continued to be important, as states began citing multiple human rights reasons for levying economic sanctions. These data show how the political salience of rights shifts over time, but also the enduring importance of norms, once salient.

Table 3 summarizes all human rights sanction episodes, with the specification of which rights were violated. Any given case may contain multiple categories of human rights violations. Consistent with physical integrity and expression rights, table 3 indicates that early sanctions episodes focused on the treatment of political dissidents and expression rights. In the 1970s, an expansion into other types of civil and political rights become the targets of sanctions, and by the 1980s, there are several demands for the restoration or respect for democracy. Note that out of fourteen total human rights-based justifications in the 1970s, all but one reflected either physical integrity or expression rights, whereas in the 1980s, ten out of fourteen did so. These demands, as table 3 shows, were also often coupled with appeals such as the right to free speech, association, and the rule of law.[15] The trend toward economic sanctions in the name of democracy increased in the 1990s, as noted by Hufbauer et al. (2007). These tendencies to equate

TABLE 3. Human rights sanctions by episode, 1910–2006

Case	Countries	Year begin	Year end	Case summary, justifications	Physical integrity, expression, or democratic rights?
62-2	UN v. S. Africa**	1962	1994	Apartheid; Namibian independence	P, E, D
65-3	UN, UK v. Rhodesia**	1965	1979	Majority rule by Black Africans	D
72-1	UK, US v. Uganda	1972	1979	Expelling Asians, human rights, destabilize Amin	P
73-2	US v. S. Korea	1973	1977	Human rights	P, E
75-4	US v. Kampuchea†	1975	1979	Human rights, Vietnam deterrent	—
75-5	US v. Chile	1975	1990	Human rights, Letelier, restore democracy	P
76-1	US v. Uruguay	1976	1981	Human rights	P
77-1	US v. Paraguay	1977	1981	Human rights	P
77-2	US v. Guatemala	1977	2005	Human rights	P
77-3	US v. Argentina	1977	1983	Human rights	P
77-5	US v. Nicaragua†	1977	1979	Human rights, destabilize Somoza	P
77-6	US v. El Salvador	1977	1981	Human rights	P, E
77-7	US v. Brazil	1977	1984	Human rights	E
77-8	US v. Ethiopia	1977	1992	Expropriations, human rights	P
78-5	US v. USSR**	1978	1980	Dissident treatment	E
79-4	US v. Bolivia	1979	1982	Human rights, drug trafficking	P, E, D
81-2	US v. Poland**	1981	1987	Martial law, dissidents, Solidarity talks	E, D
81-4	European Community v. Turkey	1981	1986	Restore democracy	E, D
82-2	Netherlands v. Suriname	1982	1991	Human rights, limit alliance with Cuba and Libya, reverse coup	P, D
83-3	US v. Zimbabwe*	1983	1988	Anti-American comments in UN, food to Matabeleland, dissident suppression	E
83-4	US, OECS v. Grenada	1983	1983	Elections, destabilize regime	—
83-5	US v. Romania	1983, 1990	1989, 1993	Human rights, emigration restrictions, democracy	P, E, D
85-1	US, British Commonwealth v. S. Africa	1985	1991	Apartheid	P, E, D
86-2	US v. Angola	1986	1992	Cuban troops, democracy	D
86-3	Greece v. Turkey	1986	1999	Renounce claims to Aegean island, leave Cyprus, improve human rights	—

Case	Countries	Year begin	Year end	Case summary, justifications	Physical integrity, expression, or democratic rights?
87-2	US v. Haiti	1987	1990	Human rights, democracy, drug smuggling	P, E
87-4	India, Australia, New Zealand v. Fiji	1987	2001	Democracy, minority rights	D
88-1	Japan, W. Germany, US v. Burma	1988	—	Human rights, democracy	P, E, D
88-2	US, UK, UN v. Somalia	1988	—	Human rights, end civil war	P
89-2	US v. China†	1989	—	Tiananmen Square, human rights	E, D
89-3	US v. Sudan	1989	—	Human rights, civil war, democracy	P, E
90-2	US v. El Salvador	1990	1993	Human rights, civil war	P
90-3	US, Western donors v. Kenya	1990	1993	Political repression, democracy	P, E, D
90-4	US, Belgium, France v. Zaire	1990	1997	Establish democracy	P, E, D
91-3	US v. Thailand	1991	1992	Restore constitutional regime	D
91-4	US, Netherlands v. Indonesia	1991	1997	Human rights, East Timor	P
91-5	US, UN, OAS v. Haiti	1991	1994	Restore democracy	D
91-7	USSR/Russia v. Turkmenistan	1991	1995	Rights of Russian minority	D
91-8	US v. Peru	1991	1995	Human rights, democracy	P, E, D
92-2	EC/EU, France, Germany v. Togo	1992	—	Democracy, human rights	P, D
92-3	US, UK v. Malawi	1992	1993	Democracy, human rights	P, E, D
92-4	EU, Spain v. Equatorial Guinea	1992	2000	Democracy, human rights	E, D
92-5	EU v. Algeria	1992	1994	Promote democracy	P, D
92-6	US v. Cameroon	1992	1998	Democracy, human rights	P, E, D
92-8	UN, US, and Germany v. Khmer Rouge, Cambodia	1992	—	Ban Khmer Rouge, establish democracy	D
92-9	USSR/Russia v. Estonia	1992	1999	Rights of Russian minority	D
92-13	USSR/Russia v. Latvia	1992	1998	Rights of Russian minority	D
93-3	UN v. Angola UNITA	1993	2002	Civil war, democracy	D
93-4	US, EU v. Nigeria§	1993	1998	Human rights, democracy, drug trafficking	E, D
94-2	Greece v. Albania	1994	1995	Release jailed Greek leaders	P
94-4	US, EU, Japan v. The Gambia	1994	1998	Democracy	E, D
95-2	EU v. Turkey	1995	1995	Human rights	E, D

(*continued*)

TABLE 3. Human rights sanctions by episode, 1910–2006 (*Continued*)

Case	Countries	Year begin	Year end	Case summary, justifications	Physical integrity, expression, or democratic rights?
96-1	East African members of OAU v. Burundi	1996	1999	Democracy	P, D
96-2	US, EU v. Niger	1996	2000	Restore democracy	D
96-3	US, Western donors v. Zambia	1996	1998	Human rights, constitutional reform	D
96-4	US v. Colombia	1996	1998	Drug trafficking, human rights	P, D
97-1	UN, ECOWAS v. Sierra Leone	1997	2003	Restoration of democracy	P, D
99-2	US, EU, France v. Ivory Coast	1999	2002	Democracy	P, D
99-3	US, Japan v. Pakistan	1999	2001	Democracy	D
—	EU, US v. Haiti	2001	2005	Democratization	P, D
—	EU v. Guinea	2002	2006	Democracy	P, D
—	EU, US v. Zimbabwe	2002	—	Democracy, human rights	P, E, D
—	EU, US, Switzerland v. Uzbekistan	2005	—	Human rights	P
—	Australia, EU, New Zealand, US v. Fiji	2006	—	Coup, democracy	E, D
—	EU, US v. Belarus	2006	—	Democracy	P, D

†: These are new human rights classifications in Hufbauer et al. (2007), missing in earlier versions.

§: This case, unlike many of the others, has compound demands from sanctioning parties for both a restoration of democratic processes as well as demands to allow for political dissension and free speech.

* Drury (1998) codes as "human rights," but not Hufbauer et al. (1990).

** Not coded as human rights in Hufbauer et al. (1990) or Hufbauer et al. (2007).

democracy with human rights, which started under Reagan in the 1980s, were emblematic of US foreign policy. However, starting in the late 1980s other countries and groups followed suit with demands for democracy via economic sanctions.

Table 3 includes sanctions that are "human rights" based, accounting for a total of sixty. As mentioned above, a broader definition of "human rights" has been used to include democracy-based sanctions for two reasons: (1) to increase the number of cases that are human rights related to reflect the trajectory of human rights norms and to show the changes in human rights norms over time; and (2) because expression rights, and to a lesser extent physical integrity rights, are part of the definition of "democracy." Although the electoral process is the common indicator of democracy, freedom of belief and expression, and freedom from arbitrary imprisonment are hallmarks of democratic regimes. And finally, including democratic rights shows the evolution of human rights norms from one that was much more limited to physical integrity and expression rights in the 1970s and 1980s to a gradual expansion to democracy more generally by the 1990s. Together, tables 2 and 3 show the changes in international human rights norms based on the pattern of which rights states chose as justification for sanctions. Economic sanctions are used for a very limited repertoire of rights. Because sanctioning is a very public act, designed to attract attention at the international and domestic levels, the selection of only a few rights for economic sanctions makes those rights politically salient.

What becomes clear is that not all rights form reasons for why states sanction one another. In fact, states use a very limited subset of human rights to impose sanctions on one another. A further pattern is that states tend to stick to this limited repertoire over time. As they include more types of rights into their justifications for sanctioning another state, those rights become sticky as well. Thus what we see is the pattern of introduction (e.g. physical integrity and expression rights in the early 1970s), extensive use (throughout the 1970s and 80s), and then, a less intense, but still present, use of the same reason for sanctions. In fact, in the 1990s we see states bundling physical integrity or expression rights concerns with attention to democracy rights. These trends in the reasoning for economic sanctions show that over time states accept more rights as normative, and thus, take costly actions to regulate those norms. Such actions signal the political salience of physical integrity, expression, and democracy rights over other kinds of rights in particular eras. In future years, other categories of rights may also become part of what states deem unacceptable and therefore worthy of condemnation via economic sanction as well. This expectation is consistent with observed patterns since the end of World War II.

One criticism of these data is that they reflect the politics of the powerful, since economic sanctioning only works if sender states can threaten to or actually hurt the economies of target states. This is true, however, for many other types of measures that try to change state behavior, such as offering aid in exchange for good actions. Powerful states can harness more resources than weak states, making their threats credible. The United States is a frequent user of economic sanctions, although the UN has increasingly made use of sanctions since the 1990s (Drezner 2003; Pape 1997). What is interesting in the cases involving the United States throughout the years is the consistency with which sanctions were applied, despite the fact that each administration from Carter to Clinton had different human rights foci (Sikkink 2004). Furthermore, power matters for international relations more generally, as the logic behind setting up international institutions follows a "lock-in" logic: states want to create rules, but they also want to preserve power relations (e.g., the Security Council's permanent five members and their veto power).

Another important criticism of putting the focus on the United States is that this approach misses an explanation for why other countries did not make use of economic sanctions to the same degree until the 1980s. In particular, why did the European states, whose commitment to human rights surely cannot be overlooked, neglect to apply sanctions against human rights violators? The European continent has, since 1950, institutionalized the protection of human rights through the European Convention on Human Rights. This convention established the European Court of Human Rights, which has allowed Council of Europe states, and individuals living in them, to bring cases before the court against violating states.[16] Outside of European targets, the US-heavy presence for economic sanctions prior to 1989 likely reflects Cold War dynamics. European states may have been reluctant to sanction given the fact that economics were so dichotomized between the United States and USSR that states would be unlikely to respond to threats from Europe regarding human rights. Economic sanctions from either of the two superpowers would be far more effective. Moreover, the tendency for European governments to follow consensus-based models of governance (Lijphart 1999) may have also encouraged such states to use more "carrot" rather than "stick" tactics to get human rights compliance—buying off violators of human rights norms, rather than punishing them. European states would incur costs in doing so, but different kinds of costs. There are two possible explanations for why USSR did not use economic sanctions to enforce human rights. First, as economic sanctions are costly, Soviet leaders may not have considered human rights important enough for commitment.[17] Second, the rights commonly attributed to the Soviet Union—economic rights—could mostly be resolved through institutions such as the Council for Mutual Economic Assistance, or Comecon.

Nonetheless, the US-centric question remains important. According to one strain of hegemonic stability theory, leader states can accede to costly behaviors by providing public goods; in doing so, they benefit themselves (Lake 1993). The United States often acted alone early on in the 1970s,[18] providing in a sense, the public good of protecting human rights. As human rights norms solidified in the 1980s, more states began shouldering the burden of taking on costs to protect human rights consistently with the rights initially targeted by the United States, as table 3 shows.

Using economic sanctions as an indicator of international human rights norms has one major drawback, which also happens to be its major advantage. Rarely do NGOs ask states to use economic sanctions as a part of the package of policy recommendations they make. NGOs do not demand economic sanctions. In this sense, it is hard to assess what the NGO is "doing" in the decision for states to use economic sanctions against one another. Put simply, NGOs are not directly involved, if they are even involved at all in the process of using and implementing economic sanctions. Our existing models of norm change, such as the spiral model (Risse, Ropp, and Sikkink 1999), presume the existence of NGOs that target states. NGOs reveal abuses, and states either deny them, explain them, or end their norms-violating behavior. NGOs socialize states to international norms through combative challenges, and we see them as successful when states accede to their demands. If states do adhere to norms, or if some rights are politically salient, they should also exhibit norms-abiding behavior in noncombative situations, in the absence of actors demanding that they change. This expectation comports with Krasner's classic definition: "[Norms are] standards of behavior defined in terms of rights and obligations" (Krasner 1983, 2).

Another way to observe whether human rights are politically salient, then, is to see whether states take the "lessons" offered them from human rights NGOs and their own international institutions and translate them into actions. The pattern of economic sanctions using human rights justifications reflects a different way to observe the internationalization of norms that scholars have theorized (Finnemore and Sikkink 1998). If states have internalized human rights, we should be able to see them used in contexts outside of human rights-specific law, or in instances in which NGOs name and shame state behavior. The effect of NGOs, in other words, can be observed indirectly through other types of political action by analyzing the justifications states use in the name of human rights. The pattern of economic sanctions in the twentieth century is just one way to test the effect of NGOs outside of a direct, confrontational relationship.

Conclusion

Norms are tricky to discern, particularly for human rights. So many organizations, individuals, and governments use the word with relative ease in contemporary politics that extricating "what counts" as human rights, and what ideas are more salient than others becomes a difficult task. I have suggested using the term *political salience* as an alternative and supplementary approach. In this chapter, I have provided three different approaches to assessing political salience. Despite the problems with using law as a guide for political salience, legalization is a tremendously helpful and desired process for many NGOs, which seek to use the power of legal status to shame states into compliance with human rights. This chapter does not seek to discount this. Far from being irrelevant, legalization is very much part of the NGO political process.

Because NGO seek legal tools, it is hard to assess the political salience of a given idea. The plethora of UN-level human rights agreements (there are currently nine) speaks to the breadth of human rights law, but it does not necessarily speak to the depth of the acceptance of that law. Studies have confirmed the skepticism with which some approach international law: human rights instruments do not seem to actually prevent human rights violations or improve human rights respect (Keith 1999; Hafner-Burton 2008). Thus, although NGOs have seen success in expanding legalistic protections for human rights, the actual implementation of that law has been less triumphant. Furthermore, the complexity of international human rights law, the scope of issues it covers, and the way it has expanded to include more recognition of group rights sends an unclear signal as to which rights matter more and which are politically salient.

Using ideas that are prominent in the NGO network itself to probe political salience serves as a problematic alternative to legalization. Despite the fact that NGO advocacy matters, and does have effects on other types of political actors, taking what they deem to be important is just one part of process. After all, NGOs' primary targets remain states. They want states to stop abusing rights and fulfill their obligations to respect them. Knowing what NGOs want, and understanding the underlying dynamics that surround how issues become salient among nonstate actors clarifies how and why certain rights receive support, but it does not actually address the effects of NGO efforts. Reporting does not automatically lead to state action. To understand the effect of NGO efforts, we must look to another facet of state behavior, beyond creating international law on human rights, that could be influenced by the rallying cry of transnational activists congregating around different rights.

Thus, economic sanctions, or more specifically, the reasoning behind the use of economic sanctions, provide a better method of assessing the political salience of rights. First, economic sanctions in the name of human rights are not voluntary for the targeted states, and implementing them does not necessarily yield a benefit for either state. Thus sanctions differ from the ratification of international human rights law, which in some cases lead directly to trade or foreign aid benefits. Second, because sanctions are costly on sanctioner states as well, the reasons used by states to implement them shows a commitment beyond the relatively costless signing of an international treaty. Finally, economic sanctions are not solely concerned with human rights. They are a form of statecraft states can levy for a wide variety of political concerns. NGOs rarely advocate for economic sanctions because of their humanitarian consequences. Thus, if the logic behind the five-stage spiral model (Risse, Ropp, and Sikkink 1999) is true, using human rights as a reason for economic sanctions is consistent with the last stage of human rights change: rule-consistent behavior. In the final stage, not only have states ratified relevant human rights treaties and applied those practices domestically (stage 4), but they behave in other areas consistently with human rights prescriptives. That is, not only do states talk human rights, they also take on political and economic risks in support of such ideas. Thus, we can see how the reasoning behind economic sanctions helps reveal the degree of political salience of a given human right.

One additional benefit of using economic sanctions as the lens of analysis for the political salience of human rights is that it signals the limited value of emphasizing the nature of issues as the primary reason for their success at the international level. The fact that states resort to using economic sanctions for such "basic" human rights as physical integrity and expression indicates that achieving protections for these rights is by no means given. Levying such a harsh punishment implies the salience of such issues at the *domestic* level such that leaders can levy sanctions for *international* political ends. States utilize NGO reporting to justify their use of economic sanctions, and NGOs provide the details with which states choose to act (or not). When states use economic sanctions, they use them knowing the costs—economic, humanitarian, political—and use them for reasons that they can justify for domestic and international audiences.

Physical integrity, expression, and democracy rights dominated the justifications for economic sanctions in the latter half of the twentieth century. This trend may hold for the new century as well, or it may not. What this trend indicates is the effect of NGO advocacy throughout the post–World War II period. As early efforts pushed physical integrity and expression rights in particular, states were compelled to respond to those demands. Over time, states began applying NGO lessons to their own interactions with other states. We should expect, then, that as other types of issues, namely economic, social, and cultural rights, become more politically salient, states will eventually use those rights as justifications for implementing economic sanctions against other states.

In the rest of this book, I will evaluate how we can think about political salience using the three perspectives introduced in this chapter as a way to compare NGOs based on their organizational structures. As will become evident, all three conceptions of political salience provide insight into how we can assess the value of human rights NGO work, which is an important theoretical and policy-related concern. The contribution of this book is to unite characteristics of NGOs' internal structures with their external influence on human rights politics.

2

The Importance of Organizational Structure

It is clear that NGOs do affect the political salience of rights in international politics; NGO persistence on various human rights issues since the end of the Cold War has raised the profile of certain rights over others. But why some organizations and not others? The answer in this chapter (and book) is the variation in the ways that NGOs distribute agenda-setting power. The theory is inspired by the efforts to seriously engage organizational structure and network theory within international relations. Given the spate of interest in organizations beyond the state that also have a stake in global politics (Avant, Finnemore, and Sell 2010; see Barnett and Finnemore 1999) and the power of networks (Keck and Sikkink 1998; Khagram, Riker, and Sikkink 2002), international relations theory benefits from a serious consideration of the variations among "like" political actors. By contrast, organization theory gains from a serious consideration of the implications of organizational survival. I am motivated by questions of why NGOs succeed in their advocacy as enabled by organizational characteristics that make them more likely to become politically salient actors in the first place. In the last chapter, I discussed the work of Bob, Carpenter, and Murdie and her collaborators, which firmly establishes that there are more and less important NGOs. Here, I offer an explanation as to *why* Amnesty and Human Rights Watch have claimed top status among human rights NGOs, and also, why their status may change over time.

The transnational dilemma motivates NGOs in two ways: how to secure support and funding in an increasingly globalized political world while also influencing international norms. A few NGOs in the past and today have figured out just how to be the focal point of the human rights debate. Even as the number of NGOs grows, only a few can command a global audience. This differential effect of NGOs, in which the political salience of some rights gains traction over others, is a direct consequence of their organizational structure, as defined by the centralization or decentralization of agenda-setting power. If political salience is defined as the degree to which there is international coordination around a political issue, "effective" NGOs are salient both as organizations, and by extension, create salience for at least part of their agendas. Organizational structure can increase or decrease the likelihood of an NGO's ability to create salience for itself and the rights it advocates.

In political science, we often overlook the organizational structure of entities we study in the excitement of explaining their relevance, their effects, or their prominence. And yet, sociologists and business scholars have revisited this question repeatedly over the years, giving us accounts that focus on choices made by individuals, their environments, or an interaction between the two. Extensive reviews of the literature summarize the tremendous scholarship on the topic of organizational choice and the effects of structure on organizational success, growth, death, and influence (Scott 1998, 2007). Unlike political scientists, scholars engaged in organization theories tend to focus on survival and not effect.

Pulling insights from the entirety of organization studies is a vast enterprise, and although the question of why organizations choose the structures they do is an interesting and relevant one, it is not directly related to the interest I have in the consequences of different organizational choices. It is my sense that early human rights and humanitarian NGOs chose structures largely for perceived expedience and/or the personal tastes of leaders. Consequently, this chapter largely delves into the consequences of organizational choices, rather than the motivation behind those choices. Much of the work evaluated here has success as its dependent variable. Success for an organization, of course, can be identified as survival (longevity) and/or effect.

As a caveat, most efforts in organization theory examine businesses. There is a substantial literature on the theoretical differences between nonprofit and for-profit entities (Hansmann 1980; James and Rose-Ackerman 1986; DiMaggio and Anheier 1990) and the structure of nonprofit organizations (Lindenberg and Bryant 2001; Young 1989, 1992). Notably, this research does not find too many notable differences between for-profit and nonprofit enterprises. Although there may be normative reasons to prefer one over the other, empirically, the distinction does not bear substantive differences.[1] Although I see the efficacy in pointing out how pursuing profit might be a different enterprise from pursuing donations and moral good, I follow the lead of some political scientists in deemphasizing the differentiation between NGOs and business (Sell and Prakash 2004), conceiving of NGOs as agents of collective action (Johnson and Prakash 2007). Thus many insights are in fact culled from the business-oriented literature. I assume that NGOs, while possibly motivated by calls for social justice or the respect for rights, nonetheless have some of the same kinds of goals that businesses might have: establishing a market niche, surviving in a world of competitors, and creating an enduring and recognizable brand.

Organization theory has much to add to our understanding of why some nonstate actors seem to be better at changing international norms and the political salience of human rights than many others. Nonetheless, where organization theory falls short and its spin-off, network theory, picks up is in identifying the informal aspects of interaction. Thus, beyond the formal rules of how things are done (which is the focus of organization theory), network theory gets us to other aspects of NGO structure, and perhaps puts us closer to what we think of when we contrast the corporate world from nonprofits. Network theory forms the basis of the critique in this book, but my argument is less of an application of network theory than an extension. I use the contributions of network theory to conceptualize how agenda-setting power might work through informal as well as formal channels in organizations.

This chapter proceeds first to outline why structure is an important variable to consider in evaluating the influence of NGOs. I review various alternative explanations, all of which offer good reasons for organizational salience but are all inextricably tied to the effects of organizational structure. I then elaborate on the mechanisms of agenda setting: proposal power, enforcement power, and implementation power, demonstrating how this book extends current organizational and network theories to produce an account for the political salience of transnational NGOs. I then show how other intuitive explanations, such as the quality of leadership and staff, the amount of and sources of funding, geographic location, and the nature of the issues an NGO advocates, although certainly also important to creating salience for NGOs and their campaigns, cannot be easily disentangled from the effects of organizational structure. Because agenda setting and implementation shape so much of what happens in an NGO, politically salient NGOs centralize agenda setting and decentralize agenda-implementation to become influential as political actors shaping the politics of international human rights.

Navigating the Transnational Dilemma: Differences in Organizational Structure

Scholars have noted both the great variety and explosion in the number of international NGOs as an international trend, particularly since the end of the Cold War (Smith, Pagnucco, and Romeril 1994; Keck and Sikkink 1998; Smith, Pagnucco, and Lopez 1998). Even though most accounts are optimistic about the effects of "global civil society" (Brysk 2002; Lipschutz 1996; Price 1998), others have cautioned that NGOs are simply responding to market conditions that facilitate their founding (Cooley and Ron 2002; Luong and Weinthal 1999). In fact, some find evidence that NGO efforts are often clustered where work is already being done by other actors and NGOs (Koch, Dreher, Nunnenkamp, and Thiele 2009). Nonetheless, it is incontrovertible that NGOs have helped promote human rights internationally, most notably through the promotion of law (Korey 1998; Sikkink 1993) or influencing how the UN defines human rights (Clark 2001; Clark, Friedman, and Hochstetler 1998; Gaer 1995). The success of human rights as discourse, for instance, can be seen in localized interpretation of international standards, as "nonhuman rights" campaigns adopt human rights language and tools (Goodale and Merry 2007). Nonetheless, very few of the rapidly proliferating NGOs receive global recognition of their political efforts (Boli and Thomas 1999), and only a few are recognizable household names.

Efforts to discover the key characteristics of success in an NGO have largely been descriptive (Lindenberg and Bryant 2001; Welch 2001), rather than a theoretical linking of how organizational structure influences the work of NGOs. As some have pointed out, the term *NGO* can mean any number of things—from community-based, local groups to transnational organizations split into country-level offices—but they are always non-profit organizations (Charnovitz 1996). But even among the most successful and the largest—that is, the household names—there is a great deal of variation in how they choose or have come to organize themselves.

What is it about some international NGOs that make them more successful than others? All transnational organizations, whether NGOs, multinational corporations, or intergovernmental organizations, face the fundamental struggle, what I call the "transnational dilemma," of striking a balance between centralization and decentralization. On the one hand, centralizing, or minimizing the number of participants that can influence the agenda makes for a more efficient model. The agenda for an NGO consists of decision-making on strategy, advocacy for topics, and implementation of key issues. On the other hand, decentralizing, or allowing for greater participation in agenda setting, can gain for an organization greater legitimacy, sensitivity to local dynamics, and organizational transformation. Too much centralization leads to stasis; too little of it leads to a lack of leadership. Similarly, too much decentralization can lead to an inability to hold parts of a transnational NGO accountable; too little can result in fading support or political irrelevance. All transnational NGOs must make decisions about the degree to which they centralize and decentralize core functions. This balancing act results in the NGO's organizational structure, or the way that agenda-setting power is distributed among the NGO's parts. The formula for how much agenda-setting power, and what aspects of agenda-setting power need to be centralized or decentralized might vary over time as international frameworks evolve. Those NGOs that successfully navigate the transnational dilemma have a far greater chance at landing their advocacy issues on the international stage.

The way NGOs find their sweet spot in organizational structure is similar to how groups in other fields face their own institutional obstacles. Part of the interest in balancing centralizing and decentralizing forces lies in disaggregating the notion of "authority" in organizations and understanding what positive and negative consequences arise from distributing some agenda-setting powers widely (Aghion and Tirole 1997). For corporations, organizational choice is fundamental to whether a business will survive expansion in the domestic market, and if truly successful, whether it is able to reach global customers. The recent interest in knowledge management, for example, demonstrates how businesses have started to ask themselves the same questions that the leaders of DuPont and General Motors did a century earlier (Chandler 1969)—how centralized should decisions be? Is the most effective way to organize employees in regionalized or programmatic groups, or should all decisions go through a central leadership structure?

One of the most successful historical social movements, the rise of state socialism and the Bolsheviks in Russia in 1917, can be looked at from an organizational perspective (Fitzpatrick 2008; Malia 1995; Pipes 1991). By adopting a centralized decision-making core and a Party presence at all local-level gatherings, the Bolsheviks were able to instill their system into broader Soviet society, essentially replacing all of the structure that had existed before the Russian Revolution. More important, the Bolsheviks infiltrated popular and community organizations, using local knowledge to their advantage to spread their version of communism.

Intergovernmental organizations have taken similar tactics. International financial institutions in recent years have adopted structures that can take into account ground-level variations when implementing policy. The World Bank, Asian Development Bank, and Inter-American Development Bank have all adopted programs that account for policy sequencing in development projects (Hausmann, Rodrik, and Velasco 2005). The move away from one-size-fits-all mentality of the Washington Consensus to one with an ability to account for local variation is reflective of a general change in the organizational structuring of economic development that allows for flexibility in implementation of an overall agenda. Across the spectra of major fields—business, politics, economics—leaders and analysts have begun questioning the organization of people into strict entities without organic, ground-up contributions.

In international relations, scholars of other subject areas, such as sovereignty (Cooley 2008) and nonstate violent resistance (Asal and Rethemeyer 2008; Sinno 2008) have examined the effect of structure on the capacity to control parts of an organization and the consequent effectiveness of different organizational forms. For human rights, as much as there has been theorizing about the normative differences between NGOs, scholarship has ignored the crucial question of structural variations between different organizations. Though some have pointed out how North-South linking in networks have often been rife with incompatibility issues, these insights have not been carried forward to a serious discussion about the effects of organizational variability. A recent study found that NGOs create political change when they were tied with localities and fostered political hubbub within communities (Brown, Brown, and Desposato 2008). If we think that NGOs have influence over the content and trajectory of human rights norms, and if we think that norms drive states to take on costly human rights behavior (Busby 2007; Hawkins 2004), the question of how structure makes some NGOs more powerful than others in their activities is an area in need of the theory discussed here.

Alternative Views

This discussion of organizational structure illustrates the unique properties of some organizations, but do these characteristics explain the greater salience of some organizations? A number of other factors—quality of leadership and staff, the amount of and sources of funding, geographic location, and the nature of the issues an NGO advocates—provide an intuitive basis by which to evaluate NGO salience. While these qualities certainly matter for the salience of NGOs and their advocacy, the outcomes that these alternative explanations produce are largely products of, or at least strongly influenced by, organizational structure. I review each of these arguments in turn to show how organizational structure actually informs many of these factors.

One reasonable inference from examining salient NGOs is that they must have all had competent staffs and extraordinary leadership. Clearly, successful organizations need accomplished individuals leading them and enough support to help them achieve their goals. Considering the importance of organizational structure does not preclude the critical role that leaders play in the life of organizations. However, it must be pointed out many of the NGOs detailed in this book all began with highly capable, perhaps even charismatic leaders in the classic Weberian sense: leading based on the strength of character, rather than the strengths of rules that legitimated their leadership. Henri Dunant, the founder of the International Committee of the Red Cross, was extremely gifted at publicizing his cause for more ethical treatment of soldiers on the battlefield but had no administrative capabilities. His role was diminished by the creation of rules that truncated his role and put agenda-setting power in the hands of a committee. Peter Benenson, well-known for his role as the founder of Amnesty, led the organization for many years on (at times) sheer will, persevering in pushing the rights of prisoners, even in the days of nearly no money and no formal office space. Eventually, Benenson was removed because his efforts nearly drove the organization into the ground, and it became evident that more institutionalization was necessary if the NGO would persist beyond its founder.

Leadership for both the ICRC and Amnesty played a significant role in putting the two organizations on the map and earning them their initial recognition in promoting humanitarian and human rights causes. However, leadership without rules could not endure in either case. The reorganization of agenda setting and implementation rules after the founding leadership shaped how the NGO would be able to come up with new causes to advocate, and in both cases, reformers hoped that the rules would capture the *je ne sais quoi* of the founders in a more systematic and less charismatic way. Therefore organizational structure is a way for NGOs to continue the enthusiasm of the early days without relying on personal leadership capabilities. Organizational structure also gives various staff functions; in the absence of defined roles, even the most capable staff would not necessarily be able to help an organization thrive.

A second argument might be that the more funding an NGO has, the better it will be able to use the funding to become prominent as an organization, thus making its advocacy agenda salient as well. The intuition is clear: rich NGOs can hire more staff, do more research, gain the ear of the media, and in fact, funding can be seen as a way that organizations can claim legitimacy. After all, how could an illegitimate NGO garner funding successfully? While money is certainly something that helps NGOs gain influence, it is not the only factor. In fact, money often comes after initial success. For many years, Amnesty struggled to keep its budget balanced, and until it figured out how to generate income without creating bastions of volunteers needing resources, Amnesty had continual financial worries.[2] In fact, both HRW and Amnesty became more financially secure after they had each established footholds in human rights politics, and the relationship between money and NGO success might run in both causal directions. Obviously, money matters, but it may not matter for achieving initial political salience, and in fact, political salience might be realized prior to funding success.

A third factor analysts have pointed to is the global North-South divide (Bandy and Smith 2005; Hertel 2006; Joachim 2003). NGOs with bases in the North are more likely to have access to international power centers, and thus can move policy more ably than those in far-flung locales in the South. Certainly, being in the global North provides a boost for human rights movements in terms of resources and access. Yet Northern NGOs are not unaware of the disparity between themselves and their colleagues in the developing world, and the shift to encompass more economic, social, and cultural rights since the end of the Cold War in part reflects this sensitivity (see Chong 2010). Furthermore, all of the NGOs in the book are definitely Northern. All of them have headquarters in the developed world, and even as many have reached quite extensively in the developing world, they are far from being an NGO from the global South. If we take critics' claims seriously about the disparity between North and South, then limiting the study to only Northern NGOs should give us a sense of why some NGOs make it and become so influential among NGOs worldwide.

It is a priori very difficult to determine what kinds of issues resonate internationally. Much of the success of an issue has as much to do with its nature as with the way NGOs frame it, as we see with HRW's attempts to pitch economic, social, and cultural rights into a similar frame that it uses for other kinds of rights (Roth 2004). One can imagine making the case that some issues certainly might more easily elicit sympathy than others. For instance, torture victims harness disgust far more readily than even civilians in wartime distress (Luban 2007). But what about issues such as economic inequality, or women's rights? NGOs must frame issues to create links to preexisting norms (Finnemore and Sikkink 1998; Keck and Sikkink 1998), often through a process of grafting new ideas to existing ones (Price 1995; Acharya 2004). How issues get framed is a function of organizational structure. Whether each country chapter follows a given formula for promoting an issue (e.g. women's rights), or whether each chapter can take into account national preferences in their positioning of the issue, is restricted by organizational structure. Having one agenda setter lessens the ambiguity of an NGO's framing of an issue, whereas more agenda setters lead to greater diversity among messages from the "same organization."

An important example from this book is the choice made by Oxfam to pursue rights-based advocacy. Many other development NGOs have taken up the rights-based approach as a defensive measure to protect their respective niches and to remain relevant (Nelson and Dorsey 2008). Issues that might be viewed as "traditional" development issues still inform Oxfam's work—poverty, inequality produced by trade—but these pursuits now require an "explicit reference to internationally recognized human rights standards and principles and to their expression in national constitutions and statutes" (Nelson and Dorsey 2008, 93). The way that rights-based approaches infuses the agenda of a particular international NGO, however, still depends on organizational structure. Whereas Oxfam is increasingly centralizing many of its agenda-setting functions, other organizations, such as Save the Children or ActionAid, remain decentralized in the distribution of agenda-setting powers (Nelson and Dorsey 2003, 2008, 111–115). This can be seen in how individual chapters can opt for or avoid using rights-based advocacy approaches.[3] Choosing the "right" issue depends in part on how an NGO frames it. Furthermore, given the variance in the distribution of agenda-setting power, some NGOs have an advantage in terms of spreading a coherent message about rights-based advocacy, for instance, over others.

Although each of the factors discussed above should, and do, influence the prominence of international NGOs, the argument here is that none of them preclude, and in fact, many of them necessitate, the explanatory power that an analysis of organizational structure provides. For some factors, such as funding or location, organizational structure is an antecedent consideration: these are choices constrained by agenda setting and implementation power. For the case of leadership, it is true that strong leadership can precede organizational structure, but rarely is organizational structure irrelevant, especially in the aftermath of charismatic leadership. Finally, in the case of an issue driving the salience of a cause, I would caution putting the proverbial cart before the horse. After all, the issues that are selected and framed are mediated through organizational structure. How constituent parts of an NGO can take on new topics, which parts of the NGO implement the agenda, and how ideas get packaged and distributed for public consumption are all key choices made by international NGOs, but the way they make those choices are clearly structured by the formal and informal distribution of agenda-setting power. Thus, to understand NGOs and their salience, we need to seriously analyze their structures, using tools from organization and network theories.

Organization Theory

Organization theory encompasses a large, interdisciplinary field and has spawned a vast variety of studies that have explored the relationship between environment and organization. Its major strength is the consistency of its findings (Haveman 2000). Many organization theorists are interested in the question of efficacy of organizations, whether this means profitability, influence, or survival. For contemporary studies of international NGOs, organization theory offers a sense of how to begin, but is inadequate when it comes to accounting for informal relationships. Although there are many explanations available from this work, the bottom line about organization theory is not what it tells us, but what is missing: a consideration of informal as well as formal rules and a good explanation for how the internal worlds of organizations have consequences for their external political power.

The most relevant studies for this book fall roughly into two camps: those who are concerned with organizational survival and those who are concerned with why an organization chooses (or comes to) the organizational structure it does. Organization theory is therefore quite helpful in understanding the way that institutions order themselves without distinguishing the consequences of different types of ordering. The dominant metaphors, in other words, have been organizations as machines and organizations as organisms (Morgan 2006). Very bluntly stated, organization theorists have focused on either the organization as a phenomenon to be studied as one of a management problem in getting the structure "right" (Chandler 1969; 1981; Taylor 1911) or they have focused on the environments around organizations (Freeman and Hannan 1989; Hannan and Freeman 1977, 1988; Hannan, Pólos, and Carroll 2007; Singh and Lumsden 1990). Theories have modeled the relationship between environment factors and the capacity of certain organizational forms to cope with changes in those environments through the delegation of power to department managers (Siggelkow and Rivkin 2005) or how environments differentially affect specialists versus generalists ("niche") (Freeman and Hannan 1983). Most arguments assume long timelines in terms of environmental and organizational change, but shifts may occur suddenly, challenging structural and cultural pliability of firms (Tushman, Newman, and Romanelli 1986; Tushman and O'Reilly III 1996). Some have even posited a life cycle of organizational form, whereby firms might transition from form to form as they mature (Harris and Raviv 2002).

In terms of cross-fertilization, some have looked at the reaction of the organization to external changes, that is, how agency interacts with environment (Selznick 1984; Thompson 2003; Weber 1978). Aldrich notably developed a three-stage model—variation, selection, and retention—that explains not just the effect of environment on organizational survival, but also how organizations might shape their environments (Aldrich 1979). Contingency theory is an example of this type of theorization, which conceptualizes the interaction of structure and environment, thereby supplanting the organization-environment distinction. That is, organizations will seek structures that work for their given environments (Donaldson 2001; Lawrence and Lorsch 1967). Transaction cost theories are another example, in which rational organizations pick hierarchy to account for the tendency for defection, or the costliness of multiple renegotiating transactions in the context of a given environment (Coase 1937; Williamson 1983). Why some structural characteristics seem effective whereas others do not work, therefore, is a function of fit with the external environment. Many of the above works observed corporations or organizations that provide a tangible product (dynamite, health care, etc.).

One of the key notions to emerge from the study of organizations and their environments is the organizational niche, which has been defined as "all those combinations of resource levels at which the population can survive and reproduce itself" (Hannan and Freeman 1977, 947). Determining an organization's niche relies on an analysis of both environmental qualities (competitors, resources) and the characteristics of the organization (Hannan, Carroll, and Polos 2003). Longitudinal research indicates that in industries in which scale matters for survival and success, the few firms that become dominant tend to also expand their niches (Dobrev, Kim, and Carroll 2002, 234). Studies of voluntary organizations have found that because of the narrowness of their audiences, they tend to be homogenous, and their membership can vary depending on the degree of niche overlap between competing organizations (Popielarz and McPherson 1995). The tendency toward homophily (McPherson and Rotolo 1996; McPherson, Smith-Lovin, and Cook 2001), or flocking with others like oneself, can be countered with strategic decisions.

Transnationalism is one such decision organizations might pursue to increase heterogeneity. A growing awareness about the effects of globalization gripped organization theory in the 1990s, reenergizing the discussion of intangible benefits provided by firms. Responding to the new pathways of innovation and competition opened up by technological proliferation, scholars stressed the importance of knowledge within firms to reduce complexity and create comparative advantages for firms (Leonard-Barton 1998). The emphasis shifted from one based on hard outcomes to one that placed an emphasis on the benefits of the process of acquiring knowledge, as a number of Japanese academics introduced notions from manufacturing in their home country to consider the implications for industry in an information economy (Nonaka 1991; Nonaka and Takeuchi 1995). Business became not just a for-profit enterprise, but engaged in the process of knowledge creation (Nonaka and Toyama 2007), and thus, scholars posited, firms should move to "create, safeguard, and put to use a wide range of knowledge assets" (Hasanali 2004, 57). As such, globalized corporations need to incorporate local knowledge or cultural norms (Short 2004) into their global strategies rather than push a globalized vision onto localities (Gilbert 2007).

Globalization, however, requires the ability for firms to balance two competing needs: centralized decision-making and decentralized markets. Because they are moving into different markets and cultures, firms need to consider carefully what transnational strategy they choose to adopt. Bartlett and Ghoshal describe three different structures that corporations might adopt in managing their resources across transnational borders: the multinational, international, and global organization models (Bartlett and Ghoshal 1991, 50–52). These models vary in terms of how they consider local input, the management of personnel, and how they distribute assets. Global organizations run on a centralized model of maintaining key assets in one place, funneling profits back to a headquarters, viewing presence in other countries as a pipeline to access global markets; the multinational model, on the other hand, accommodates much more independence in

terms of the branches on the ground, the informality of management relationships, and the location of assets in multiple locations. This framework
echoes findings that underscore the benefits of taking into account a diverse set of perspectives before enforceable decisions are made (Rivkin and
Siggelkow 2003). Put succinctly, the lesson from corporate organization
theory is that the transnational dilemma requires input from a wide range
of sources before agendas are set and implemented.

What insights might the aforementioned scholarship on the *for-profit*
industry have on NGOs, which are defined as nonprofits? NGOs are often
viewed as value-driven actors that lack a material profit motive.[4] Organization theory has also considered entities that do not produce market
goods. Many prominent theories evaluate the role of organizations in
producing cultural or institutional products, or intangibles that cannot
be measured in quite the same straightforward way (Berger and Luckmann 1967; DiMaggio and Powell 1983; Meyer and Rowan 1977; Powell
and DiMaggio 1991; Scott 2007). Organizational structures are adopted
not because they are more efficient, as earlier theorists concerned with organizational choice argued. Instead, the structure may be seen to be more
legitimate for a particular type of organization, becoming institutionalized
via coercive, mimetic, or normative mechanisms (DiMaggio and Powell
1983). A similar observation has been made about norm change more generally (Schelling 2006), as changes occur when more and more agents view
a certain way of doing things as correct until the perspective cascades. For
example, NGOs concerned with social change shifted from philanthropic
and extensions of for-profit enterprises to nonprofit models in an effort to
seem more legitimately committed to a cause.

The study of nonprofits has largely taken the frames laid by corporate
theories. Scholars have looked at differences between international and national nonprofits, finding that their structures are analogous (Young 1989;
Zald and Denton 1963). Increasing professionalization in nonprofits in the
United States, for example, has resulted in the transformation of a largely voluntary sector into one with rationalized practices and the capacity to provide
routinized employment for those seeking to "do good" (Hwang and Powell 2009). Both international and large national NGOs with many branches
tend to adopt a federated structure, in which autonomous local units operate with direction from a central office (Hudson and Bielefeld 1997; Provan
1983; Young 1992). Very few studies systematically compare international
NGOs working on a particular issue, but an investigation of the major

development and relief organizations confirmed many of the earlier studies' conclusions (Lindenberg and Bryant 2001). In their work, Lindenberg and Bryant (2001) formulate a typology of structures, in which they place various international NGOs and track changes over time. They find that many international NGOs adopt middling structures (not too centralized, but not too loose either) through an evaluation of formal rules and operations. Studies of international or domestic NGOs, however, do not adequately capture the interdependence of international NGOs, whose struggles over the right structure and authority between sections falls outside of a strict typology based on formal rules. Many international NGOs are actually also the product of bargaining between formerly independent NGOs, and thus informal understandings should inform our analysis. Informal decision making affects how advocacy NGOs create and pursue their principles politically. Both formal and informal relationships can create interdependence.

While organization theory can tell us quite a bit about what seems to work for firm survival and explicates quite a bit about how environment shapes firm decisions and vice versa, it does not do as adequate of a job in discussing two interrelated factors that matter for managing the transnational dilemma. The first is the importance of informal ties *within* organizations. Formal and informal structures both matter (Selznick 1996); the formality of structures and their permanence is often mythologized (Meyer and Rowan 1977). The second is the notion of interdependence of parts within organizations, especially in conceptualizing power as a consequence of informal exchanges. Network theory, discussed below, is a helpful beginning for knitting power to formal and informal structures, but as we will see, is an approach limited by its extensive data thresholds and ambiguity in the definition of "network" as form, method, and process. Nonetheless, it provides a lens through which we can view the interconnections between parts of an organization, and why the distribution of agenda-setting power has such important consequences for the ultimate influence of an NGO on international norms.

Network Theory

Network theory provides an avenue by which we can examine the notion of centrality, through an analysis of the relationships between actors. Networks have become a topic of scholarly and general interest as notions of interdependence and interconnectivity have grown in influence (see for instance Christakis and Fowler 2009). Network analysis, correspondingly, starts from the insight that actors are defined in terms of interdependence and that relations makes network analysis unique (Wasserman and Faust 1994).[5] Networks can be evaluated as distinct objects or used as a method of analysis (Dicken, Kelly, Olds, and Yueng 2001; Hafner-Burton, Kahler, and Montgomery 2009; Thompson 2003, 6). These two approaches are complementary, and together produce a range of implications for the way to understand political relationships and the consequences of those relationships.

Definitions of networks range from typologies to very general definitions, which simply state that networks are created when actors, whether individuals or organizations, interact (Salancik 1995). Network theory begins from the assumption that structures shape social (and political) interactions and are not inherent characteristics of the actors involved (Wellman 1983, 156–57). The insights of network theory expand the basic tenets of organization theory and help explain why some human rights NGOs have built better networks to facilitate international advocacy. In particular, the notion of structural centrality highlights how formal and informal relationships between networks have important implications for organizations. Organizational structure affects how information moves within and outside of networks.

At a basic level, all networks are composed of actors, called nodes, whose connections to one another are variously called links, edges, ties, or vertices. Any two nodes linked directly together are called adjacent. Nodes are "visible" when they are more prominent than others in a network, which means they are more involved (Wasserman and Faust 1994: 172–73). One of the ways that nodes can be visible is by being central.

Centrality of various nodes is one of the most measured and most significant measures in social network analysis (Everett and Borgatti 2006). Since his seminal paper, Freeman's (1978) three criteria have been the mainstay for succeeding scholars who have refined his concepts for measuring centrality.[6] These three centrality measures assess distance (closeness), adjacency (degree), and whether a relationship between two nodes must go through another (betweenness) (Freeman 1978). A network characterized by short paths between all of the nodes is closer and thus more centralized. Ideally, a centralized network has a node with a high degree, sits between all or most of the paths between nodes, and has short connections between its various nodes. A decentralized network is the opposite:

nodes with low degree scores, little betweenness, and long links between all of the various nodes.

One of the pitfalls of using network theory in international relations is the inappropriateness or incommensurability of available measures (Hafner-Burton, Kahler, and Montgomery 2009). The notion of a link between two nodes, for instance, can mean anything from trade agreements, mutual membership in intergovernmental organizations, or diplomatic relations. Even identifying these links, however, often tells us very little about the strength or direction of that relationship, and thus, what the purpose of the connection is, and the benefits of networking to one another. What is intended to be a dynamic way of thinking about relationships can often be reduced to static representations of "networking"—lists that document linkages without a theoretical framework for assessing the content of those links. Furthermore, network scholars tend to concentrate on methodological and measurement issues, as the number of recent textbooks on the subject attest (Carrington, Scott, and Wasserman 2005; Jackson 2008; Knoke 1994; Knoke and Yang 2007; Newman 2010; Scott 2000; Wasserman and Faust 1994), rather than the substantive implications of network analysis to advance the field (Hafner-Burton, Kahler, and Montgomery 2009).

Defining where networks begin and end and how we detect networks in an important pursuit (Marsden 1990). The importance of network analysis for international relations, however, is the implication of differences in network structure, including the notion of centrality and its implications, and the way that networks can measure both formal relationships (rule-bound) and informal relationships (ad hoc or de facto). We need to come back to the original intentions of network analysis intervention, which is to help us understand the effects of interdependence and the implications of the variations in structure (Emirbayer and Goodwin 1994; Wellman 1983). Thus I take network theory as the starting point to remedy the focus on formal aspects of organizations in organization theory and to provide a way to talk about centrality.

Applying Network Theory to Organizations

The publication of two generally accessible texts, Barabási (2002) and Watts (2004), underscored the ubiquity of a certain type of network, called scale-free networks, in social and political change. Scale-free networks are networks that follow a power law distribution, that is, very few nodes link to a large number of nodes, whereas a great number of the nodes in the network link to very few others (e.g., airline hubs).[7] In scale-free networks, very few nodes can command a great deal of attention (central nodes), whereas less-well-connected nodes cannot influence as many others simply from a structural point of view. Networks can be hierarchies too.

Watts and Barabasi stand in stark contrast to other popular constructs of networks. Since 9/11, many have claimed that the relatively flat structure (its network) of al-Qaeda led to the destructive attacks on the United States in 2001.[8] Nonetheless, the evidence shows that any concerted attack by nonstate actors requires central coordination (Eilstrup-Sangiovanni and Jones 2008). A pervasive sense of the power of decentralization, however, runs into everyday constructs of what benefits decentralized networks might bring for political, social, and economic ends (Brafman and Beckstrom 2006). Say "network" and many think that that implies horizontal, rather than vertical, patterns of association. Much existing scholarship posits the "flatness," reciprocity, trust, and spontaneity of networks as alternatives to hierarchical and stodgy firms (Powell 1990; Burt 1995; Podolny and Page 1998; Vertovec 1999; Castells 2000). These perspectives view random distributions and perhaps even "small world" distributions as the emblematic and ideal network formations. In a random distribution (e.g., the national highway system), nodes are connected by roughly the same number of linkages, forming a latticelike structure or grid. In a "small world" distribution, nodes are connected in clusters; only one of the nodes within each cluster has links to other clusters. This is the phenomenon of running into friends of friends at parties where guests remark "what a small world" it is.[9]

Claiming that networks are flat, however, misses both the structural diversity of, and the importance of, structure on effecting political outcomes. Not all networks are flat, just as not all firms are necessarily hierarchical. Over time, moreover, networks may become more set in their ways as they find that certain ways of doing things yield desired results. Networks, as such, like firms, may change over time to adjust to changing environments, or they may struggle with adapting to new challenges. The ability of networks to react to new stimuli and situations is in large part determined by network structure. Unlike small world and distributed networks, scale-free networks allow their central nodes to limit access to information, influence, or other nodes, all mitigated by differential positions within the network.

The truth is, in both "real life" and in terms of politics, scale-free networks offer much more than their counterparts. Scale-free networks centralize the distribution of links. Because all links go to it, central nodes can exert quite a bit of power over agenda setting. Central nodes have access to information first and are more likely to be early adopters of new ideas and technologies (Powell, Koput, and Smith-Doerr 1996). This fact has many advantages but also one great disadvantage. A scale-free network is both most powerful at its central node, and most vulnerable.[10] In terms of political mobilization and advocacy, building a scale-free network requires low levels of investment for potentially large return. Organized around a central actor, scale-free networks can help transmit ideas widely while limiting the ability of those in the periphery (i.e. noncentral nodes) to dilute or alter the overall agenda. For agents of social and political change whose purpose is to generate attention and visibility, scale-free networks represent an ideal functional form for generating a coherent agenda and fomenting widespread adherence to that agenda.

Scale-free networks form under two conditions: low barriers to entry and preferential attachment (Barabási 2002). Low barriers mean that there are either no or low prerequisites to join the network, in other words, support of human rights versus having expertise in international law. Preferential attachment means that newcomers to the network will forge links with central nodes, rather than other nodes. Central nodes create value for the rest of the network by setting the agenda. They are powerful in the sense they control which principles are salient, de facto silencing others (Schattschneider 1960; Bachrach and Baratz 1970). Agenda setting is not the same as persuasion, which involves convincing others of the rightness of one's point of view. In networks, agenda setting operates to truncate the menu of principles from which to choose (proposal power); to find other principles to support, nodes may exit the network but are unlikely to change the central node's agenda without large-scale collective action (enforcement power).

For the most part, network theory has not bothered to examine closely the effects of different network structures on power, in large part because political science has only recently begun to consider the tractability of its insights. Recent, notable exceptions include attempts to model the effects of new entrants into the life sciences field (Powell, White, Koput, and Owen-Smith 2005) and state membership in intergovernmental organizations (Hafner-Burton and Montgomery 2006), to understand how some NGOs prevent advocacy topics from entering the international agenda (Carpenter 2010, 2011), and to predict conflict in international relations (Maoz 2006; Maoz, Kuperman, Terris, and Talmud 2006).

Many international human rights NGOs are more appropriately thought about as networks with both formal and informal aspects, rather than more cohesive organizations. This is true of corporations that adopt more decentralized mechanisms of agenda setting and distribution as well, following Bartlett and Ghoshal's (1991) conception of multinational networks, where each branch responds more to local conditions than to some generalized global plan distributed from headquarters. But thinking about networks also requires a shift in mindset from thinking about different organizational forms as discrete categories. Organizational forms run along a continuum of more to less centralized, and the tools provided by organization and network theories give us with a kit with which to discern and evaluate variations in organizational structure.

In many contexts, we observe the importance of centrality. Network analysis gives us a vocabulary with which to explore the nuances of centrality that allows us to focus on both formal and informal rules. I use the formal rules of an organization to understand basic agenda-setting relationships, but then I examine how other factors that are relatively informal actually explain agenda setting and agenda-implementation outcomes. We know for a fact that organizational flowcharts represent an ideal in management—knowing the formal rules of accountability can only get us so far. Formality, on the other hand, provides an easy metric by which to "count" ties, but on the other hand, tells us only part of the story of how organizations function. People interact with others in way that cannot be captured by boxes and arrows. I am interested in exploring how informal links and formal relationships provide a more complete understanding of how the distribution of agenda-setting powers determines the political salience of NGOs and their human rights interests. Network theory's basic insights provide a method to consider how we can think about which tasks an international NGO might want to centralize or decentralize, and the implications of those structural decisions on the efficacy of the NGO in making human rights politically salient.

Agenda setting is what advocacy NGOs do. Without the ability to change international discourse on human rights, NGOs would lose their raison d'être. Yet not all NGOs agenda-set in equally effective or prominent ways. Using network analysis in particular for international NGOs is appropriate because many of them actually resemble transnational networks. They tend to be more informal than their logos and slogans might suggest. Different national sections may have opposing views of a situation or a campaign that have resonance with the rest of the organization. This dissent may have real effects on the ability for an international NGO to advocate on an issue. Thus, looking at the relationships between the national sections, both formal and informal, can reveal the dynamics involved in creating norms from shared principles within organizations.

Network analysis on its own, however, does not complete the picture. Why NGOs have begun to move toward a more "scale-free" structure that centralizes certain aspects of agenda setting and decentralizes implementation is another puzzle this book addresses. Visions of a coming democratization of power, while cautiously optimistic (Florini 2000), leave out the fact that even if NGOs are poised to take over some of the tasks that, since the early twentieth century, have gone to states, there will be some that will be much more likely to be picked for these duties than others. In recent years, international human rights NGOs have faced an onslaught of competition as funding for global civil society has increased. HRW has, for example, has been selected by George Soros to receive $100 million, in part to build support for human rights outside of North America and Europe.[11] Competition in the form of the use of rights language by "non-human rights" NGOs—e.g. social justice, humanitarian aid—also contribute to shaping the definition of human rights (Chong 2010) but might limit the effect of purely advocacy oriented, human rights only NGOs. What separates advocacy NGOs from one another, and how does organizational structure play into these distinctions? Organization theory tells us that any group in any field competes with others for survival and in building their respective niches. The expansion of these niches grows as NGOs pursue transnational advocacy strategies, but at the same time, NGOs need to maintain a centralized agenda in order to be successful at securing political change.

Building a Better Organization for Advocacy

Organizational structure can be deliberate or incidental, but initial choices are sticky. Centralizing agenda-setting power has advantages. It allows a few actors, or perhaps one agent, to set the parameters of advocacy and provide a clear set of advocacy issues for anyone who might have interest in joining an organization. Centralized agenda-setting powers also makes the NGO more efficient by cutting out potential veto players. However, centralizing agenda setting also has the effect of stifling creativity, or perhaps disallowing dissent from a variety of perspectives. Local initiatives, which may add nuance to an overall objective, might be silenced. Only one viewpoint has legitimacy, and thus centralized agenda setting might dissuade new joiners to an NGO. There are trade-offs to allowing only a few to provide the advocacy direction to the network of activists. Although centralized agenda setting is efficient and results in clear directives for others to follow, it also generates a unilateral view that potential supporters might find unacceptable and stifling.

Having some aspect of decentralization gives international NGOs legitimacy in domestic contexts. While advocating for universal human rights is necessarily abstract and divorced from "reality," practically speaking, advocates still need to garner support from individuals living in states, to whom human rights might speak for other types of issues they encounter locally. On-the-ground advocacy creates support, and that support translates into international political power in terms of funding, people to assign campaign work to, and a legitimacy of having adherents in many places besides where the headquarters is located.

Scale-free networks occupy a distinct organization niche; they also provide a useful metaphor to consider NGO structures. These types of networks allow them to be both centralized in proposal power, enforcement power, and control of information while decentralized in implementation of that agenda. Similarly, others have identified characteristics of firms that resemble the structure of scale-free networks: wide reach, but a centralized power to make decisions that stick. The choice for centralization-decentralization in any organization is about balance and desired outcome. As Bartlett and Ghoshal put it: "The central process is usually associated with...[the mentality] which sees diversity...as an inconvenience whose effects must be minimized.... The local innovation process...sees conformity to local needs as the unavoidable price of admission to the market" (Bartlett and Ghoshal 1991, 116). They also point out, however, the move toward balancing these centralizing and decentralizing tendencies, finding ways to leverage local contributions at the global level and use the benefits of coordination for corporate gain (Bartlett and Ghoshal 1991, 115–133). This they term *transnational innovation processes.*

For advocacy NGOs working on international standards, a scale-free-like structure, or one that uses transnational innovation processes, is one that accommodates transnational differences while preventing alternatives to the agenda set by the designated actors. Because their product is ideational and not tangible like a washing machine or baby formula, the emphasis on the same advocacy messages across borders is ever more important. Everyone's conception of torture or political dissident needs to be the same. However, the implementation of those ideas must oblige local differences if the ideas are ever to gain traction in domestic politics.[12] The following three mechanisms of agenda setting within organizations—proposal power, enforcement power, and implementation power—provide the key for understanding why organizational structures that employ centralized agenda setting and decentralized agenda-implementation techniques tend to fare better in affecting the political salience of human rights norms. These types of organizations share some of the characteristics of scale-free networks: low barriers to entry, expansive membership at the periphery, which is all linked back to a central actor(s).

There are two important notes of caution. First, centrality is a continuum, rather than a state of absolute being. Therefore, international NGOs can be more or less centralized networks of advocates, according to the agenda-setting criteria underlined here. Centrality (or decentrality) is always relative. Second, centrality can be thought of in terms of persons, but more often, should be thought of in terms of offices or positions, as international NGOs tend to be highly professionalized. Below, I outline the process by which NGOs translate benefits of scale-free network structure into an advantage in international human rights politics. Those organizations whose internal structures are most productive for creating norms through their advocacy will be centralized in agenda-setting powers, but also be decentralized in implementation.

Proposal Power

The organizational structure of NGOs creates proposal power for some actors and not others. Proposal power is the ability to create agenda items. In the study of the US Congress, this is referred to as positive agenda-setting power (Cox and McCubbins 1993, 2005). This is contrasted with the ability to veto, or block policies in the legislative houses. The more diffuse proposal power is in a network (i.e., the more actors or nodes have the ability to raise agenda items), the less centralized it is. Conversely, when organizations limit the power of actors, whether collective or individual, to bring items up for consideration in decision-making forums, the more centralized agenda-setting power is.

When proposal power is limited to one or a few actors within an organization, these few can suggest changes for the rest of the organization to approve or disprove. The power of agenda setting lies in determining what goes up for consideration, and also who can block ideas from taking hold (veto power). In other words, the content of proposals is just as contentious of a situation as actually agreeing to proposals (Kingdon 2002). If few actors can suggest agenda items, those actors will be able to shape the direction of the rest of the organization by truncating the alternatives. More concretely, if something never appears for consideration, it cannot be part of the agenda for the NGO.

Proposal power literally allows actors to prevent an item from reaching the agenda. Unlike a veto, therefore, proposal power is more subtle in the sense that things get taken off of the agenda before it goes to a broader audience of decision-makers. Thus the fewer actors who have this capability, the more centralized agenda-setting power is. The more dispersed this power, the more actors can propose alternatives for consideration, and the more decentralized an organization is. Centralizing agenda-setting powers allow for quick changes in the direction of an NGO's strategies and advocacy scope at the same time, reflecting the capacity of a few nodes to dominate the rest of the network's principles. However, centralization also tends to eliminate contention, and by extension, representativeness. The trade-off, therefore, for smoother functioning and fewer debates simultaneously removes dissent and opportunities for changing the direction of a network.

The ability to determine the frame of particular human rights abuse, and how the NGO plans to pursue the issue internationally, is also part of proposal power. Information is paramount in human rights NGOs. After all, they are engaged in the business of providing an alternative account regarding the adherence of states to international principles and norms. Information is the value added by NGOs, and as such, they work to ensure the accuracy and speed of their reporting. The framing of the issue changes the perception of its importance (Gamson and Meyer 1996; Nelson and Oxley 1999; Druckman 2001). Maintaining control around the frame is paramount for an advocacy NGO working to create international norms. Human rights violations happen; if one was truly looking, states of all types have transgressed any number of rights defined by international law. The trick, then, is to choose which of those violations to highlight— what principles of human rights to which states have agreed are the most central? What are the rights that states and individuals should care most about protecting? Defining this through their reporting and advocacy is the task of human rights NGOs. What an NGO advocates, and how it goes about doing so changes the way policymakers and individuals, supporters and opponents, think about human rights alike.

Centralizing agenda-setting power restricts the number of proposers. De facto, this leads to control of the overall message, or universe of messages, from which an NGO's leadership will select. Centralizing agenda setting can eliminate principles before they get proposed to the network more broadly. That is, even if there might exist a multiplicity of ideas, a centralized actor(s) can eliminate some principles from consideration altogether. At the same time, because of the centralization of proposal power, these centralized actors are able to disseminate their own ideas as definitive and set the agenda for the rest of the members of the organization.

Enforcement Power

Organizational structure also affects who can say no, or veto, a decision made within an international NGO. What I call enforcement power is the ability to veto proposals once they are on the agenda *and* to ensure that those vetoes are followed. Borrowing from the literature on US presidential power, vetoes can affect proposals in three different ways (Cameron 2000). First, vetoes can be used to kill bills, or proposals in the case of NGOs. Second, the threat of a veto may push actors to change their proposals so as to be "veto-proof." Third, vetoers can force proposers to change the proposal once it has been vetoed, promising to support the idea if the right concessions are made. We can figure out the ability for policy to change by looking at the number of veto players in any given political institution (Tsebelis 2002). Veto players are the actors whose approval must be garnered in order to change a given policy, which Tsebelis differentiates from proposers (he calls those agenda setters) (see (Tsebelis 2002, 2). These insights can be applied to the study of NGOs.

Organizations that have many vetoers are decentralized relative to those with few or even one vetoer. Organizations with many veto players do not have the luxury of deferring to one or a few decision-makers; they must conciliate multiple parties, which leads to few changes in the status quo or many concessions in order to fulfill the desires of all of those who could possible veto. The threat of a veto can similarly encourage proposers to change their original idea so as to be more inclusive or less strident. The more concentrated veto power is, the fewer the veto players. Having concentration of veto power means having to make fewer concessions, but it also means that the decisions taken by a network of activists may not be as representative of the international nature of NGO that it could be. At the same time, concentrating veto power allows an NGO to move quicker.

Veto power is less useful if it does not come with the ability to enforce. Thus I have moved from a conception of vetoing to one of enforcement. To have enforcement power means that actors must not only be able to block an agenda item, but to ensure that others cannot go ahead with it in spite of the veto. For governments with institutionalized police power and the recognized ability to enforce decisions, this is less of a concern, and therefore plays a minor role in the influential arguments on veto power. For an international NGO, however, the capability to make sure that vetoes do not continue as policy for other parts of the network is not a given, and in fact, is not always part and parcel with veto power. International NGOs with independent national sections can come to an agreement not to go forward with a particular message or advocacy perspective, but no part of the network can actually prevent an enterprising (or defiant) national section from pursuing a campaign. One of the cases from this book, Médecins sans Frontières, has struggled with precisely this point: the notable case in the mid-1990s of two MSF sections departing Zairean refugee camps despite the veto of a third created huge rifts in the organization. To be meaningful, veto power has to be enforceable. Different parts of the network, including the central node, need to be able to ensure collective agreements and hold others accountable when vetoes are given for changes. Though this intuition is straightforward, it is not always possible.

Enforcement power is determined by organizational structure. Centralizing enforcement power means that decisions go through the limited members of an organization, and therefore those members can veto proposals. Adopting a scale-free network structure creates the optimal conditions for the enforcement of vetoes, particularly if resources must travel through the central node before being redistributed to the rest of the network. If nodes choose to go it alone in spite of opposition by veto players, central actors can pull financial or human resources, or can denounce or even exile national sections. This is the ultimate enforcement capacity. However, in less punitive ways, central actors can regulate the enforcement of vetoes by shunning certain parts of the organization, or denying them access to information if parts of the network choose to ignore the veto of the rest. The more actors who have veto power, the more dispersed but the harder to enforce disapproval. Having a few vetoers with the power to enforce characterizes the centralization of agenda-setting power in an NGO.

Implementation

After the principles and strategies of a network are established, NGOs need to go about making things happen according to their agendas. Unlike the other criteria outlined above, implementation tells us about changing hearts and minds. More centralization of the implementation of tasks is actually counterproductive to an effective international NGO. The strength of a transnational network of advocates is the locality of their experiences, and their ability to support the international NGO's efforts domestically. Advocates can lobby their government leaders directly, stage petitions and protests, or launch campaigns with a more homegrown tilt. The largest international NGOs capitalize on the fact that they have access to local politics and governments precisely because they have members from many countries. This logic reflects the finding that successful transnational advocacy requires the cooperation of domestic elites and NGOs (Burgerman 2001; Risse 2000b).

As such, decentralization of implementation, or allowing for local and grassroots level advocacy to happen, triggers the adoption of an NGO's principles more effectively than just concentrating on top-level politics, such as the UN or state levels. A decentralized execution mechanism is actually more effective than a centralized procedure. This finding is analogous to Chandler's 1969) argument about unitary versus multidivisional structures.[13] Chandler finds in his examination of major American corporations of the early twentieth century that many of them switched to the more decentralized multidivisional structure, where a central office delegates to divisional offices (based on region, function, or product). The divisional offices all have their own respective departments for product creation, marketing, finance, and so on. Each of these divisional offices executes according to the general plan given by the central office, but each division leader is responsible for the outcomes in her sector. As corporations diversify their investments in the market, there is a need to decentralize operations to accommodate the increasing demands for coordination and planning that, in a centralized, unitary organization, would be handled by a central office.

Correspondingly, in international advocacy, decentralization at the implementation or execution stage of advocacy allows for an NGO to better tailor messages to different domestic contexts. Lobbying at the international level, whether at intergovernmental organizations or before the media requires one set of strengths—a unified set of principles and a consistent set of strategies to convince international diplomats, journalists, and state leaders of the importance of a particular set of human rights. At the domestic and local levels, many international NGOs struggle because they do not have an indigenous base from which to lobby legislators and lower-levels of government. Their ideas may not take hold locally because of a lack of representation in-country. Those NGOs that have a grassroots-level capacity rely on this network to work in communities and in governments to advocate for the principles of the organization.

A scale-free network model helps us understand how grassroots implementation can be achieved quickly and across borders. Because of preferential attachment and low barriers to entry, scale-free networks are likely to form in such a way so that agenda control is maximized through the centralization of proposal, enforcement, and information while taking advantage of the large number of members that they are likely to attract. Scale-free networks centralize the agenda-setting and informational capacities of organizations without losing the crucial advantage of having decentralized implementation via individual members based around the world. Using a model from the firms literature, we would expect that organizations would want to be able to capitalize on its reach in relevant markets to attain the most profits or come to the right answers about knowledge management (Bartlett and Ghoshal 1991; Rivkin and Siggelkow 2003). Centralizing the other mechanisms—proposal and enforcement powers—enables organizations to limit access to the agenda, while allowing for innovation at the margins in different social, political, and cultural contexts.

Conclusion

In reality, very few NGOs map perfectly onto the ideal types discussed here, whether it be a scale-free network or a multinational corporation, but there are some that evince the key qualities that allow for centralization of agenda setting with decentralization of agenda implementation. Maintaining absolute centralization of agenda, and especially as an NGO becomes successful and expands to more states, is a difficult task. Sometimes NGOs expand geographically, or even topically, more quickly than their structures can practically handle, and rules change over how the allocation of tasks and agenda setting are handled. Thus, over time, dynamics may change as former central actors become more peripheral, or alliances form between national sections vis-à-vis the international office. When that happens, the various mechanisms of agenda setting and implementation will change, affecting the influence the NGO has on the political salience of human rights.

Adopting the balance between centralization and decentralization described here provides an incentive to maintain the structural and advocacy status quo. Having a definitive vision of human rights that results from centralized agenda setting creates value for the rest of the human rights network. It also facilitates membership to one's organization. Following the insights from network theory, low barriers to entry into a scale-free network contributes to the size to which such networks can grow, but growth also requires central coordination. Without a minimal standard of the types of participants an NGO attracts, many activists come to human rights as novices in the countries in which abuses occur or to human rights as a concept. The clarity of an NGO's advocacy agenda makes joining easy: NGOs, if they centralize enforcement power and proposal power, should have cohesive "templates" of human rights advocacy. Too much restriction of the members as they join can cause some to leave. Decentralizing implementation helps build in some level of flexibility for the NGO, helping members feel part of an overall network of activists and contributing "their part" to human rights politics.

The importance of centralizing proposal and enforcement power increases as membership rises. However, growth works against centralization, as discussed above. Thus, as the scale or scope of the organization increases, the job of actors who oversee enforcement and proposal power is to limit changes to the distribution of these powers and to funnel new members to implementation tasks. This is easier said than done. An alternative might be to limit the organization itself and occupy a niche of smaller, more nimble transnational advocacy NGOs, as Tarrow suggests (Tarrow 2010). However, Tarrow's example of small groups linking Sudan to the 2008 Beijing Olympics is just one campaign in a myriad of human rights campaigns. The small group strategy works for singular cases, but for creating widespread, longstanding political salience of rights, NGOs necessarily must draw in as many advocates as they can. The bigger the network, the more potential the NGO has for political change.

In the twentieth century, the stakes for many human rights NGOs was quite high, particularly in the charged environment of the Cold War. To earn credibility, NGOs had to appear unbiased, neutral, or impartial while enforcing a political agenda. Through advocacy efforts such as naming and shaming campaigns, backroom negotiations at diplomatic meetings, or grassroots protest, human rights NGOs pursued their agendas, trying to get states to change their abusive behaviors. Although each individual effort may not have been successful, those NGOs that were able to centralize agenda-setting powers confronted states time and again over the same issues, often the same state. Decentralizing implementation furthered the repetitive nature of creating norms—getting on-the-ground supporters who could convince their governments to either change their behavior, or push other governments to change their behaviors. NGOs that tried to pursue too many things, or concentrated their efforts on only the highest international offices, lost influence. The politics of human rights and norm change are not simply about having the best idea, or the most "right" rights. These sentiments have to be cultivated on multiple levels in multiple forums. Structure, while a background variable, has an important role in the foreground in the politics of norms: shaping the terms of debate and how activists go about pushing their agendas.

3

AMNESTY INTERNATIONAL

The NGO That Made Human Rights Important

Although Amnesty has been the darling of analysts and the target of critics for many years, not many have actually endeavored to scrutinize, through an organizational lens,[1] the continued success that the NGO has had in promoting its cause, its frequent citation in the media and by world leaders, and its influence over the course of human rights. The fact of its "bias" in its reporting of human rights speaks to the very nature of the politics around the concept. From 1961 to 2001, Amnesty remained steadfast in its commitment to a narrow conception of its organizational mandate, long deflecting challenges from development, women's, and LGBT groups that clamored to have their cause be part of Amnesty's human rights agenda. For many years, and arguably still today, Amnesty has provided a basis for our understanding of what human rights are and has consistently supplied a growing global public with information about human rights abuses. How Amnesty's organizational structure enabled it to become a household name, why it endures as a part of the human rights landscape, and how a British organization came to define the political salience of human rights in the twentieth century is the subject of this chapter.

Amnesty's ascent was both rocky and meteoric, shaped by its attempt to balance centralized agenda setting with a member-centric implementation method. The infrastructure for centralized, international leadership was put in place by 1968. Thus the International Secretariat (IS), from very early on, has served as the focal point of the organization, providing information through meticulously researched reports and statements, deciding who constituted "Prisoners of Conscience" (POCs), and coordinating the national sections in international campaigns. Nonetheless, the NGO also very seriously believes in the power of membership (Thakur 1994), which contributes to both its struggles and its triumphs. Members held the key to Amnesty's early popularity, wealth of resources, and global diffusion, but members also have held back the move to "full spectrum" rights and the spread of its agenda beyond (until the 2000s) the old stand-ins of human rights that Amnesty helped make salient: freedom of expression and religion, freedom from torture and arbitrary arrest, the right to a fair trial. Membership propelled torture to the top of the international agenda in the 1970s, and by 1984 Amnesty had successfully lobbied the United Nations to pass the Convention Against Torture. Nonetheless Amnesty's membership has challenged to the direction of the organization as it faces more and more competitors in the business of human rights that have moved to the frontiers of advocacy, innovating their agendas in much quicker ways than Amnesty can because of its formal inclusion of membership in decision making.

Amnesty's significance in the international politics of human rights continues to be its structural capacity to harness the strength of international mobilization while controlling the fundamental content of what their supporters say about the issue. Thus, while Amnesty, like other international NGOs, provides information on human rights, it also successfully spins that information in a way that revolves around a core set of issues set at International Council Meetings (ICMs), as interpreted by the IS. The centralization of proposal and enforcement powers and the decentralization of implementation power has given Amnesty a distinct ability to make the rights it advocates salient in international politics.

In this chapter, I discuss how the choice for an organizational structure that embraced both centrality in agenda setting—by endowing the IS with nearly complete control over research and its distribution—and decentrality in implementation—through the efforts of its membership—led to the dominance of Amnesty as *the* human rights NGO in the period between the ends of World War II and the Cold War. Though there were other NGOs that provided alternatives to Amnesty's way of doing human rights and organizing itself, such as the International League of Human Rights, Anti-Slavery International, the International Commission of Jurists, PEN International, and the Fédération Internationale des Ligues des Droits de l'Homme, none of them really managed to challenge Amnesty's ability to make certain human rights salient. It was not until the Watch Committees came onto the scene in the late 1970s and 1980s that Amnesty faced major competition for the first time. Other NGOs that have now come to be part of the human rights conversation, such as Oxfam, were not the advocacy-oriented organizations they have been since the turn of the twenty-first century.

I focus on the role of centralizing proposal power and enforcement power at the IS and within the structure of the biennial ICMs and the contribution of membership throughout Amnesty's existence. In addition to this rightful attention to Amnesty's centralized structure (Stroup 2010), I draw attention to the other major factor in the NGO's early success at propagating its vision of human rights: the membership. The role of the broader network of advocates who tapped into Amnesty's vision of human rights and believed in how it pursued them politically also played an integral role in creating the political salience of those rights at the international level. The network that formed around Amnesty's version of human rights enabled the rapid spread of its ideas and ensured that these ideas would endure prominently as focal points in international human rights.

Many observers have credited Amnesty's choice of human rights issues to advocate (Kaufman 1991; Larsen 1979; Power 1981, 2002), or the narrowness of its mandate (Baehr 1994) to explain its political salience, fitting into the body of theories that focus on issue-driven explanations (see chapter 1). Other plausible explanations might be tied to the significance of Amnesty's charismatic leadership in its early days, and the dedicated efforts of its volunteers, whose participation Amnesty proudly touts to this day. These two alternative accounts do indeed matter, but the decisions of the leadership to pursue certain types of human rights issues are shaped not just by timing, strategic framing, and certain personal attributes. The importance of organizational structure becomes apparent in the story of how Amnesty came to define human rights in the twentieth century precisely because its distribution of agenda-setting powers shaped and diffused a certain set of human rights ideas, packaged in a certain way, across many international contexts. The story of Amnesty's political salience points to its organizational structure, and as such, is much more than the content of its advocacy and the personal characteristics of those who make up its ranks. Rather than seeing Amnesty as an idiosyncratic NGO, an organizational perspective shows that political salience is transferable through organizational choices and structures.

This chapter is organized into roughly three major parts. The first two sections offer a broad-stroke history of the NGO and analyze the basic organizational choices made, and the reasoning behind those decisions. The second part of the chapter discusses how proposal, enforcement, and implementation powers are distributed among different actors, demonstrating how Amnesty has centralized proposal and enforcement power at the IS while decentralizing the implementation of its agenda. The discussion of the distribution of agenda-setting power in this particular NGO demonstrates how alternative, organization-level explanations, as discussed in chapter 2, form only part of the explanation for why Amnesty has become salient. In the third part, I discuss two major campaigns, the death penalty and the Campaign against Torture (CAT). Using these two campaigns, I assess the relative strength of organizational structure as an explanation for the political salience of rights at the international level versus alternative international level explanations.

The Roots and Rules of Amnesty International

Origins

Amnesty claims 2.2 million members in more than 150 countries and regions,[2] a dramatic leap from even the grand visions of its founder, British barrister Peter Benenson. As the apocryphal founding story goes, in 1961 Benenson came up with the idea of adopting "Prisoners of Conscience" after reading about two Portuguese students who had been arrested because they toasted freedom under a dictatorial regime. This perceived injustice, among other instances of nonviolent resistance, led Benenson to write the London *Observer* article on May 28 about the "Forgotten Prisoners," which launched a year-long campaign called "Appeal for Amnesty,

1961." The article quickly caught fire, and what began as a modest campaign involving Benenson and his barrister peers grew very quickly into an international phenomenon, with participants all over Europe eagerly responding by forming groups to adopt these POCs. Benenson himself engaged in tours of European countries to rile up support for the young movement. Very soon thereafter Benenson established the headquarters (née the Library) in his barrister quarters in London, which eventually became the IS. At the time, Amnesty was the first of its kind to internationalize a prisoner adoption model and use a membership-based model of advocacy for human rights work. It also distinguished between violent actors (non-Amnesty cases) and those who resisted nonviolently (POCs). These two factors contributed to how the NGO would choose its structures and prioritize centralized proposal and enforcement powers.

The funding scheme that would sustain Amnesty until the 1980s emerged from the response to the Appeal. The NGO carved its niche by relying on small donors, many of whom had first been inspired by Benenson's article and responded with cash, time, and in-kind gifts. Because of the success of the Appeal, therefore, Benenson was able to build on the support of volunteers and create an NGO independent of government or foundation funding (Buchanan 2009). Amnesty became an international NGO, organized into national sections that consulted IS and contributed to its coffers. Volunteer adoption groups, now called "Threes,"[3] were given prisoner dossiers and asked to continue supporting prisoners until a situation changed, a process that often took months or years of letter-writing and follow-up of efforts. National sections and Threes reaped the benefits of having the IS, which researched and distributed human rights information and organized the prisoner cases for groups to adopt.

The basic principles for Amnesty were a strict impartial and apolitical stance (Wilson 1997; Winston 2001) that blended volunteerism and professionalism (Korey 1968; Cook 1996) and focused on a particular slice of human rights from the Universal Declaration of Human Rights, namely the freedom from torture and arbitrary (political) imprisonment; the freedom of expression, conscience, and religion; and the right to a fair trial.[4] Government funding was avoided, both because of the Cold War–fueled desire to remain "apolitical," but also because Amnesty was able to sustain itself by drawing on member donations. These fundamental principles would inform Amnesty and its choice of what issues to include in its agenda until the twenty-first century, and it was these principles that time and again prevented new issues from being added to the Amnesty agenda, as resistance came from both the IS and national sections at ICMs (see Hopgood 2010).

Basic Structures

Early on, Benenson and his supporters underlined the importance of information in securing Amnesty's place among other human rights activists. Two parts of the organization were to be permanent: "the Library"[5] and the information newsletter.[6] The Library in particular, founders felt, distinguished Amnesty from its human rights NGO peers:

> After discussion about the main function of the movement, particularly with reference to relations with other groups in the Human Rights field, it was decided that the principal work of AMNESTY would be the collection and dissemination of information about Prisoners of Conscience. For this purpose the growth of the Library was all important.[7]

Amnesty's founders realized the contribution that the nascent organization would make, and structured functions so that research came from a centralized actor. Whereas the membership provided money, manpower, and a source of legitimacy for early efforts, their role as agenda setters within the organization itself was determined to be secondary from the beginning. Powerful national sections, such as the British, German, Dutch, Swedish, and later, the United States, at varying times worked out their differences with the IS, and over time, national sections (especially those in Western countries) have succeeded in gaining concessions to determine the research and advocacy agendas. However, the IS to this day controls much of the research and advocacy agenda. National sections can choose to highlight certain aspects of Amnesty's overall program and strategic plan, but they cannot ignore IS decisions.[8] Centralizing research functions helped to ensure the accuracy and consistency of Amnesty's message.

Nonetheless, Amnesty formally operates on a democratic model, governed by its organizational statute. The current system operates with regular ICMs, to which each national section sends delegates, and national sections organize their own annual meetings and subnational gatherings,

when applicable. In 1968, Amnesty decided on a statute that would become the foundational document for the post-Benenson organization. The
membership of Amnesty is the first entity within the organization that the
statute mentions, and it is the membership that funds the organization and
makes the ultimate decisions on changes to the mandate. Decisions made
at ICMs are the policies of the organization: the "directive authority for
the conduct of the affairs of the Amnesty International is vested in the
International Council."[9] Members of Amnesty include national sections,
affiliated groups, individuals, and corporations. The International Executive Council (IEC) serves the role of executor between ICMs, "responsible
for the conduct of affairs of Amnesty International and for the implementation of the decisions of the International Council."[10] The IEC is made up
of members elected by the International Council, with renewable terms. It
must meet at least twice a year, and it sets its own schedule. Though by the
statute both the International Council and the IEC take the lion's share of
policymaking capacities, the day-to-day decisions come from the IS. The
IEC appoints the head of the IS, the secretary general, but s/he is free to
appoint executive and other staff "as appear to him to be necessary for the
proper conduct of the affairs of Amnesty International."[11]

The structures outlined here were set up largely in reaction to the first
five years of Amnesty's history. Even as the basic organizational structure
of the central office, the national sections, and the volunteer groups was
established very early on, Amnesty remained a one-man show throughout
Benenson's tenure. Benenson was no accidental activist, and many of the
ideas he pushed as the leader of Amnesty he advocated earlier in his life.
He had a long history of trying to bridge political differences between bar-
risters, though he himself was partial to the Labour Party. He long felt
that one could not just let others suffer, that activism and helping others
was an important, human thing to do. After his conversion to Catholicism,
he wanted to find something secular that would help others experience
that sort of profound change, and he thought political activism was one of
the vectors by which to do so. The profundity of Benenson's influence reflects how central he was as a node in the Amnesty network. Even in the
last couple of years of his formal involvement with Amnesty as his health
deteriorated and those who supported him began looking elsewhere for
leadership, he was still considered as a central, and indeed, necessary figure in Amnesty's network. Benenson was at the center of several scandals

after he resigned from formal day-to-day operations in 1964, the details of which can be found elsewhere.[12] After Benenson, the organization plowed on following many of his original ideas, even if the leadership now shifted hands (Buchanan 2004, 287).

The change in leadership created the office of secretary general, headed in the interim by cofounder Eric Baker, and later taken up by British activist Martin Ennals, who led Amnesty from 1968 to 1980. The secretary general was charged with administering the IS, and in effect, became the face of Amnesty in-between ICMs and IEC meetings. Indeed, in the post-Benenson era, Amnesty's leaders sought precisely to create a more heavily rule-bound, abstract, and less "sacred" organization.

The 1968 statute was a critical juncture for the NGO, marking a turn from a personalized organization closely associated to Benenson to an international organization with specific principles and structures. In terms of creating a common purpose for the organization, the 1968 statute defined Amnesty's mandate in reference to other statutes of the UDHR (Articles 5, 9, 18, and 19)[13] and put opposition to the death penalty on the table.[14] Thus, in 1968, leaders paved the path that Amnesty would doggedly pursue until 2001.

However, another commonly overlooked, enduring feature of the 1968 statute was its effect on defining the structure of the organization. The 1968 changes had the effect of centralizing proposal and enforcement power in the London office of the IS. Though by the charter of the organization, the IS plays a very minimal policymaking role, the revised responsibilities of the IS led to a day-to-day administration that allowed it to make a larger contribution than anticipated to Amnesty's human rights policies. De facto, the IS fields thousands of alleged human rights violations, and it must comb through these to decide (1) whether they are legitimate claims and (2) the strategy by which the NGO should address a legitimate claim.

Whether a case gets treated individually in the form of prisoner adoption/letter-writing campaigns or whether it becomes part of a broader report or a press release are all decisions made within the IS, under the auspices of the relevant research team. As a consequence, the IS serves as the central agenda setter for the NGO. The IS, however, does not do everything—much of the campaigning takes place in national sections and local groups, with the IS coordinating a broader international network. As such, the implementation of the agenda largely takes place beyond the direct action of the IS. Below, I evaluate how proposal, enforcement, and implementation powers were and are currently distributed throughout the Amnesty network, and demonstrate how organizational structure reinforced the narrowness of the 1968 statute and how the IS's control over proposal and enforcement power made mandate revisions difficult.

Using Organizational Structure as the Lens

Centralizing Principles: Proposal Power

Amnesty's membership has constrained the capacity for the IS to change the agenda quickly for all but the first years. During the initial period under the founder from 1961 to 1967, when the organization was quite small and composed of upper middle-class European elites like himself, Benenson was able to influence the agenda quite dramatically. Staff at the office in London (what would become the IS) catered to Benenson's inability to "stop making the revolution" (Buchanan 2002, 587). A few other leaders, dubbed "The Godfathers," also had some proposal power over the organization's principles and frequently advised Benenson on projects he pursued via Amnesty. By and large, however, many of the ideas that carried forth, such as the notion of adopting political prisoners, writing letters demanding their release or a betterment of their treatment, or the organization of the world into Threes when it came to advocacy originated from Benenson. The London office also made decisions on who could be adopted by Amnesty according to its mandate, and whose cases required further investigation before group adoption.

After the 1968 ICM, proposal power, which had always formally rested in the annual ICMs of all national sections and IS representatives, was also allocated to the IS, which was charged with administering the decisions of the ICMs and IEC. Instead of being the projects that emerged from Benenson's constant brainstorming, then, three bodies within Amnesty were allocated proposal power after 1967.

However, in terms of day-to-day decisions, of which there were many, and particularly as the organization grew in membership in the early 1970s and the IS launched the Campaign to Abolish Torture in 1973, the IS remained ascendant. In the words of several former Amnesty staffers, the

NGO was a centralized research organization with a decentralized action function.[15] Though national sections' representatives continued to make proposals at ICMs, the increasing number of proposals at each meeting, coupled with the change from annual to biennial meetings, eliminated many of the opportunities national sections had to exercise their formal proposal power. Charged with implementing ICM and IEC directives, the IS had to create rules to manage their fulfillment. Moreover, the primacy of research as the raison d'être of the NGO led to the continued delegation of research to the IS, as it is the only consistent, day-to-day link that holds national sections together. This resulted in an internal controversy in the late-1980s and into the 1990s that was resolved in part by giving some research functions to more developed national sections (Hopgood 2006). As an Amnesty executive characterizes it: "Right now the International Secretariat takes most of the decisions on where do we do research, what do we do it on and so on. And sections have, try to get their input into it but they're not on an equal level [with the IS]."[16]

Through its administrative role, the IS extends its influence over proposal power because most of the time, it is the only actor within the statute that has the duty to do so. Even though the ICMs serve as a way for national sections to assert their collective will against IS policies when necessary, it is difficult for national sections to get their agendas agreed to at the international level. For instance, the Mexican section continually fought for increased Amnesty attention to migrants' and refugees' rights throughout the 1970s and early 1980s, but was thwarted in its efforts.[17] Although it was a small section, AI-Mexico was one of the key groups in Latin America. Even though other, more powerful national sections in Europe and the US branch can regularly get the ear of the IS, it is through the formal administrative role that the IS can make the lion's share of proposals for the rest of the NGO.

For Amnesty, the IS *must* regularly exercise proposal power. For many years, the IS was the sole producer of case sheets for the rest of the NGO—these case sheets contained the information necessary for participants to write letters on behalf of prisoners. In fact, there was a crisis during the 1980s in which the demand for case sheets could not be met by the IS researchers.[18] Thus, even though the formal rules in the statute grant preeminent policymaking status to ICMs,[19] in reality the informal importance of the IS in making sure the Amnesty network functions must be considered. All the way through the end of the 1980s, national sections relied on the IS for information, guidance, and coherence in the human rights principles Amnesty stood for,[20] because the IS was the only body charged with fact-finding. Information is never objective, and generations of researchers were able to shape Amnesty's principles on human rights much more than the relatively infrequent ICMs and IEC meetings could.

Two factors made expanding Amnesty's list of rights an unlikely event for forty years. The first is the role of the IS in controlling the flow of information between various parts of the network. As any good bureaucrat understands, implementing the rules always requires interpretation. The IS's job was to evaluate cases and deem them appropriate for Amnesty or not. It also zealously guarded this power; Hopgood (2006, 105–145) documents the challenge posed by upstart Amnesty USA (AIUSA), newly flush with cash in the late 1980s. In the early days of Amnesty's network, the US sections amounted to very few members—though some, such as the Riverside group in New York, were quite outspoken. As AIUSA grew in monetary and membership power through a shift in leadership, it demanded concessions from London, in particular in terms of doing research and working on domestic cases, which hitherto had been a shunned practice. The IS's relinquishment of some research functions to larger national sections still requires that national sections follow the international plan.[21]

The second reason is actually a function of the democratic nature of ICMs. Those national sections that did want to advocate for more rights continually encountered resistance from other members. Adding gender concerns or sexual orientation to the list of rights led to struggles between larger, European sections that wanted to work on those issues and objections by smaller national sections in Muslim and Catholic countries that found supporting those types of rights objectionable. Amnesty's sensitivities to its Northern-centric membership made it more likely to respond to demands from smaller Southern sections. Both of these dynamics ensured that change to Amnesty's agenda of fighting against torture and arbitrary arrest, as well as protecting expression, opinion, and religion—protecting "conscience"—would be conservative and narrow. The inability of ICM participants to overcome collective action problems thus ensured the primacy of the formal and informal aspects of the IS's proposal power over the formal authority of ICMs as the primary policymaker.

Getting Compliance—Enforcement Power

Enforcement power includes both veto power and the ability to make sure that others comply with the veto. Amnesty's enforcement power comes from two bodies within the network: the IS and the IEC. Technically, neither of these bodies can veto decisions made at ICMs, but they are the only two that can act on (or not) the policies set by the ICM. In other words, even though the ICM can veto, it is very difficult to enforce that veto because of its infrequent meetings and its collective nature, as a body representative of all of Amnesty's national sections.

In its quarterly meetings, the IEC discusses solutions to the requests and decisions of ICMs, often pushing for more, rather than less, pondering. Past IEC members see the body as an intermediary between the membership and the IS, representing the interests of members, while at the same time being a much smaller body that can work toward bringing ICM decisions to fruition.[22] Without enforcement power, ICMs, and by extension national sections, have very little opportunity to exercise a veto and see those vetoes through. At the national section level, many leaders face a collective action problem with getting enough national sections to agree on a single solution at the biennial ICMs in order to overturn existing policy. As such, blocking or changing policy through the meetings is at best difficult, and often time consuming. The fact that the IS and the IEC meet much more regularly in comparison to the ICMs in effect dilutes the power of national sections to enforce vetoes and follow through on their proposals.

Amnesty highlights the importance of looking at enforcement power, rather than just veto power by itself. The infrequency with which the ICM meets makes it difficult for vetoes to be implemented effectively. One central Amnesty issue that became controversial in the 1980s was the process by which borderline adoption cases would be handled. Amnesty has always wrestled with its rejection of perfectly good candidates for POCs because of its refusal to advocate for those who have supported or used violence. Beginning with the 1979 ICM, national sections began demanding more transparency in decisions on borderline cases.[23] A series of reports followed that outlined the procedure by which borderline cases would be decided—essentially delineating that cases would largely be resolved by the IS, and any dissent over IS decisions would be handled by the IEC.[24]

Perhaps more clearly articulated, a memo from 1982 simply states that borderline cases could be resolved by the IS, IEC, or the ICM, effectively negating the role of the ICM in having substantive input in deciding all but the most problematic cases.[25] Decisions to not adopt borderline cases, the stickiest situations in applying decisions made by ICMs, could not wait for the infrequent gatherings of national sections for resolution. Even if national sections did not agree with the adoption (or rejection) of a particular prisoner case, there was very little they could do in spite of increased monitoring on IS actions by the IEC.

Given the IS's role in proposing and enforcing the agenda in the organization, it is logical to expect that its importance grows the larger the network of Amnesty activists. Conversely, the relative power of the national sections and ICM go down as the membership of Amnesty increases. With more national sections, the relative proposal and enforcement power decreases, as more sections need to agree in order to change policy, and the ICM's collective action problems intensify. Because of the difficulties national sections face in coordinating action at the international level, the ability of the IS to forward its vision of the mandate grows in importance. With the expansion of the mandate to "full spectrum" to accommodate all of the rights mentioned in the UDHR, proposal power increases for the IS. The breadth of the new imperatives from ICM meetings and the ambiguity of programs such as "Demand Dignity" gives the IS more control over deciding what cases and countries fit within the rubric. Enforcement power also increases for the IS, since it has more ways to justify its actions as falling within mandate. Conversely, as the network expands and as membership grows, the IS has more individuals and groups to rely on to implement its agenda. This decentralization of the agenda, of course, creates more coordination work for the IS.

Proposal power determines the way that issues are framed, whether in Amnesty or another NGO. Enforcement power, on the other hand, removes items for the agenda. The two powers work in tandem to shape how a potential topic for advocacy gets introduced, and the packaging that surrounds it, depends on who exercises proposal power in the organization. Thus the attributes that other scholars have focused on as the main source of Amnesty's salience as an organization—POCs, limited to a selection based on the violation of civil and political rights—emerges from the distribution of agenda-setting power. Amnesty could have easily expanded its scope of activity, and in fact, until 2001, ICMs had time and again visited the question of whether to embrace economic, social, and cultural rights, or even other civil and political rights, in its campaigns. Formally, this should have been easy, as a response to membership demand. But the diffuseness of the ICM's proposal power, coupled with the informal exercise of proposal and enforcement powers by the IS and the tendency of the IEC's involvement to opt for more research, rather than action, kept Amnesty's repertoire relatively limited. This characteristic, which others have pointed to as causal for Amnesty's political salience, is actually a product of organizational structure and not foresight.

Implementing the Agenda

Amnesty's agenda is implemented by its greater network of staff and volunteers beyond the IS; advocacy efforts at the local level, then, are often the product of homegrown ingenuity, such as bake sales, protests, and other types of fund-raising and awareness-building activity. If anything defines Amnesty, it is the practice of letter-writing. Sending correspondence is foundational to the NGO's identity, as it differentiated Amnesty from other human rights NGOs before and after it. It is also the hallmark of how membership organizations might involve individuals in the business of human rights advocacy. Amnesty's founders made membership meaningful by designating letter-writing as both a primary advocacy output and one that could not possibly be completed without the assistance of the ever-growing ranks of new activists who committed themselves to the cause. As the second ICM in Geneva reaffirmed, Amnesty was an organization founded on the logic that individuals could lobby governments in support of prisoners, and that letter-writing and adoption were an integral part of the NGO's work.[26] Few of Amnesty's goals through the end of the Cold War could be met without the greater network of volunteers and national sections, and the IS remained central in coordinating volunteers' efforts through its case selection, research, and information dissemination capacities. In its formative days, letter-writing was coupled with the notion of prisoner adoption by volunteer groups. That is, groups would maintain a steady stream of correspondence with prisoners, even when months would go by without answer or reaction from officials in an effort to "hold a candle to the darkness": the idea was to let those being held know someone was aware of his/

her plight, and over time, win a war of attrition with state officials. Obviously, many adopted prisoners were never heard from, or news was infrequent and sporadic. Group morale was a continuous concern in London.

One of the historical innovations of Amnesty's advocacy model was the formation of Threes groups.[27] The idea was to have each adoption group work simultaneously on one prisoner from each part of the world to demonstrate Amnesty's impartiality. The IS issued case dossiers to Threes groups as needed. One of the dilemmas that Amnesty faced over time as it gained members was a continual shortage of case sheets.[28] IS staffers worked to keep up the supply of case sheets for traditional adoption, but it became clear during the 1970s that the adoption group model was not sustainable as the NGO's reach grew. The IS came up with other types of methods of engaging the membership, such as case dossiers, which were more generalized campaigns against countries, rather than directed in support of certain individuals.

Decentralization goes beyond merely writing letters. Volunteers who came to Amnesty often had regional or country expertise as well, and aided the IS in finding out conditions on the ground for endangered populations, or provided London with more contacts. Entities such as Regional Action Networks, for instance, amplified the professionalized research functions of the IS, but they also provided researchers in London with additional links to countries with human rights abuses. Maintaining regular contact with expert volunteers opened the way for more ways to engage in advocacy, but also gave Amnesty further ways to leverage the knowledge of the membership. There are also more ad hoc networks that have formed over time, specializing in legal issues, medical issues, and other areas as the need arises. Thus volunteering as a member can mean more than writing letters. The coordination of the network comes from the IS, but involvement in fundamental tasks of advocacy comes from the membership.

The fact that Amnesty decentralizes advocacy functions complicates the usual simple dichotomy between professionalized staff and amateur volunteers. Both adoption groups and more specialized groups such as Regional Action Networks contribute to the central functions and identity of Amnesty. Despite the fact that the IS does collect and redirect information found by volunteers, the research done by volunteers is sometimes irreplaceable. Following from this issue of the quality of research conducted by non-IS sources, Amnesty struggled with the role of national sections in the role of research and implementation. Although national sections contributed information to the IS, the IS was encouraged to find corroborative evidence independent of the national section contributions.[29] Implementation was another story. For many years, it strayed away from allowing national sections to work on cases in their own countries for fear that the organizations in each country would become too parochial in focus, stressing only cases in their own parts of the world, rather than the broader international movement, the so-called WOOC policy (Work on Own Country) (Winston 2001). Thus, the emphasis in terms of implementation of the overall Amnesty agenda was to stray away from situations in which representatives of the movement in any given country would be seen to be too parochially focused.

The tension between centralized agenda setting and decentralized agenda implementation creates somewhat of a balancing act for the IS vis-à-vis the membership and vice versa. Both elements rely on one another, and this mutual reliance creates incentives for the IS to push its agenda unilaterally. After all, national sections, local groups, and individual volunteers depend on the IS to administer the decisions made by the ICM, and without its guidance, the millions Amnesty currently counts within its ranks would not have a central direction. However, the IS has to tread carefully as well, since its financial well-being still largely rests on national section contributions. Exercising excessive proposal power might discourage national sections and lead to membership attrition. Hence, the distribution of proposal, enforcement, and implementation power, although stable, is an arrangement of tweaking and negotiation, compromise and flexibility. The distribution of implementation power, and its ability to maintain its network over the years is the primary reason why it has found success in creating political salience as an organization. This has not necessarily translated into obvious victories for the norms it advocates at the international level, as the next section demonstrates.

One clear emphasis in Amnesty has been on the role of membership, rather than leadership, despite the fact that all of Amnesty's secretary generals have hailed from activism or international service, and they have all received recognition for their many achievements. Early on, the salience of the NGO was certainly enhanced by the involvement of international politician Sean MacBride, among others, and Benenson himself, who was quite prominent among lawyer activists in England. Nonetheless, telling the story of the accomplishments of Amnesty's early and later leadership misses part of the puzzle for why the NGO has remained politically salient through so many different trends in international human rights. Leaders come and go, and they excel in some areas and not others. What has stayed constant, since 1968, is the organizational structure. Furthermore, the emphasis, at least rhetorically, has been on the power of Amnesty's membership in producing political change. I would contend that the NGO's leadership has undoubtedly helped Amnesty stay politically salient, but I would add that it has been the distribution of agenda-setting powers that has kept it at the forefront of human rights politics. The membership, composed of ordinary people, not professional staff, and not leadership, carry Amnesty's message widely. Without the centralization of proposal and enforcement powers, Amnesty may not have been able to produce the consistency of message others have underscored as the NGO's uniqueness; without the decentralization of implementation power, it may not have been able to spread its message as widely, in spite of the merits of its leaders. Thus, without the underlying organizational structure, the most capable leadership could not have established Amnesty's salience as an internationally recognized human rights monitor.

Discussing the merits of Amnesty's organizational structure in the abstract yields insights into why the NGO dominated human rights politics for so many decades. Nonetheless, Amnesty has not always been successful in its international campaigns, and despite its organizational strengths, it has struggled with convincing states to change their behaviors in certain areas. In the following section, I take a closer look at two campaigns: the CAT and Amnesty's opposition to the death penalty.

International Campaigns

Though they were both launched in the 1970s, Amnesty's campaigns against the death penalty and torture (CAT) display remarkably different attitudes toward proposal and enforcement power, and for this reason alone, makes a comparison between the two fruitful. Torture was much easier to define as an international issue, framed as something no state should do and supported by the UDHR and its status as a nonderogable right in ICCPR. To take on torture was no stretch for Amnesty, and fit neatly into its model of centralizing the research and framing, allowing the membership to pick up where the IS left off. Effectively, CAT reinforced the model of centralizing proposal and enforcement powers, and in a sense, the torture issue *necessitated* centralized information and agenda setting. For the death penalty, the priority on centralized proposal and enforcement powers shifted. While there were certainly economies of scale for the IS to produce research on the topic, and Amnesty did in fact issue internationalized statements about the death penalty, the ambiguity about the death penalty as an international human rights issue at the time made the decision less straightforward. The death penalty then and now is still seen as a domestic issue. Amnesty's work helped internationalize the death penalty, but unlike POCs, the innocence of those condemned to death cannot be assumed. This complicated Amnesty's reasoning to taking on the death penalty in the first place. Amnesty responded to the domesticity of the issue by allow national sections to work on death penalty without central coordination. These two campaigns, therefore, though linked by time and explicit decisions for the death penalty work to follow some of the tactics of the CAT, are marked by differences in both how the NGO chose to pursue the issues, and the differential level of formal abolition by states.

The effect of NGO activity must be weighed against the two alternative explanations introduced in chapter 1: American hegemony and political opportunity structures. Neither of these accounts alone can fully explain why the international norm against torture remains one of the steadfast components of the human rights regime. The American hegemony perspective can elucidate some aspects of the death penalty's continued existence in the United States, China, Iran, and a handful of other countries, but it cannot account for the international climate against the death penalty *in spite* of continued US opposition to changing its domestic practices. Likewise, political opportunity structure theories can only get us so far in terms of understanding why rights become salient when they do, and why human rights norms get reinforced by state practice. There was nothing about the early 1970s that made it a particularly convenient time for Amnesty to start pursuing the torture issue. Torture was prominent in several Latin American dictatorships at the time, but torture had been a widespread form of political control, even after World War II, such as the British treatment of prisoners in Aden. Similarly, the death penalty had been in international discussion since the UDHR (Schabas 1993), and has been developed by both regional institutions such as the European Convention on Human Rights (ECHR) and the American Convention on Human Rights.

For the death penalty, Amnesty created political opportunities for itself and like-minded groups. The major changes on the delegitimation and abandonment of the death penalty came in the late 1970s through the current day. The Second Optional Protocol of the ICCPR, dealing specifically with the abolishment of the death penalty, was enacted in 1989. Zimring (2004) argues that the 1970s was a watershed decade for anti–death penalty positions, but it was only within the past twenty-five years that the death penalty became an international norm, especially in Western Europe, that helped transform practices of former Soviet states (Zimring 2004, 16–41). In the case of the death penalty in particular, political opportunities came after Amnesty's initial actions, and continued US adherence at the domestic level signals that both American hegemony and political opportunity structure explanations require additional elaboration.

Consequently, the focus should be on the qualities of the agents working within the overall international structure. Thinking about the qualities of organizations and their agenda-setting powers can help clarify the timing of the global antitorture campaign, which happened several years before US president Jimmy Carter made human rights a major plank of his election platform, and the flurried success of the Convention Against Torture, which went into force a mere three years after its initial signing. The organizational perspective, moreover, tells us why both death penalty and torture are politically salient rights in international relations, notwithstanding American resistance to the banning of the death penalty and the renewal of torturelike practices after 9/11. This view also highlights how organizations do not grow by accident, and that their choices to centralize agenda setting and decentralize agenda implementation led to the expansion of Amnesty as an NGO and Amnesty's ideas about human rights. In examining Amnesty's campaigns against torture and the death penalty (which occurred in rapid succession), we not only see Amnesty's role in pushing an overall human rights agenda beyond its original conception of political prisoners, but also its growth from a small British organization with transnational ties to its more modern form of an international NGO run out of a prominent British headquarters. Early efforts by Benenson and others created national sections in Europe, building an international presence; the two campaigns discussed here, and especially the CAT, helped reinforce the viability of Amnesty's methods, which would persist well in the 1990s as its modus operandi. Without a careful analysis of how agenda setting is structured, not only do we lose out on a key piece of the puzzle of how norms emerge, but we also do not catch the organizational reasons why some NGOs become prominent international agenda setters and succeed at making rights salient.

Campaigning against Torture

The CAT, which involved a massive worldwide campaign, demonstrates the central role of IS, as well as the need for decentralized implementation of some of the most important aspects of the campaign. The CAT resulted in the signing of the Convention against Torture in 1985, but the convention capped off, rather than ushered in, the norm against torture. CAT was also auspiciously timed from an organizational point of view. One of the ways Amnesty dealt with rapid expansion in the 1970s was to shift its advocacy model from Threes adoption groups to more massive scale letter-writing techniques and alternative actions that exploited the growing popularity of the network and saved money.[30] As the number of adherents grew, it became obvious that expansion of the structure of adoption groups with the IS in the center was not only going to be costly financially, but adding more groups simply was not going to address the administrative burdens of trying to appropriately distribute prisoner cases.[31] The goal of expanding Amnesty's reach worldwide, moreover, was of prime importance, since more national sections and more individual adherents meant more exposure and possibilities to pressure states at home. The most viable option and blueprint for the future turned out to be connected to AI's move to eradicate torture.

The CAT was launched at the end of 1972.[32] The first stage, which took place between 1972 and 1973, raised public awareness of state practices and rallied for an international normative consensus against torture. It was a call for states to abide by the principles to which they had all agreed in article 5 of the UDHR, which explicitly states: "No one shall be subjected to torture or to cruel, inhuman or degrading treatment or punishment." Like the origins of the Amnesty itself, the CAT was designed to be a year-long campaign to eradicate torture, but was instituted as part of the IS as a permanent function a year later. The CAT became the most visible part of Amnesty's work, fulfilling the dual role of diplomacy at the UN and intergovernmental levels, while publicizing Amnesty's work and presence in the field of human rights advocacy.[33] It successfully lobbied for two General Assembly resolutions in 1973 and 1974 (3059 and 3218, respectively), which forwarded the UN agenda in formulating a convention concerning torture and the maltreatment of prisoners.

In December 1973, the CAT organized the Paris Convention, which gathered representatives from sixty-nine NGOs and established four different goals to stop the practice of torture: (1) identify individuals and institutions responsible for torture; (2) establish social, political, and economic background to torture; (3) discuss international, regional, and national legal factors affecting torture practices; and (4) determine the physical, psychological, and emotional effect on victims and the role of doctors in torture sessions.[34] The *Report on Torture,* which was released shortly before the Paris Convention, nearly derailed the meeting because of its impact on the media and the public, causing UNESCO sponsors of the conference to momentarily pull support because the report criticized member states (Huckerby and Rodley 2009, 17–18). In the *Report,* Amnesty researchers catalogued practices in sixty-five countries, providing the most comprehensive coverage at the time about domestic torture practices. CAT also engaged in a number of large-scale, country-targeted campaigns: torture and misuse of police power in Spain, denial of right to trial in the Philippines, observing the trials of the Greek junta concerning their use of torture, a country campaign against Uruguay, and encouraging a Danish medical study in how physicians could help prevent torture and deal with its aftereffects.

Although there was initial resistance from the IS in making CAT an integral part of the Amnesty agenda, these doubts quickly dissipated when it set up a full-time Campaigns Department (Huckerby and Rodley 2009, 19). As part of the second stage of CAT, Amnesty initiated the Urgent Action (UA) program. UAs were a modification of the old adoption model: a quick and large campaign designed to last only four to six weeks, mounted on behalf of a prisoner who was a victim of torture. Neither groups nor long-term commitment, therefore, were necessary. The UA campaigns employ the tactic of immediate inundation: letters, faxes, emails, and telegrams are sent to relevant personnel in countries where a certain prisoner's rights are neglected. By contrast to the old adoption model, UA campaigns were not as well researched (Clark 2001, 48) because time became a factor in many torture (and disappearance) cases. The first UA was issued in reaction to the unexplained arrest and subsequent disappearance of Brazilian economics professor Luiz Rossi in 1973. The success of this campaign led to the proliferation of the UA program, expanding its original mandate to other types of cases in 1976: death penalty and the denial of access to the judicial process or medical treatment. Thus, contrary to the Threes model, individuals could rally behind victims of torture without the infrastructure of the group, because in many cases the process of group adoption might take longer than the actual duration of the torture suffered by the individual prisoner. Letters could be generated by individuals willing to act very quickly in reactions to bulletins from the IS.

Another innovation of the CAT was the type of evidence used. To campaign against torture, Amnesty not only relied on personal accounts and information about specific cases but also brought in medical expertise. The campaign was thus transformed into not only one about the wrongness of torture from political and moral standpoints, but also brought in medical evidence as a way to systematize arguments against the practice. Bringing in physicians on torture led to later innovations of having medical advisory groups for other issues as well.[35]

The informal importance of the agenda-setting power of the IS became more evident as the network itself expanded into a greater number of advocacy types and issue areas. Though the statute rearticulated the importance of the membership in making decisions about the trajectory of the organization, as Amnesty grew larger in size, it necessitated more and more full-time staff to supply the crucial weapon of information to the rest of the network. To run a global campaign such as CAT, the IS needed to control information so that all national sections were on the same page on the issue of torture, in accordance with WOOC. Running an international campaign requires coordination; the natural focal point was the IS, which had already by the 1970s developed a Research Office and membership management capacities. The IS also continued its influence on Threes groups and UA volunteers, providing assistance with cases and exercising proposal power through the distribution of prisoners and cases. UAs were expanded to accommodate more cases as it became clear the technique worked. As this happened, the IS, which had served at the center of the original adoption group method, became more significant in coordinating further types of grassroots politicking. The IS's proposal power and control over information, which had characterized dynamics between the London office and national and local sections, intensified as a clearly international effort emerged from CAT. Campaigns, as well as organized letter-writing, became the mainstay of Amnesty's work.

The consequences for the success of the CAT reinforced the importance of centralizing agenda setting at the IS, but also highlighted the significance of the broader network in gaining traction on the "torture issue." The leadership provided by the coordinators at the international level enabled the same message to be delivered in local, national, and global contexts, whether facing domestic politicians or international bureaucrats. Nonetheless, without its growing membership and the conundrum of not knowing what to do with the number of activists dedicated to Amnesty, a program such as CAT could never have succeeded. Implementing an anti-torture agenda, which up until this point had been a nonissue among states at the international level, required not just a coherent agenda, but an army of all sorts to battle it out at multiple levels of governance.

The CAT also substantiated a more interesting dynamic that had been implicit since the end of the 1960s of centralizing agenda-setting power, namely proposal power, in the IS. The power of the IS increased vis-à-vis other parts of the network because the rest of the network needed its research in cases of human rights violations, and as the network grew, needed more productivity out of its central informational node. IS filtered this information in its London office through its daily activities: who was a Prisoner of Conscience, who would be the subject of a UA, which countries to do research on, how to distribute cases to the Threes groups, how better to utilize the increasing support it was garnering. These activities led the IS to increasingly assert day-to-day power over the activities of the organization, which allowed it to set the agenda for the rest of the network. The IS added value to the network by guiding volunteers (and donors) to a specific set of goals. The IS decided who counted as an Amnesty adoptee, and therefore, who had their rights violated (and who did not).

All of this centralization of agenda-setting power did not go unnoticed. In a letter to Secretary General Martin Ennals dated February 17, 1979,[36] Paul Lyons, executive director of AIUSA, critiqued the role of the IS in the network, stating that the politics of the central node caused errors in some of its Prisoners of Conscience (adoption cases) selections. By selecting prisoners, the IS engaged in policy decisions, which Lyons argued was overstepping the bounds of its duties of research. Also, the IS's procedures were not transparent, and the reasons for its decisions were not always made known. In his letter, Lyons challenged both the role of the IS in making decisions about Prisoners of Conscience and the reliance on letter-writing campaigns, thereby questioning the original advocacy model altogether. Lyons's critique focused on the fact that many of the IS's tasks involved not just following through with agenda decisions made at the ICMs, but actually agenda setting through its administration. Put differently, Lyons questioned the growing informal importance of the IS while its formal role was rather limited.

His critique was well placed. It highlighted the tension between membership and professional staffers. The 1977 ICM, for instance, showed a turn toward monetary participation, rather than activism. Urgent Actions led to increased engagement with the membership, but there was also a turn toward having members who simply paid without participating. The debate about "real" members—whether members could just give money or whether they had to be active—continued well into the 1990s. For the IS, increasing membership (i.e., money) without adding to the volunteer corps gave it access to more resources as the national sections became richer, without needing to deal with the demands of activists at the day-to-day level. The IS could concentrate on campaigning rather than gathering cases for letter-writers. Other parts of the network, namely AIUSA, chafed at this arrangement, and by the late 1980s, began wresting for control over the agenda and information under IEC chair Peter Duffy. Even though the number of members went up, no corresponding shift of proposal or enforcement powers to national sections followed.

The CAT was monumental for Amnesty as an organization in several ways. First, it made Amnesty a politically salient NGO. Second, it changed the way that its members could take on cases. Under the old rubric, Threes groups adopted individuals. Under the new UA formula, no one adopted anyone, and the commitment to freeing prisoners went only as far as the first letter and any follow-ups issued by the IS. Second, the CAT solidified the informal powers of agenda setting that the IS held and set them very clearly into relief (to the chagrin of some parts of the network). Third, the dual-pronged strategy of having centralized agenda setting with decentralized implementation produced its first widespread and tangible outcome. Agenda setting by the IS led to clear principles regarding the banning of the practice. Using national sections and individual members to spread the antitorture message on the ground and through letters gave the network a broader reach and forced states to reckon with not just demands from London, New York, and Berlin, but also from individual citizens of those places. Finally, the CAT culminated in a convention against torture. Amnesty's efforts made the issue politically salient in a number of ways, and states began pursuing antitorture and anti–political prisoner positions through other practices as well, such as implementing economic sanctions.

Opposition to the Death Penalty

Many times, critics of human rights NGOs point to the persistence of the death penalty in the United States as a giant chink in the advocacy armor. If NGO cannot convince the leader of the free world to abandon capital punishment, after all, how can it claim success? The answer is to target the United States with an extensive campaign hostile to the death penalty, against which the United States argues that democratic processes have legitimized the practice (Bolton 2000). Observers also often champion sovereignty as the explanation and justification for why the United States rejects international pressure to revise its stance on the death penalty (Spiro 2000; Rothenberg 2003). Despite the fact that it is the big fish and the major exception among liberal democracies (and many nondemocracies) in persisting with the use of the death penalty, appraising the value and efficacy of NGO action against the death penalty using only the American case fails to account for the general shift against the death penalty both at the international legal level and in domestic politics. Even in the recalcitrant United States, we find a growing number of states with moratoria or outright banning of the practice, and increasingly the notion of innocence has confronted the finality of death sentences (Baumgartner, Boef, and Boydstun 2008).

All of this leads to the question of the role of NGOs, and particularly Amnesty, in advancing this anti–death penalty agenda at the international level. Opponents of the death penalty were strongest in religious circles, with abolitionist roots from the mid-1800s, when a handful of states— Michigan, Rhode Island, and Wisconsin—succeeded in abolishing the practice altogether (Bedau 2004). Domestic religious groups have continued working on the issue, but the first, and only international actor (besides Pope Jon Paul II) continually working on the campaign since the 1970s has been Amnesty International (Bedau 2004; Zimring 2004). Amnesty's reach, which went beyond the United States to a much wider global audience, made the death penalty politically salient. Thus Amnesty's participation in the anti–death penalty movement classified the importance of the issue as a human rights issue, and furthermore, complemented the movement at the UN and in Europe to cast the practice in unfavorable and unacceptable light (Hodgkinson 2000; Schabas 2004).

The death penalty campaign started as an offshoot of the CAT. It began as a special campaign, designed for the short term, but eventually took off because of demands by the membership.[37] Campaigning against the death penalty was also a project that (eventual) Secretary General Thomas Hammarberg had been keen on for many years and had pushed when he served on the IEC in the 1970s (Thompson 2008). As outlined above, ICMs had moved to consider the death penalty even before that, deciding as early as 1968 that Amnesty could take on death penalty cases. In 1973, it decided that Amnesty would expand its mandate as a statement of opposing the death penalty in all circumstances (Thompson 2008).

The difficulty with taking on the death penalty was that it was in many ways orthogonal to the other campaigns that Amnesty had run and would run in that the victims of the death penalty often had been found guilty of committing violent acts to receive such a punishment in the first place. In short, members were concerned with the tacit approval of violence in supporting campaigning against the death penalty when the main criteria for declaring an individual a POC or not was whether the person had participated acts of violence.[38] This unease contributed to the pause with which the NGO took up the issue.

Perhaps felt more acutely within Amnesty at the time was the struggle about how to campaign about a topic in which the line shifted from the traditional Amnesty argument about the innocence of POCs, or the unjustness of using torture as a technique of social control and weeding out opponents, to one in which they acknowledged the guilt of an individual, but nonetheless opposed the domestic policy of the state. In other words, Amnesty rejected the way that states decided to treat people they had convicted through their own domestic institutions, and this marked a huge step, "in many ways a trial balloon to see to what extent world public opinion and nongovernmental bodies can affect the behavior of individual states" (Kaufman 1991, 341). Though there was general agreement on expanding the mandate to include the death penalty, the British section cautioned against both telling governments what to do with their violent criminals and also the risks of expanding into an area that was not, at the time "a human rights issue" (Thompson 2008).

After the decision to include the death penalty in its work, Amnesty followed a similar model as the strategies employed in the CAT. It hosted a conference on the death penalty in 1978 in Stockholm, Sweden (Power 2002), to generate support in a similar way to its conference on torture in 1973. Amnesty also issued a comprehensive report called *The Death Penalty* the next year, which, similar to the report on torture, described the practices and pitfalls of states using the death penalty. The most active national section, as one might assume, was the American section, AIUSA. Driven by the membership in the United States, cultural and political understandings, and geographical proximity, the IS decided to allow AIUSA to break its previously incontrovertible WOOC policy.[39] Working on the death penalty became a major draw for building up AIUSA's membership,[40] which changed the politics within the organization.

Amnesty's move to work on the death penalty marked it as an NGO on the forefront of human rights. At the time, the death penalty was not necessarily considered a human rights issue. Even though many European states had, by the 1970s, de facto discontinued the death penalty, European institutions did not formally adopt a ban against the practice. The ICCPR and the ECHR had both been reluctant to ban the death penalty outright. Article 6 of the ICCPR specifies that the death penalty only be applied for the most serious crimes, that an appeals process be made available, and exempt juveniles and pregnant women from capital punishment. Until 1983, with protocol 6, the ECHR actually allowed states the right to use the death penalty (Hodgkinson 2000). Amnesty's contribution to the salience of the death penalty, therefore, was twofold. First, it linked the death penalty explicitly to human rights law, making it an issue that could be attacked using the same set of rules and norms it used for its other work. Put differently, it changed a largely domesticized conversation into one about international norms. Second, its multipronged strategy of allowing intense domestic lobbying by its national sections and building up international support through its broader network gave Amnesty (and death penalty opponents) more leverage. The decision to decentralize research functions on the death penalty was seen as a tactical advantage and a way to draw in more members. Although it was the beginning of a loosening of IS control over proposal and enforcement power, thus far in the organization's history, it has not led to widespread revolt against the IS's research functions. Increasingly, the NGO has come to understand that while there are benefits to delegating most agenda-setting powers to the IS, in some instances, such as the death penalty, the intimacy and local expertise of national sections leverages Amnesty's capacity to gain attention at the domestic level. Giving in for some of these instances, furthermore, helps the IS solidify its relationship with powerful national sections in particular, helping ensure cooperation in future campaigns.

Discussion

Juxtaposing Amnesty's death penalty and torture campaigns presents an interesting story of organizational choice and influence. Without question, Amnesty was an early mover for both of these issues, creating political salience at the international level and salience for itself as an organization. For torture, the case was much easier, but nonetheless, the inclination of states to ignore human rights violations in the first period of the Cold War was interrupted by Amnesty's tenacity in pushing the torture issue and bringing in new standards of human rights abuse evidence. The culmination of Amnesty's efforts with a Nobel Peace Prize in 1977 to award its efforts in Latin America to document torture, disappearances, and extrajudicial executions,[41] and a UN convention banning torture and other cruel and unusual punishment, capped off CAT. The CAT helped solidify the IS's position among the national sections, in terms of the Research Department and its role in coordinating international campaigns. The success of the CAT led to the death penalty campaign.

    In some ways, the effect of Amnesty's work on the death penalty is much harder to measure because of the entrenchment of the death penalty in domestic law. In other ways, however, it is easy to credit Amnesty with internationalizing opposition to the death penalty, even if its campaign did not lead to its abolishment in the United States. Raising the political salience of the death penalty, and indeed, making it an *international* human rights issue, rather than a domestic politics issue, cleared the way for regional agreements to make firm declarations against the death penalty, and eventually, gave states the necessary justification to give UN statements some legal legs via the Second Optional Protocol of the ICCPR. Despite the recalcitrance of the United States toward international efforts to change its behavior, the undertakings of the NGO and specifically AIUSA in creating the salience around the death penalty issue provides an international focal point for advocates. Amnesty's comprehensive investigations into the death penalty, similar to the effect of its torture reports, had the consequence of linking state behaviors to one another in comparative fashion.

The two alternative explanations to the organizational structure argument, American hegemony and political opportunity structures, provide lenses through which to understand state behavior. In the case of torture and the death penalty, however, states did not provide much of the impetus for international movements against either practice. Nonstate actors, of which Amnesty was the most prominent actor in both instances, did. Certainly the effect of American hegemony shaped the way that especially the death penalty campaign turned out, but the fact that Amnesty's push through its network led to an increase in the domestic abolition and international attention to the issue *in spite* of American resistance demonstrates the ability of NGOs to shape the political agenda.

There remains another explanation not yet covered. Did the nature of the violation in question create a causal impetus for the uptake (or not) of human rights norms? Keck and Sikkink argue that two aspects of issues— bodily harm to vulnerable individuals and legal equality of opportunity— explain why some ideas stick at the international level and others do not (Keck and Sikkink 1998, 204). Certainly one can see that some types of issues find a natural resonance for a broad audience, as the depiction of suffering arouses sympathy from others (Boltanski 1999), and this sympathy can be used for political ends. However, it is more useful to view bodily harm and injustice as enabling conditions, rather than sufficient or necessary. The lack of an international norm around children born of rape (Carpenter 2010) or the weakness of rules on the use of child soldiers (Achvarina and Reich 2006) demonstrate that vulnerability and injustice do not automatically lead to norm adoption. Furthermore, the growing prominence of resistance to the death penalty belies the emphasis on suffering and victimhood. While opponents of the death penalty argue that it constitutes cruel and unusual punishment, it is undeniable that the death penalty is used on individuals who have been found guilty of crimes, in the West oftentimes heinous crimes. Thus the emphasis Keck and Sikkink place on the nature of the issue needs further elaboration.

In the case of both torture and the death penalty, Amnesty created its own political opportunities. Foundational documents had been laid, but states up until the end of the Cold War approached human rights very tentatively and reluctantly. Amnesty's effort through globalized campaigns helped shift states' focus, making at least torture, the death penalty, and POCs focal points and sites of future coordination by states.

Conclusion

Organizational structure has real consequences for the political salience of NGOs and their effectiveness in making rights salient at the international level. In Amnesty's case, its organizational structure has enabled both kinds of salience, but not without cost. It has been able to limit access to proposal and enforcement powers relatively easily in its near fifty-year history, but this led to a constriction of its advocacy agenda for forty years. For several decades, Amnesty remained at the forefront of defining human rights, using a formula that seemed to work quite well. Its success at making human rights salient in influencing the behavior of states at domestic and international levels, however, inevitably led to more attention to human rights generally. In all three ways of thinking about political salience, Amnesty has affected the politics of international human rights. Amnesty's efforts led to new international law, the Convention against Torture. These efforts also affected the way other NGOs acted as human rights advocates, shaping for instance the decisions of HRW in a very direct way. Amnesty remains very central to the international human rights network and sets the tone for other NGOs to act. Finally, if we revisit the pattern of justifications for economic sanctions, we can see that, indeed, Amnesty's core set of rights—physical integrity, religious and expressive freedom—formed many of the initial reasons for why states acted in the name of human rights. States rely on Amnesty reports to inform their policies, and Amnesty's focus on a slim set of rights early on helped shape why states would sanction one another.

Nonetheless, the Amnesty model has encountered many challenges. Because centralizing proposal and enforcement power worked so well for so long, it was slow to pick up on new possibilities in human rights in a way that HRW was not. The incredible success of the Amnesty concerts in the 1980s, coordinated by AIUSA despite the unease of other national sections and the IS, propelled human rights into the public imagination (Weinstein 1989). The benefit of these concerts, which generated enormous attention to Amnesty and the cause of human rights, was increased awareness and publicity. The drawback, however, was insularity, ensuring that Amnesty would not change its formula, at least in the short term, as it enjoyed its success as a human rights organization interested in a very narrow swath of the broad human rights agenda, as articulated in the UDHR and other documents. Into this vacuum would step, among others, HRW, a trend that would intensify after the end of the Cold War.

4

OTHER MODELS OF ADVOCATING CHANGE

The Cold War constrained how NGOs acted and their influence over human rights issues of the day at the formal, institutional level. Among its peers during the Cold War, Amnesty stood out with its unique structure because it actively sought to activate grassroots networks through emphasizing membership. It is the combination of centralized proposal and enforcement powers and decentralized implementation power that led to Amnesty's political salience as an organization and, furthermore, gave the NGO its influence on human rights politics. Many other NGOs opted for a more typical model of elite activism that targeted domestic leaders and international bureaucrats, and some have become politically salient as organizations. The goal of this chapter is to explore the different organizational structures of NGOs and to show how these structural choices matter for organizational salience.

Though rights organizations existed between the world wars, they were mostly parochial, aiming their efforts at domestic audiences (Burgers 1992). One exception was the Fédération Internationale des Droits de

L'homme (FIDH), founded in 1922. Humanitarian NGOs were much more common in the interwar years—CARE International, Catholic Relief Services, Oxfam Great Britain, Save the Children—but these organizations were mainly about relief at the time. Aside from the International League of Human Rights (ILHR)[1] (discussed below) and the International Commission of Jurists (ICJ), founded in 1952, postwar human rights politics was quite barren. Early human rights work tended to focus on rule of law at the domestic or international levels, and the ICJ also worked to ensure fair trials through observations.

One closely related field of international law and concern to human rights is humanitarianism. Although there are those who wish to draw hard distinctions between these two different approaches (Forsythe 2005b), in the most significant respects, human rights and humanitarianism are both fundamentally concerned with maintaining human dignity. HRW, under Aryeh Neier, made explicit reference to their compatibility, and the evolution of international human rights and humanitarian law has coalesced in recent decades. The erasure of the distinction between the two fields has increased in part because of NGO action (Barnett 2005; Osiatynski 2009).

One of the primary objections to evaluating humanitarian organizations with the same lens as human rights groups is that the former are foremost service providers and the latter are chiefly advocacy providers. Service provision might require an altogether different prioritization of agenda setting, thus resulting in inept structures for effective advocacy. Furthermore, because the raison d'être of service providers and advocacy providers differ, the comparison is naught.

I disagree with this view. It is true that many service providers do not "advocate" in the way that naming and shaming NGOs do. But it is also untrue to claim that humanitarian groups simply bury their heads in the task of saving lives without taking a stance, á la the classic Dunantist model of humanitarian work (Stoddard 2003). In the cases of Médecins sans Frontières (MSF) (examined in this chapter) and even the International Committee of the Red Cross (ICRC) (examined in chapter 5), advocacy, and at the very least, speaking out regarding the atrocities and suffering they witness, is something that is no longer alien to their routine.[2] I also argue that in the cases of MSF and ICRC in particular, advocacy has been very much a part of the implicit identity of these organizations, even if they subvert them to provide services. The ICRC created the Geneva Conventions through an impressive international campaign. MSF's témoignage (explained below), although a rough approximation of the advocacy human rights NGOs use, nonetheless explicitly identifies wrongdoers, victims, and the mechanisms that cause unnecessary suffering. Even if advocacy is not consistently a part of all service-provision organizations, it certainly plays a role in their international profiles.

As a further point, I have also included in this chapter an NGO whose reputation is built mainly on its development and humanitarian work, Oxfam International. Where the implicit identities of the ICRC and MSF were built in protest to state neglect or cruelty, Oxfam, in the beginning, sought to provide goods and services in the absence of state support. In recent years, however, scholars and activists working in this area have linked the language of human rights to the work of development (Alston 1998; Sen 2000; Sano 2000; Nelson and Dorsey 2003, 2007, 2008). Oxfam is not the only NGO moving in this direction—in fact, many of its peers are—but it is, to date, the only development NGO that has fundamentally redistributed agenda setting and implementation powers to meet its new goal of rights-based development, premised on advocacy and project-based strategies.

Each of the NGOs studied in this chapter use advocacy. Some of the NGOs have built their political salience through service provision, but this is different from their political salience as advocacy NGOs. Using organizational structure as the lens, I look at how the distribution of agenda setting and implementation shapes their salience as advocacy groups. What the cases in this chapter—HRW, MSF, ILHR, and Oxfam—demonstrate is that informal agenda-setting powers matter just as much as formal powers. NGOs that have many formally defined responsibilities on the one hand create a system with common expectations to which all can refer. On the other hand, excessive formalization can indeed lead to overlap in responsibility and authority, and can generate perverse outcomes in the case of conflict.

While there are certainly merits to how all of the NGOs here have chosen to distribute agenda setting and proposal power, they are not all uniformly well-positioned to generate political salience for themselves as organizations. This chapter proceeds through a brief history of each of these organizations, followed by a cross-organizational comparison along the three aspects of agenda setting to argue that the political salience of organizations is established through both formal and informal rules that centralize proposal and enforcement powers and decentralize implementation power. I then explain why alternative explanations are insufficient in elucidating the reasons for why NGOs become politically salient. I conclude with remarks on how these NGOs have affected the political salience of human rights, and why a shift in their organizational structures in campaigns (chapter 5) has helped most of these organizations generate political salience around the rights they advocate.

Organizational Histories

HRW: Defending Soviet Dissidents

Helsinki Watch was established by Random House publisher Bob Bernstein, known in its earliest days as the Fund for Free Expression, which was run by a lone staffer, Jeri Laber. Bernstein was eager to support the dissidents in Russia and the rest of the Soviet Union in holding the government accountable to the Helsinki Accords signed in 1975, as it had become clear that Moscow was not going to hold up to its agreements. The accords had included human rights provisions, which were insisted on by Western European countries, but Soviet negotiators had seen these as nominal, and after unsuccessfully fighting them, agreed to them but then continued the repression on critics of the regime. Bernstein founded the first of the regional Watch groups, Helsinki Watch, in New York in 1978, as a support group for the indigenous Watch groups in the USSR. Over time, however, the tactics of Eastern European governments and Moscow dispersed many of the dissident groups based in the Soviet Union. Under the aegis of Executive Director Aryeh Neier, Helsinki Watch expanded into Americas Watch (1981), Asia Watch (1985), Africa Watch (1988), and Middle East Watch (1989), adopting the name HRW in 1988.

It is worth mentioning that in some respects that HRW and Amnesty have common histories. Amnesty and Helsinki Watch focused early on particular prisoners. Both groups wrote letters in support of political dissidents, raised issues about their treatment, and formed groups around the world to advocate on behalf of those who were fighting in repressive countries. While Amnesty groups adopted prisoners, Helsinki Watch formed the more formalized International Helsinki Federation for Human Rights, which recruited prominent Western Europeans to help Helsinki groups in the East fight on against Soviet governments. Both organizations wrote reports based on country visits, and both NGOs lobbied Western governments to take action when faced with rights-violating regimes. Thus the early days of HRW reflected where the broader international human rights movement was, which in turn reflected how Amnesty's efforts had influenced the politics around human rights and which rights were established about political salience.[3]

Nonetheless, HRW is a distinct organization. HRW emphasizes its professional focus: paid, on-the-ground researchers with international outposts in international capitals and major cities.[4] It is not a grassroots-based movement, and therefore claims a much more modest footprint, both in terms of staff (275) and international reach.[5] HRW has also traditionally relied on big donors, whether foundational or politically and economically well-off individuals. It started with seed money from the Ford Foundation (Laber 2005), and Ford has remained an integral part of the organization. For example, it provided the impetus for an internal review that unified all of the various Watch committees under the umbrella HRW in the late 1980s. Without needing to rely on a dispersed membership for funding and manpower, HRW formed as a streamlined and professionalized organization with an ability to make bombastic statements and challenge the US government precisely because its funding came from a left-leaning foundation. In 2010, the NGO received money from the philanthropist George Soros for a ten-year project to build its presence globally.[6] As part of its ongoing strategy since 2008, HRW has contended with the need to build beyond its American offices in response to an increasingly regionalized world.[7]

ILHR: Supporting Human Rights

In 1894, Alfred Dreyfus, a member of the French General Staff, was accused of treason. As one of the first Jewish members of the army's highest command, he was in a vulnerable position. Until 1906, when he was pardoned, the so-called Dreyfus Affair roiled French politics, engaging members of the elite such as Emile Zola and demonstrating the rampant anti-Semitism of the time (Rabben 2002). It was during Dreyfus Affair that Ludovic Trarieux founded the Ligue des Droits de l'Homme et du Ci-toyen.[8] This organization became the precursor to Roger Baldwin's[9] Inter-national League for the Rights of Man in the United States, which revived the movement in 1942.[10] In 1976, the NGO changed its name to the ILHR. On its website, the ILHR claims:

> The International League for Human Rights has worked to keep human rights at the forefront of international affairs and to give meaning and effect to the human rights values enshrined in international human rights treaties and conventions. The League's special mission for 65 years has been defend-ing individual human rights advocates who have risked their lives to pro-mote the ideals of a just and civil society in their homelands.[11]

The NGO maintains consultative status with a number of IOs, includ-ing the UN and the Organization for Security and Cooperation in Eu-rope. Nonetheless, from both historical and contemporary perspectives, it remains difficult to discern the agenda of the ILHR. The principles of the NGO, in other words, have never been clear, in large part because its or-ganizational structure, strategies, and overall mission have precluded a de-finitive statement of human rights principles that is distinctively ILHR's.

A challenge to examining the ILHR is that there is relatively little re-search that has been done on such a long-standing organization, and all of it comes from the 1970s and early 1980s; there does not exist, to my knowl-edge, any current research on the work of the NGO in the past twenty-odd years. In fact, it is often mentioned as one of the NGOs that was around before Amnesty came onto the scene (Clark 1999, 314), but its own role in changing the tenor of the human rights world since the 1970s has at best been undetected, with the rise of other like-minded organizations. None-theless, several very sympathetic pieces offer clues as to why, in spite of its presence at the early human rights debates and its support for some of the most important human rights instruments we have today, the ILHR re-mains a small and unassuming NGO when compared to giants HRW and Amnesty, and also the smaller (but more media-savvy and salient) Physi-cians for Human Rights and Human Rights First.[12]

The ILHR is an organization and a larger network of federated NGOs—it is both a network of affiliate, independent organizations,[13] mostly concentrated in the West, and is also a part of the network itself. The organizations that have joined the network are mostly civil rights groups with prominence in their home countries, such as the ACLU in the United States and the National Council of Civil Liberties in the United Kingdom. Surprisingly, then, its scope is the entirety of the UDHR, as well as other international treaties (Shestack 1978). The ILHR leverages its links to domestic civil rights groups, taking advantage of their links when necessary in cases (Clark 1981) and otherwise using national-level groups as conduits of information (Ray and Taylor 1977, 480). In an unprecedented move, the ILHR decided to officially link to a non-Western human rights organization behind the Iron Curtain, called the Moscow Human Rights Committee. This was not just any Soviet NGO: it was headed by noted dissident Andrei Sakharov (Wiseberg and Scoble 1977, 307). This affiliation and effort to connect Soviet dissidents to freedom of expression, speech, and religion movements in the West came several years before HRW would start its fight against the USSR suppression of such rights.

Oxfam: Food and Health

During World War II, citizens of Oxford, England founded the Oxford Committee for Famine Relief ("Oxfam") in 1942.[14] Eventually the Oxford Committee became Oxfam Great Britain (GB), formally establishing branches in Canada in 1966,[15] and Belgium in 1964. Other branches soon built up in the United States, Australia, and Hong Kong. The degree to which the different branches of Oxfam were independent varied; Oxfam GB as the original, and as the largest, served as the center of the network of Oxfam organizations because it had created several of them.

In the early 1990s, then-CEO (executive director) of Oxfam Great Britain, David Bryer, in conjunction with Oxfam Belgium, had discussed the possibility of uniting Oxfams in Europe to create a bigger voice in Brussels, where the European Union was just starting to come together.[16] Oxfam leaders also saw the Rio Earth Summit of 1992 as a catalyst for uniting the Oxfams formally—if they had the same policy for that meeting, why not cooperate on other issues? Processes of increasing globalization after the Cold War made it clear to Oxfam leaders that having a unified advocacy stance among the Oxfams would be useful.

By 1994, the two Oxfams had made initial moves to partner with Dutch development giant Novib and the Australian organization Community

Aid Abroad, as well as existing Oxfams in Asia (Hong Kong) and the Americas (Canada, Quebec, and the United States).[17] In 1995, the newly incorporated Oxfam International came into being, headquartered in Oxford, with offices in Addis Ababa, Brasilia, Brussels, Geneva, New York, and Washington, DC. It is currently a confederation of fifteen independent NGOs. The purpose of Oxfam International is to avoid duplication of efforts on the research, advocacy, and eventually, on-the-ground project levels. Oxfam International gives the movement coherence and the ability to advocate an Oxfam position before intergovernmental organizations—the World Bank, the International Monetary Fund, the United Nations, the EU—as well as in grassroots efforts, such as the campaign in favor of debt forgiveness for very poor countries. Oxfam is also making moves toward the consolidation of funding local development projects, which had to date been at the discretion of individual Oxfams.[18] In recent years, Oxfam has moved toward a model of rights-based development, which naturally requires more advocacy and fewer programmatic (development) projects.[19]

Oxfam International's International Secretariat, led by its own executive director, works in conjunction with the executive directors and boards of the sister organizations through the formal governing bodies of the Oxfam International Board and the executive director meetings. Its role is seen as both facilitative and leading.[20] But because the Oxfams came together rather late in their history, when each national section had established its own domestic fund-raising, footprint, and distinct identities in both their own countries and in the developing countries in which their projects have taken place, the process of unifying those distinct NGOs has been gradual. National section executive directors take the lead with decision making, though as more aspects of Oxfam's work go to the international level, this dynamic may change. For instance, there are many multilateral working groups that operate much more informally that help synchronize international campaigns.[21]

MSF: Doctors with Critical Voices

MSF's founders were French radicals in the 1960s—it was established in December 1971 when a group of medical doctors and medical journalists gathered to form a "core group intended to change the way humanitarian aid was delivered" (Phelan 2008, 1) after witnessing the complicity of both the media and the International Committee of the Red Cross in the deaths of a million Biafrans in the Nigerian civil war. As a consequence, MSF was founded in part on the notion of "témoignage," or (roughly translated) "witnessing." The reputation for speaking out against atrocity has established MSF as a "maverick" NGO among its humanitarian compatriots (Bortolotti 2006). It also established a basis from which MSF could advocate on behalf of beleaguered populations, in addition to providing them with life-saving services,[22] in part reflecting the political bent of its founding corps (Barnett 2009). In 1999, MSF received the Nobel Peace Prize "in recognition of the organization's pioneering humanitarian work on several continents."[23] It made the decision to use the winnings from the Nobel Prize to establish its first full-time advocacy campaign, the Access to Essential Medicines campaign (discussed in chapter 5), marking a turning point in the NGO's self-identity in which advocacy gained a more permanent, institutionalized place in its work beyond the ambiguity of the témoignage response.

MSF-France was the first of the national sections established, followed by MSF-Belgium in 1980, MSF-Switzerland in 1981, MSF-Holland in 1984, and MSF-Spain and MSF-Luxembourg in 1986.[24] Under the old model, France, Belgium, Holland, Switzerland, and Spain were the original "operational sections," supported by fourteen "nonoperational sections." Each operational section had a different number of nonoperational sections tied to it, depending on the extent to which they had expanded. Operational sections sent medical missions, whereas nonoperational sections performed administrative tasks, such as fund-raising, recruitment, and publicity. However, by the 2000s, it became clear for a number of the operational sections that nonoperational sections were contributing much of the money and manpower for the missions; nonoperational sections in some cases, such as those tied to MSF-Holland, demanded more accountability and inclusion.

In response, "operational section" was replaced with an "operational center" (OC), signaling a change from subordinate to associative partner. "OC" designates the partnership between the former operational sections and the other national sections. However, the degree to which the former nonoperational sections participate in managing missions varies from OC to OC. OC-Amsterdam (OCA) is the most decentralized of the larger OCs—OC-Paris (OCP) and OC-Brussels (OCB)—having signed a

Memorandum of Understanding about the power sharing between OCA members.[25] The variation between OCs is unchecked—the international structure of MSF does not allow for OCs to require changes in any other OC. This means that each national section has its own funding, advocacy, and marketing priorities. Each section makes its own rules (Dechaine 2006). Until very recently, international-level agenda setting was not very robust.

On June 27, 2011, MSF's national sections adopted a new statute that reformed existing international governance structures. With an eye toward strengthening the international bodies, the new International General Assembly (replacing the Council), along with the International Board, will "be responsible for safeguarding MSF's medical humanitarian identity and mission."[26] The intention behind these changes reflects the growing realization that had been growing since the La Mancha agreement in 2005—MSF has expanded far beyond the developed world, extending its reaches into countries such as South Africa, Brazil, Argentina, and the Czech Republic (Jayawickrama 2010). With this expansion, proponents within the organization felt that the international structure needed reconsideration.

Until the most recent changes were made, international structures were often overridden (Jayawickrama 2010), in some ways speaking ambiguously about the importance MSF placed on the "international" part of the organization. The International Office was founded in 1990 (Tanguy 1999). The office was composed of the International Secretariat and the International Council. The council was made up of all of the presidents of the boards of each MSF national section, with the international president, and is the highest international governing body in MSF. It has been replaced by the General Assembly with the hopes of making it more representative of more diverse interests.[27] A smaller body, called the International Council Board, oversees the work of the office. The Geneva-based secretariat supports the work done at the international level. Prior to 2011, there were many other formal groupings at the international level, called platforms, of which the more general ones are: the RIOD (Restricted International Operations Directors), composed of the operational directors of the five OCs; the ExDir, a group of all of the general directors of each national section; and ExCom, which only includes the general directors of the five OCs. There are also platforms that make fund-raising, communications, and medical decisions. With the 2011 changes, however, the importance of these other groups might wane in favor of shifting more proposal and enforcement power to the General Assembly and Board. Because of the newness of the reforms, and thus, the difficulty with assessing their effects and the extent to which MSFs come to embrace these changes, this chapter discusses how the International Council, OCs, and other international platforms have affected MSF's advocacy abilities prior to 2011.

The Role of Organizational Structure

The distribution of the three dimensions of agenda-setting, proposal, enforcement, and implementation powers, can vary from NGO to NGO quite dramatically. This becomes especially apparent when we distinguish between informal and formal ways to distribute agenda setting. Given the importance of organizational structure in shaping NGO influence over international norms, I do want to discuss some caveats. First, it is probably fair to say that those international NGOs that did not start out as international—that is, the "international" aspect came about after at least one of the members had already reached prominence on its own—tend to have a greater number of formal rules as a function of the need to define new roles after creating a transnational organization. It also has something to do with organizational values, about which I do not go into much detail here. Some organizations desire dissent, whereas others seek conciliation. Some are concerned about defining a unified front, whereas other NGOs might not see that as an absolute need while simultaneously recognizing that coherence in advocacy does have its merits for influencing international policy.

Furthermore, when comparing advocacy NGOs, especially those that are not explicitly "human rights" groups, it is important to state that there is variation in how much NGOs want to frame their work as advocacy. Some organizations, such as MSF, tread carefully when speaking of their advocacy work, believing that an overemphasis on "political" work might compromise its humanitarian operations. This stands in contradiction to its founding charge against the International Committee of the Red Cross's refusal to speak out against the government's abuses of civilians during the Nigerian civil war (1967–70). Other NGOs are less reluctant to admit their roles in changing human rights, or in generating change in the political salience of certain types of rights that they argue human beings need.

Proposal Power

Proposal power is the power of suggestion, which accounts for both creating agenda items and keeping alternatives from reaching the agenda. Those with proposal power also hold the power to frame issues as they see fit, and which ones to highlight as human rights abuses that an NGO might pursue. As outlined in chapter 2, the fewer proposers there are, the more centralized this power is and vice versa. The NGOs in this chapter differ in the number of proposers they have, which can affect the diversity of views that get aired and the degree to which the process is participatory.

The early history of HRW was characterized by the ability to change advocacy directions quickly, precisely because proposal power largely lay in the hands of two offices: the executive director and the relevant regional or thematic director. Despite the fact that the Watches were nominally separate organizations, by the founding of Middle East Watch, they had clearly become part of an overall grander scheme headed by executive director Aryeh Neier.[28] Early on, Neier harnessed the power of the media in facilitating political change, provocatively taking on the US government for its tolerance of obvious abuses in Latin America. The story of a little NGO named HRW taking on the leader of the free world generated tons of press. This media savvy has continued to play a big role in the NGO and is something that leaders must balance with the desire to expand the scope of HRW's human rights coverage.

The director of each of the regional and thematic programs retained tremendous proposal power in deciding cases that researchers would investigate, and how the information would be presented in reports. They also suggested the policy recommendations that accompanied the reports. Rarely would the executive director stand in the way of a well-conceived proposal brought forth by a regional or thematic director, since they were the known experts in their respective regions and issue areas.[29] Throughout the interviews I conducted with HRW staffers past and present, many of them point to the deference with which they treat researchers' expertise. Informally, therefore, researchers and thematic or area directors gain support because other staffers prioritize the quality and correctness of information.

Under Neier, both he and the regional and thematic directors retained proposal power. Though he gave directors a fair amount of leeway, Neier also had a clear sense of how he thought human rights advocacy should progress. For example, he spearheaded the integration of international human rights with international humanitarian law (Neier 2005). Founded clearly after Amnesty had established an influential position in human rights politics, Helsinki Watch, and more importantly, Americas Watch, needed to tread new ground. The desire to be different from Amnesty was both conscious, as Neier and other leaders in Americas Watch were well aware of Amnesty's accomplishments and shortcomings,[30] and unconscious, as the focus of HRW was bound to be different given that those who took up its cause (New York lawyers)[31] and the structure of the organization, focused on Neier's and the directors' research agendas and expertise. For much of the earlier period of HRW's history, then, the topics of advocacy came from two sources, the executive director and the regional or thematic director.

After Neier's departure in 1993, the NGO went through a review that was spearheaded by one its main funders, the Ford Foundation. As the organization had grown both in the number of programs and in its international presence, the new (and current) executive director Kenneth Roth decided that it was time to implement a different apparatus that would unify the advocacy agenda of the NGO. With the program and thematic directors given so much leeway in the past, reigning in their agenda-setting power proved to be a somewhat difficult process, as many long-time directors balked at the restrictions on their proposal power. The creation of the senior management team (now called the Leadership and Management Team—LMT) and several offices designed to coordinate the various programs' efforts—the establishment of the General Counsel and Program Director, more specifically—forced researchers and their directors to go through an additional review process of their reports. These two offices curtailed the relative freedom of the directors to propose new projects, as they had to be consistent with existing and past work that some had seen as the strength of HRW.[32] Since the establishment of the LMT in 1994, proposal power has increasingly moved from the program directors to the coordinative bodies in HRW. Thus, though there is still room for creativity and new project directions, directors and researchers alike find themselves reigned in in an effort to maintain consistency across the multiple programs. The LMT also decides where new offices are built and controls the expansion of HRW.

HRW has historically been able to maintain proposal power among few actors. Nonetheless, a cross-current emphasizing the independence of researchers is also a prominent aspect of the work. There is a core belief that researchers should pursue what is the most pressing issue of the day, even if it might not be as marketable from a communications or publicity perspective.[33] Although the LMT and other central staff can propose projects and provide input at January meetings, the specific projects come from researchers and their respective directors.[34] On the outset, HRW seems to be very centralized, and in fact hierarchical, because of the formal roles of its central staff, but its emphasis on quality research informally gives researchers more discretion over projects.

Other NGOs have had quite different histories. For instance, MSF's history has been marked by various disagreements between its five main national sections. The change to the Operational Center structure created more entrenched (and formalized) proposal power for each of the OCs. In addition, the International Council serves as a further source of proposal power for MSF as an international NGO. In terms of formal international bodies, the council proposes goals for MSF overall, but such declarations remain general and gain consent precisely because they focus on things to which everyone can agree.[35] The council has the ability to make decisions about expansion—adding new national sections, changing the status of existing national sections—as it is the highest level of governance in MSF. Since its establishment, the International Office, working alongside the Council, has coordinated efforts to centralize some parts of MSF's work, such as establishing common medical protocols.[36] The international level proposal power remains limited but has grown over time and exists alongside the more-established roles of the OCs. Periodic MSF-wide meetings, such as the 2005 "La Mancha" and the Odyssey, which concluded in 2011, address issues universal to all MSFs. They also establish common rules and goals, but these remain, in large part, difficult to enforce.

Proposal power proves elusive for MSF in an additional way. How information is produced and diffused reflects the multiplicity of proposers within the NGO. One of the primary reasons is that there are simply many sources of information (each of the five OCs reports on its own missions), and there are many points along the chain where discretion over information can be exercised before it is released outside of the MSF network into the broader world. Different types of information follow different paths.

Day-to-day messaging about missions is cleared by both the people in the field and the operations managers ("desks").[37] Press releases regarding countries in which there are missions run by multiple OCs need to clear at least every Head of Mission and operations manager before being released; if there are multiple OCs involved in-country, the advocacy needs to go to the RIOD. Strategic communications within OCs is handled by a team that represents all of the interests of the national sections, making policy decisions on things like blogging. However, the content of national level advocacy for each MSF is not regulated, so MSF-Germany might have a very different webpage and representation of the NGO than MSF-Canada.[38]

Finally, MSF's operations (service provision) take priority over advocacy work, as most see service provision as the raison d'être of the NGO. Operations are controlled at the OC level. Operations directors at each of the OCs make decisions about where to go for humanitarian missions, the types of projects they take on, and coordinate the logistics. That is, OCA and OCP can send simultaneous and multiple missions to the same country with little to no coordination beyond acknowledgment. This is the modal operational method, though in extremely risky contexts, such as the current mission to Afghanistan, OCs have chosen to act together.[39] In terms of advocacy positions, these are almost always linked to situations in the field and at the discretion of the operations directors. Consequently, OCs running missions in the same country can propose different advocacy positions, depending on the particular village or region they are in, and what challenges they face.

The problems posed by the unification of Oxfam are quite different. Because not all of the sister organizations in Oxfam International were Oxfams to begin with, the initial challenge was getting everyone on the same page in terms of principles and the types of development programs that each was administering on the ground. Oxfam is formally governed by an international Board, composed of the executive directors and Board directors from each sister organization (Brown 2007) and administered by the Oxfam International Secretariat. Each Oxfam gets one vote in the Board, despite vast differences in size and resources.[40] There is also a group of executive directors; the executive director of each Oxfam holds proposal power.[41] Oxfam International cannot pursue projects (advocacy, campaign, program) without delegation from national executive directors. In addition, the executive director of Oxfam International can flag issues s/he considers important for all Oxfams, thus exercising proposal power.

The power of the executive director of Oxfam International, who heads the International Secretariat, should not be overlooked as the Oxfams move toward an ever-more unified model of operation. First, new Oxfams, previously established by existing Oxfams, are now led by the Secretariat.[42] Thus expansion comes from the collaborative effort by sister organizations, rather than singular Oxfams pursuing new strategic goals. Second, the priority placed on creating an international brand, advocacy principles and campaigns, and soon, the merging of programs on the ground, makes the position of executive director of Oxfam International increasingly important. Integration increases demand for coordination, which the international office is designed to provide. Resolving differences between Oxfams and coming to a common advocacy position, such as the Oxfam position regarding Israel and the Occupied Territories, is a challenge that falls to the executive director of Oxfam International to resolve, proposing solutions to the sister Oxfams. As of this writing, the Secretariat runs several advocacy offices: Brasilia, Brussels, Geneva, New York, and Washington, DC.[43]

However, the internationalization is not complete. The different sizes of the national Oxfams creates proposal power imbalances, as more nascent sections simply cannot dream of some of the projects that Oxfam GB (the biggest) or Oxfam Novib can pursue (Brown 2007). Within the Oxfam network, there is a tendency to defer to Oxfam GB because of its size and its capabilities, particularly in advocacy.[44] Oxfam GB therefore has more proposal power on an informal level because other sections defer to it.

By far, the NGOs with the least amount of proposal power for any of its actors is the ILHR. There are two formal leadership organs: the International Board of Directors, made up of US members, and the International Advisory Committee, with an international composition (Ray and Taylor 1977). The intention behind the different compositions was to mitigate the effect of US dominance, consciously forging an international network of affiliates with a common purpose. However, power lies with the Board of Directors. In the event of disagreement between the Board and Advisory Committee, the Board decides. The Board also has the power to approve the membership of national-level affiliates (Wiseberg and Scoble 1977, 296), which has important consequences for the ILHR's sources of information and finances.

In the late 1960s, an influx of cash allowed the NGO to develop an administrative infrastructure and expand its Board and the Advisory

Committee. Its funding structure circa the 1970s was based on individual, dues-paying members and the NGOs in its network, who were not obligated to (but could) fund the ILHR's activities (Wiseberg and Scoble 1977). Thus, even though the members of ILHR's network were quite professionalized, its own governing structure as the amalgamator of domestic efforts, was not.

From the little that is known, the ties between the ILHR and the national-level organizations were loose at best and informal by nature. Unlike the other NGOs examined here, the ILHR largely lacked the ability to see its agenda through fruition. While it had proposal power to take up new projects, funding remained a major constraint. Projects are funded in an ad hoc fashion, creating gaps between proposal power and other aspects of agenda setting.

Enforcement Power

Although linked, enforcement power and proposal power are two distinct mechanisms of agenda setting. For some organizations, these two powers are distributed to the same actors. In HRW's early days, compliance with vetoes and directives from the executive director and regional and thematic directors was part and parcel with the job. Veto power (and enforcement of that power) was given to the executive director precisely because Neier was seen as someone who could lead the NGO to success against the US government, and later in expanding the scope of human rights. Thus enforcement power was not an issue for HRW—regional and thematic directors could enforce vetoes vis-à-vis researchers, and ultimately the executive director was able to quash anything he did not like.

The shift in executive directors and the formation of the LMT added additional layers of accountability. Thematic and regional directors now have to garner approval on their reports from both the general counsel and the program director, both of whom are in place to ensure consistency across campaigns. Reports and proposals that do not pass muster do not go to publication or proceed through the next step. Thus, since 1994 and thereafter, the expansion of HRW's international profile has also made it so that the addition of LMT positions increases the number of actors who have enforcement power within the network, but this in turn serves as quality control for the information that the NGO disseminates to an increasing audience. The executive director, the LMT, and the relevant regional and thematic program directors therefore have enforcement power over any research project, though the power of the LMT and executive director is more formal and pro forma. Regional and thematic program directors work collaboratively with senior management on research directions,[45] and thus the formal veto power the executive director has is rarely used.

Because HRW historically developed from one main office, enforcement power has maintained a more or less "corporate" look in the sense that the central management has formal authority to change anything that researchers and directors do that they do not like. This power, however, is rarely exercised and de facto researchers and directors still receive assent from leaders because they are the experts on human rights cases. There is an emphasis on expertise and accuracy that stems from the long tradition of attacking the Reagan administration with facts that undermined its otherwise rosy position on questionable allies in Central America.[46] As Ken Roth sees it, the role of central management increases as campaigns develop and HRW sinks more resources into a project. The annual review process helps Roth and the rest of the LMT determine what the whole HRW picture is, and thus determine whether the NGO needs to go in different directions. Throughout my interviews with HRW staff, one of the notable things about those conversations was the emphasis that former and current staff members put on working on things collaboratively between researchers, directors, and central management, and thus, even though the LMT and most certainly the executive director have the ability to veto and enforce that veto, vetoes are not used.

Oxfam and MSF are almost the antithesis of HRW with regard to enforcement power. In both organizations, enforcement power has remained decentralized, as national sections have wanted to retain some autonomy from the international level. However, this decentralization has led to very different ends. For MSF, the decentralization of enforcement power is deliberate, reinforcing the notion of spontaneity in the field, and is consistent with MSF's ethos of airing minority views. Oxfam, by contrast, prefers to work via consensus, and thus avoids confrontations where vetoes must be exercised.

Enforcement power most evidently illustrates one of the fundamental tensions undergirding MSF today: what is the proper balance between advocacy and operations? Advocacy can be in three major forms: (1) press releases and public statements, (2) reports from the field, and (3) quiet advocacy that relies on negotiations with belligerents behind the scenes for improved conditions or access to new sites. Depending on the person and the national section, the answer can be drastically different, but two types of answers emerge.[47] The first is that MSF has a responsibility to shine a light on atrocity. The second is that MSF cannot speak if it jeopardizes the access they have been granted to patients. This tension plays itself out on a routine basis, as MSF does operate in some of the most dangerous and tenuous political situations in the world. The barrier to gaining organizational coherence is the fact that vetoers in MSF have no way to enforce their vetoes on either operations or advocacy. A concrete example is the decision to stay or leave refugee camps in Goma and Bukavu, Zaire, that were set up following of the 1994 Rwandan genocide. After discovering that belligerent Hutus were recruiting and taking supplies from the very refugees they had created, the French section balked and withdrew personnel from Goma. Belgium and Holland, however, continued to provide assistance for some time afterward. The MSF position in Goma was split: while MSF-Holland was firmly committed to providing assistance in spite of the recipients, MSF-France found its role in creating more violence reprehensible, and the French section denounced the situation publicly.

On both operational and advocacy levels, the operations directors in each of the OCs can veto opportunities for collective actions and decisions, though vetoing advocacy is always easier than vetoing operations.[48] Operations decisions are also decided by a combination of other formal and informal bodies, including, when necessary, RIOD and ExCom—the smaller meeting of executive directors. Veto power is particularly important in protecting MSFers on the ground,[49] but they are not necessarily enforceable. The tendency can be for advocacy to suffer—MSF essentially self-censors for fear this may jeopardize people on the ground, or risk the expulsion of MSF. The head of mission, who is the staffer who runs operations for an OC in a particular country, along with the operations director, has the final say on whether communications about atrocities on the ground can be communicated to the broader world.

The aforementioned example of the refugee camps in Zaire is illustrative of both the lack of enforcement power and the controversial role of advocacy for different MSFs. When MSF-France pulled out of the Rwandan refugee situation altogether, it did so without consensus from the other four MSFs that had people in the field. Its actions were strongly opposed by MSFs, most notably MSF-Holland (see Binet 2003). MSF-International announcements of the departure of MSF-France did not specify that it was the decision of only one national section, causing confusion over the continued work of MSF in refugee camps.[50] Just as MSF-France was unsuccessful in a bid to convince others to follow its withdrawal from the refugee camps, MSF-Holland and MSF-Belgium were unable to veto the French position. Faced with these enforcement problems, the tensions mounted among the different MSFs, and the international network nearly split over the incident.[51] Different principles of humanitarianism and the role of advocacy in helping populations in need came out during key meetings between the national sections.[52] Because of a lack of enforcement power, even when OCs or national sections disagree with one another, there is no effective system to veto opinions and enforce decisions, even when a majority agrees. Thus no other MSF, even the other four operational sections at the time, could stop MSF-France from pulling out of Zaire, which had reputational repercussions for the rest of the network.

Despite the fact that enforcement power is by and large decentralized, there is one enforcement capacity, and that is the power to pull the MSF trademark. To date, MSF has only had to do this once, in the case of MSF-Greece in the late 1990s, when the Greek section violated the fundamental tenets of humanitarianism—impartiality, neutrality, and independence—by openly supporting one side of the conflict during the 1999 Kosovo war.[53] Following the MSF-Greece incident, the MSF trademark was transferred to the International Office, which now has sole enforcement power over the brand. It remains unclear, though, under what circumstances pulling the trademark would be used, or whether an OC could ever have its trademark pulled. In more recent years, the lack of enforcement power has dogged MSF as it comes to grips with international profile and the internationalism of the network (Médecins sans Frontières 2005).

By contrast, one of the remarkable things that Oxfam members noted was the lack of major rifts between them and the ability to work through consensus.[54] This tendency has increased over time as Oxfams have grown more accustomed to working together. In case of disagreement, there are some formal rules. If any two Oxfams disagree with an advocacy position, they can effectively veto and halt the decision. Informally, Oxfam GB and Oxfam Novib need to support most projects. If either of them vetoes, most projects would be impossible to execute because they are both much bigger (money, personnel) than the others.[55] Oxfam's enforcement power is largely undefined and informal, with very few formal restrictions on the actions of different national sections. Because of the lack of formality, both the executive director and the British and Dutch sections have quite a bit of enforcement power. Oxfam GB also serves a critical function in advocacy because it has the most resources dedicated to it, and the centrality of London provides media access. Every few years, the Oxfams come together to construct a strategic plan, whose enforcement falls on Oxfam International. Although the executive director of Oxfam International cannot compel the various Oxfams to comply with their own plan, the role is facilitative and sets the agenda for international level Board meetings. Formally, the executive director has very few powers, but there is a lot of room to negotiate in the role. Particularly for enforcement, the executive director has undefined powers delegated to him through "facilitation."

One of the other tools that Oxfam International and some members have to enforce vetoes in Oxfam is the control over the brand "Oxfam International." Oxfam International controls the name and trademark for Oxfam and licenses it out to individual Oxfams. However, the original signatories to Oxfam International keep their names, should they choose to leave the network formally. The job of "policing" the brand falls on the executive director,[56] who keeps tabs on all of the different national sections.

The power of the international office to police, however, does not go unchecked. In theory, Oxfam sections can move against unfavorable international-level decisions by pulling the plug on funding. Oxfam International does not have the power to tax the national Oxfams.[57] Each sister Oxfam contributes a set percentage of its budget to the international coffers.[58] In theory, therefore, unhappy Oxfams could threaten with the power of the purse, but the equality of contributions of all sections makes it harder for any one section to credibly threaten international decisions through veto.

Although Oxfam and MSF have a multiplicity of actors with enforcement power, the ILHR does not have much enforcement power to speak of. Its reliance on national-level sections was dual: it not only needed compliance from the member organizations to find facts, the funding scheme seemed to be premised on the voluntary transfers from the member organizations. These transfers of both cash and information were not obligatory, and as such, the ILHR's reliance on its members was shaky at best. Until 1968, it operated without a full-time administrator (executive director) (Wiseberg and Scoble 1977, 296). In contrast to some of the more modern NGOs discussed in this chapter, the ILHR operated on a nineteenth-century ethic that prized amateurism: charitable efforts supplied by its members when necessary and ad hoc fund-raising supported expensive projects, such as missions. If anything, ILHR is neither able to enforce any of its decisions, nor provide itself with reliable information on a regular, sustainable basis. In fact, enforcement power ultimately rests with its member NGOs—if they do not respond to decisions made by the Board or Advisory Committee with money or support, there is nothing to obligate them to do so. A very similar dynamic repeats itself when we consider implementation of the agenda. Without formalized, or even regularized, outlets for its advocacy, the ILHR relied on the goodwill of member societies and the capacities of its executive director and staff. What this means, then, is that unlike other NGOs examined in this book, the ILHR clearly lacked a strategy for implementation. Without centralized agenda-setting power and ad hoc implementation, the ILHR's structures are clearly not designed to change international norms in any meaningful sense of the term, and it is not at all clear what kind of stamp its participation bears on international human rights law.

It seems, furthermore, that this funding scheme and the looseness of the network of civil rights organizations was precisely ILHR's problem in the past. Once it moved out of the business of law making—that is, pushing for the creation of the very legal instruments that others sought to hold states against—the ILHR was, in some sense, out of business at the international level, and with it went the incentive for its network of national-level civil rights organizations to continue supporting it. The flexibility of the network that was so helpful in earlier years in terms of securing international legal instruments and finding cases that no one else touched in the colonized world no longer helped the ILHR once those issues had been mined. Even as it turned to a new set of strategies, such as taking on individual complaints of abuses or targeting other international financial institutions (Wiseberg and Scoble 1977, 308–10), it had no army with which to pursue such goals. Other NGOs were better poised to do such work, as even its sympathetic reviewers point out. ILHR's spin-off, Human Rights First, has, by contrast, been able to weather the storm of competition with other human rights groups and has a respectable budget ($36.5 million in 2010) and niche for human rights work.[59]

Assessing Implementation and Impact

The advantage of examining such long-lived organizations is that we can evaluate their effects much more easily than more modern NGOs. A priori, it is difficult to assess the time it takes for norms to change, and it is often also murky when one is pressed to identify where and when rights have become politically salient. That is, "that one can talk about a violation indicates the existence of a norm. Many norms are so internalized and taken for granted that violations do not occur and the norm is hard to recognize" (Finnemore 1996, 23). To effectively create political salience for their advocacy, NGOs must be able to come up with cohesive principles and implement them transnationally. To become politically salient as organizations, they need both centralized agenda setting and decentralized implementation.

Historically, because HRW focused on reporting, and because its targets were largely high-level actors in the West, implementation of its agenda meant targeting the right legislators or offices with their reports (Brown 2001). The first offshoot was the Washington, DC office, set up to target the American government. The fall of the USSR and the rise of importance of European states has changed the focus somewhat. After Neier's departure, HRW also set up a UN office, reflecting both a change in the philosophy of the leadership and also the shift of the balance of power in the post–Cold War world in 1988. Finally, while the locus of HRW's operations remains in New York, it has, in recent years, established outposts in major cities around the globe, including Berlin, Brussels, Geneva, Moscow, Johannesburg, Rio de Janeiro, and Tokyo, among other places, to increase its access and profile among international organizations and developing countries.

The inevitable growth of its program and strategy has led to HRW's need to target its agenda beyond the US government. Over the years, as HRW has expanded its reach into different countries, implementing the agenda means a much more diffuse strategy with multiple targets. However, the number of staff do not come close to the other major international NGOs studied here: in 2008, it employed 275 people,[60] compared to nearly 500 in the Amnesty IS office alone. Although a growing staff and an increase in offices contribute to a decentralizing implementation process, the majority of the advocacy HRW does remains at the report level. More to the point, HRW's primary strategy does not require widespread implementation and targets elites rather than publics. Measuring success means evaluating long-term changes, which often means thinking about legal changes.[61] Although HRW can be interested in short-term outcomes, such as giving assistance to refugees, most of the time it is interested in targeting states to make commitments to more permanent policies. The complexity of post–Cold War politics means that multiple states can and should be targeted for any given campaign, but it also avails more ways to think about advocacy success.

Furthermore, HRW has implemented the strategy of setting up city committees, which are designed to provide funds, community outreach, and advocacy for the NGO. HRW generally targets influential and affluent people, whose efforts work in concert with a general advocacy strategy. These city committees, which began in 1999 with the establishment of groups in New York and Los Angeles, can help HRW pursue more locally specific strategies by accommodating access to local-level officials in human rights campaigns. They can also raise awareness of HRW in local press outlets or create partnerships with community actors. For example, in Canada, the Toronto city committee helps set up HRW's film festival and held symposia around the case of Omar Khadr,[62] who was the youngest person held in Guantanamo Bay. City committees allow HRW's New York headquarters to decentralize implementation power without decentralizing proposal and enforcement power. Thus, city committee efforts remain complementary to general HRW efforts but also give the NGO access to political and economic resources it otherwise might not have.

In evaluating the effect of early human rights campaigning, the ILHR provides us with an example of a lack of agenda setting and inconsistent implementation. Like other human rights NGOs that would follow, it is a fact-finding organization that sends missions abroad, speaks to governments, and issues reports. However, its agenda was often ad hoc and dependent on project-based donations, rather than a set budget for the year. Unlike other NGOs of its kind, ILHR never sat down and asked itself what it was: it took on projects as they came.[63] It is not surprising that it does not have a coherent advocacy agenda, but this flexibility also allowed

ILHR to go outside the "human rights" box. A distinguishing feature of the ILHR from other human rights NGOs is its concentration on colonial and postcolonial issues (Clark 1981; Wiseberg and Scoble 1977). Between 1949 and 1960, the league worked on thirty-five to forty different colonial holdings, offering assistance for resistance movements seeking an international platform (Clark 1981, 103). Put differently, the league sought standing for independence movements and colonized society's within the UN framework, that is, "it has adopted a moderate approach which emphasizes individual liberties rather than the group right to self-determination" (Clark 1981, 106). In many cases, the ILHR helped independence movement leaders gain access to international forums such as the UN in order to plead their cases, getting particularly involved in the case of East Timor. The ILHR regularly helped groups that did not have much voice gain access to international organizations through the process of affiliation.

Beyond affiliation and working with UN officials, it is hard to place a finger on the contributions of the ILHR. When money was available, it would send people to do work in the field, but by and large, even its reporting seems to have been more ad hoc than we have grown accustomed to with other human rights NGOs. Implementation was not so much decentralized as it was unpredictable. There is anecdotal evidence for the ILHR's success in bringing things to the international agenda. For instance, in 1985, UN Secretary General Javier Perez de Cuellar made an appeal on behalf of several foreigners who had gone missing in Lebanon after receiving an ILHR report.[64] The NGO has hosted speakers whose political standing might be tenuous and it also grants a human rights award whose past recipients have included former Taiwanese president Chen Shui-bian and former Irish president Mary Robinson.

Implementation faces a different set of challenges when international NGOs are fundamentally built from national-level sections accustomed to a degree of autonomy. The fact there is no central agenda setter (in terms of proposal and enforcement power) means that every MSF essentially pursues either its own agenda or the agenda of the OC to which it is affiliated. The multiple points of agenda setting correspond to the implementation of several distinct agendas, which may or may not overlap. MSF's two-headed implementation—advocacy and service delivery—go hand in hand, and both demonstrate the decentralized nature of the NGO. While decentralized service-delivery capitalizes on the creativity of the talents in the field and lets protocol arise out of situations, it also leaves the door open for exploitation by belligerents. Decentralization of advocacy, which we have already seen above, leads to empty or vague statements at best, and counterproductive actions at worst. In the most volatile—and therefore insecure—situations, the implementation of distinct agendas can have cross-cutting effects. Considering that MSF prides itself as being one of the first to any conflict or disaster situation on the ground, the decentralization of implementation can have frequent, costly effects on the organization as a whole.

MSF's multiple agenda setter and implementation structure is no secret—governments and international bureaucrats recognize this fact. The benefit for a service-delivering NGO to be able to have different agendas is the ability to adapt to different environments, even within the same state. Terrain, the challenges of fighting disease over famine, or government versus nonstate actor leadership are all factors that each team sent into the field needs to contend with in order to be able to help populations. There cannot be a centralized policy that accounts for the variety of problems that doctors, nurses, and logisticians encounter on the ground. In this sense, having context-specific implementation is a practical solution to unpredictable on-the-ground conditions. In fact, having several agendas can help some OCs stay, even as others get expelled, as shown above in the case of Sudan.

The cost of having such flexibility in the field is the collective action problem that MSF does not hide. This openness comes at a cost, as it leaves it vulnerable for others to exploit these differences and play sections off of one another. That is, belligerents may try to play different MSFs off of each other in the field, as every OC's mission has its own lead administrator (head of mission). Thus, the head of mission for OCP and the head of mission from OCA do not have to coordinate their activities, even if their project may have overlapping responsibilities or logistical similarities. Heads of mission, in particular those with OCP, consult regularly with their headquarters, relying on advice from the home office.[65] The decentralized nature of implementation at the field level means that decision-makers are faced with different incentives to act; belligerents can capitalize on these incentives to gain policy in their favor.

In terms of advocacy, the ability of local (national-level) MSFs to dictate what information goes onto their websites and how to publicize the MSF project more generally gives communications officers considerable leeway. It also creates inconsistency in messaging across MSFs, and thus it is not easy to speak of a core MSF message. Even at the OC level at the meeting of RIOD, for example, the minority clause allows one or more MSFs to disavow the "official" line on things. MSF's condemnations of the wrongdoers in political humanitarian situations becomes watered down or subject to impassioned criticisms of one OC, historically from OCP. Témoignage, which has according to one insider gone through four phases in the history of MSF (Soussan 2008), is something that staff for MSF struggle with. Whereas the more strident, maverick tone is the one that MSF might have built its reputation on, it is certainly not the character of the advocacy that the NGO uses today. Often in contemporary situations, MSF reports about what it does rather than condemns systemic or political forces. Those who have been around MSF for a long time, such as Rony Brauman, acknowledge there is legerdemain when using the term: the golden age of témoignage was in the late 1980s and early 1990s, when criticizing governments openly was more common. Nowadays, témoignage is much more self-reflective. Generalizing about MSF is a difficult task, particularly in terms of advocacy, precisely because there are a lot of agenda setters and sites of implementation of that agenda. Furthermore, the shifting tension between témoignage and activity in the field forces MSF to reflect on the role of advocacy regularly.

For Oxfam, like MSF, implementation means coordinating both advocacy efforts and programs on the ground in communities. The former has proven to be much easier and quicker to do than the latter. Early in the process of unifying Oxfams, many of the tensions lay in balancing the various "personalities" of the different sections, which had existed before the notion of a unified Oxfam had ever come about. Therefore, the job of the first executive director was to balance the needs of these formerly independent NGOs and build trust between them for future steps. Part of the job was to convince Oxfams that collaboration would, over the long run, help Oxfam International become better at advocating principles and accomplishing development goals in the field.[66] Over time, the trend has been growing formalization of shared international tasks and informal cooperation between various Oxfams. National sections still direct the implementation of the common agenda, but increasingly the benefits of scale achieved through cooperation are understood as beneficial rather than a denial of independence.

Implementing advocacy at the international level has largely taken place with the addition of the specialized offices of Oxfam International, as well as efforts at the team level between various Oxfams. International implementation has been successful in large part because the international strategic plans cover the great majority of advocacy projects. On a day-to-day level, the links between managers at different Oxfams helps bridge the differences between the national sections. These connections are informal and ad hoc, depending on the nature of the project and need, and thus create cohesive work mostly in the areas of research, fund-raising, and interacting with media to convey the Oxfam message on a particular campaign or issue.[67] The first real internationalized campaign in which Oxfams joined forces—in addition to their own national-level efforts—was in lobbying the World Bank and International Monetary Fund to forgive debts owed by heavily indebted poor countries in the 1990s (Yanacopulos 2001). With all of the Oxfams working together, lobbyists were able to reach not only national leaders in their own countries, but also a greater range of policymakers at the international level and the global media with a consistent message.

Changes are ongoing, however, in terms of implementing development and humanitarian programs. The old scheme of funding local projects, for instance, has traditionally carried a single Oxfam's label. On-the-ground work is seen as the glory-getting task,[68] so one of the difficulties facing the international-level negotiations is coaxing individual Oxfams that sharing the work in the end is more effective and more desirable than maintaining singularly managed projects. Even when each Oxfam maintains autonomous programs, they coordinate their efforts so as not to end up supporting opposite causes in the same country. As of 2009, about a third each of Oxfam programs are divided into single section sponsors, two to four sponsors, and the rest with more than four affiliates.[69] Oxfams have also moved toward joint-funding of projects and mutual monitoring of projects, usually two Oxfams reviewing a third's performance.[70] In 2010, the NGO hopes to iron out the rest of the details in merging all development programs into a single "Oxfam" banner. All of these efforts are attempts to formalize the sharing of projects that carry the NGO's name.

In spite of the need to further coordinate programmatic work, the evolution toward a more unified Oxfam international strategy comes at the expense of program work. Although Oxfam began as a charity delivering goods to the needy in Greece, they have moved progressively toward an advocacy focus. Rights-based approaches to development require both on-the-ground programs and advocacy of protecting individuals' rights. Currently Oxfam leaders have weighted advocacy more heavily.[71] This is both instrumental and philosophical. From their perspective, development organizations can achieve more through national-level and international advocacy campaigns that encourage states to protect human rights as a precursor or requirement to development. The argument also fits a shift in philosophy. While Oxfam is famous for its application of the aphorism that teaching a man to fish is better than giving him a fish, its current turn to emphasizing the causes of underdevelopment—state repression or negligence—requires that states step in and protect their citizens. The attenuation of program vis-à-vis advocacy, then, is part of both a perceived change in the international environment and also a change in the philosophical orientation of development organizations that seek to prevent man-made humanitarian disasters by going after their root causes.

As Oxfam International solidifies its expanding role in the internal politics between Oxfams, we should expect to see a change in the distribution of formal and informal duties. Oxfam International currently self-consciously views itself as a confederation, with shared and important duties carried out by the national sections. Executive directors by rule maintain a central role in decision making for their own Oxfams, as well as the trajectory of the International. Chairs of various sections decide on the policies of the International and work closely with executive directors to decide each individual section's position. Formal rules have expanded the mandate of the International as Oxfams have come to coordinate their work more broadly. However, in speaking to staff, it is clear that the ad hoc teams that form between national Oxfams to achieve specific goals or work on new projects are the engines that implement international level policies. Informal ties weigh heavily on the implementation of Oxfam International's agenda as the formal relationships that bind Oxfams become more routinized.

Other Explanations

It is clear from the case studies that organizational structure plays an important role in bolstering the political salience of NGOs. It is not the only factor, but focusing on other factors would be to ignore a critical factor to building the political salience of transnational advocacy NGOs. Centralized proposal and enforcement powers, and decentralized agenda implementation, are necessary but not sufficient conditions for salience. Importantly, the distribution of agenda-setting powers underlies how an NGO functions, and thus does shape how other factors discussed below get carried out.

All of the NGOs here are Northern NGOs, and thus the geographic location of these organizations is relatively homogenous. Nonetheless, among the cases discussed in this chapter, NGOs have chosen to distribute their offices quite differently. ILHR has one headquarters that coordinates among its partners and staff. HRW has moved rapidly to establish outposts in a variety of countries, but these newer offices still respond to the needs of the New York headquarters. Oxfam and MSF began as more decentralized NGOs, and thus, have had much more spread in terms of locations. The various branches of Oxfam and MSF differ in the level to which they can function independently, but a notable number of both NGOs' national branches can (or did) fulfill the necessities of basic operations—fund-raising, programming, and advocacy/outreach. Nonetheless, the concentration of, for lack of a better term, "major" offices in the global North does not diverge among the cases discussed here, and thus all of the cases in this chapter benefit from the boost from being Northern NGOs.

In terms of thinking about the importance of leadership and staff quality, one can look to the ILHR to demonstrate the importance of organizational structure in spite of leadership. Historically, the ILHR had prominent international figures at the helm (Baldwin), and its strategy of linking to other NGOs is one that Oxfam later adopted to grow itself into a cohesive NGO. ILHR had leadership, and it had ideas other NGOs used to fruition. In spite of this, ILHR did not grow; it currently has a handful of staffers listed on its website.[72] In terms of size, the ILHR in its modern form cannot compete with the other NGOs examined here, but this is not conclusive evidence for why it is not a salient organization. The reason why the ILHR could not take off in spite of good beginnings was its organizational structure. We can also cite HRW as an example of the role of leadership, as it has had very few leaders since its founding. Both the qualities of the leaders, as well as the benefits of consistency under such long tenures have surely benefitted HRW. However, an emphasis on leadership quality or staff cannot necessarily explain why MSF, for instance, became so politically salient. Its early leadership splintered over the decision to provide medical assistance to the "boat people" from South Vietnam. This event led to the creation of Médecins du Monde by MSF co-founder Bernard Kouchner in 1980. It was MSF's initial decision to speak out, and its subsequent (albeit inconsistent) incorporation of témoignage into its work that has led to some of its most politically salient achievements. Similarly, while leadership may have played a significant role in establishing the Oxfam sister organizations in their respective countries prior to the decision to centralize, the structural choices made by Oxfam International have contributed to how salient their campaigns have been. Without the decision to centralize proposal and enforcement powers, Oxfam's best-known campaigns would have been difficult to execute. Internationalization through centralized agenda setting and decentralized agenda implementation led to the salience for all Oxfams, particularly raising the profile for the smaller affiliates.

In terms of funding, the NGOs discussed in this book thus far have varied widely in their budget size. The only organization for which I do not have funding information is the ILHR.[73] MSF has the biggest budget, operating on nearly €617 million in 2009.[74] It allocates the least proportion of funds for awareness building, or témoignage, constituting approximately 4 percent of total expenditures, or €21.7 million. Comparing the budgets of Amnesty International (£21 million in 2010)[75] or HRW ($48 million in 2010),[76] however, makes it clear that in terms of publicizing government misdeeds and unjust situations, the numbers between advocacy delivery organizations and service delivery organizations are similar. Oxfam provides only a composite figure of €596.3 million for program expenses in 2009–10, a number that includes running programs on the ground and associated advocacy and campaigns,[77] but this figure is, again, comparable to MSF's total budget. There really is not an easy way to compare the effect of funding when all of these organizations allocate similar amounts of money to advocacy, although certainly one can argue that not spending enough probably leads to a lower profile. There is likely a spending threshold that organizations must reach, but this threshold is vague. Obviously the very poor NGOs cannot compete with leaders of the international movement, but among the leaders, there is very little variation in terms of level of funding. There is also likely a first-mover advantage, as similar spending does not necessarily mean similar salience. Amnesty and Human Rights First have comparable budgets (after conversion), yet Human Rights First does not have the network centrality or the influence over human rights politics that the older organizations does. It would certainly be foolhardy to dismiss the role of money in creating the political salience of organizations, but it is also incorrect to place too much emphasis on gross budgetary figures, and by extension, geography-driven arguments.

This leads to the final alternative explanation for the salience of organizations. Do some NGOs simply pick the right issues to advocate? Keck and Sikkink (1998) argue that issues that involve bodily harm, along with clear causality, or issues involving legal equality, are more likely to be affected by transnational actors. By now, it should be abundantly clear that many NGOs pick very worthy causes—development and poverty, access to essential human necessities such as healthcare and food, political prisoners. Most human rights claims involve at least a wrongdoer and a victim, often include some measure of bodily harm, and do involve claims of legal inequality that demands rectification. One would expect that general harkening to "human rights" generates more support, in part because of the importance of the term in contemporary politics. What we see here, however, is that NGOs vary quite a bit in the topics that they choose, and that as a field develops, NGOs develop niches for which topics they support. As we shall see in the next chapter, NGOs that pick up on causes that generate lots of support, such as the abolitionist movement, can fall apart organizationally. Similarly, NGOs such as HRW or Oxfam have successfully framed issues that find widespread enthusiasm, such as the International Criminal Court or Fair Trade, just as they have had campaigns that did not find such adherence—the small arms campaign.

Disentangling the effects of the issue from the effects of organizational structure, furthermore, is not feasible. How NGOs select, frame, and promote human rights is a function of the distribution of agenda-setting power. One cannot simply separate the effects of proposal, enforcement, and implementation power from the nature of a given issue, for the NGO fundamentally shapes the perception of any given topic. Although there is not a clean way to distill the effects of structure from issue, it is reasonable to argue that even if an NGO picks the "right" issue, it still requires agenda setting and implementation to generate support for the organization. The ILHR provides a good example of this. It promotes human rights but has struggled to become politically salient, even though it purports to espouse similar principles to other, more prominent NGOs.

Conclusion

In the four NGOs reviewed in this chapter, formal decentralization of proposal and enforcement powers led to an incoherence of the agenda unless informal powers were granted to an actor that could create consensus. Oxfam International's executive director serves this role when sister Oxfams disagree, finding points of compromise. Similarly, HRW's deference to human rights expertise means that formal enforcement and proposal power are exercised relatively infrequently compared to informal agenda setting by researchers and their program directors. Such an informal system does not exist in MSF. A profusion of formal rules among the OCs and various intersectional platforms means that a variety of actors might have overlapping duties that come into conflict when tough decisions need to be made. Without a tendency toward using informal, conciliatory measures to resolve standoffs between MSFs for proposal and enforcement issues, MSF's advocacy strategy is inconsistent across its national sections. Furthermore, this lack of need to agree also means that operations—that is, service delivery—might be impacted as well, as multiple OCs can run missions in the same country, creating redundancies and different priorities, on the one hand, but increased coverage and the opportunity to learn from mistakes, on the other.

Of the three agenda-setting powers, implementation power seems to be the one most subject to change, and this can result in great swings in political salience for an NGO. Particularly when we consider the campaigns of HRW and MSF in the next chapter, we can see that NGOs can make quite conscious efforts to change the way their agendas are implemented, and this can have enormous consequences for the political salience for their advocacy campaigns. If an NGO centralizes proposal and enforcement powers, it is relatively easy to shift the decision to distribute implementation responsibilities of a particular campaign or project more widely or not. In the next chapter, furthermore, we can see more clearly the relationship between organizational salience and campaign salience—to what extent do organizations make issues, and vice versa? Can having the right structure for a campaign lead to salience for an organization?

The take-home point of this chapter is that organizational structure is a choice, one predicated on many different factors, including organizational purpose, characteristics of founders, and decisions to "internationalize," among other things. No matter the reasoning behind the decisions to distribute agenda-setting power, these initial decisions are sticky, and have unanticipated consequences for advocates down the road. MSF's vacillation between actively practicing témoignage and subsuming its role to operational needs, for example, changes as the context in which the NGO operates shifts, from Cold War to post–Cold War, from a US-centric economy to one that encompasses many more actors, such as China and the European Union. Although actively changing the distribution of proposal, enforcement, and implementation powers is possible, the more formalized these powers were to begin with, the more difficult it may be to do so, as interests become entrenched over time. Specifically, proposal and enforcement powers may not change without dynamic effort by different parts of the NGO to restructure international agreements, such as Oxfam International in the mid-1990s in rebuilding its organization from the ground up. Navigating the transnational dilemma, as well as altered political and economic conditions, is a fundamental challenge for many international advocacy NGOs today. Generating political salience around an NGO today requires targeting many more actors than it did in earlier eras, as the loci of power shift from a few states to many, and from just states to intergovernmental organizations and multinational corporations. Thus the distribution of agenda-setting power matters even more as NGOs face an increasingly complex set of audiences for their advocacy efforts.

5

USING CAMPAIGNS TO EXAMINE
ORGANIZATIONAL AND IDEATIONAL SALIENCE

Thus far, I have established the importance of organizational structure for the political salience of organizations. NGOs that govern through centralized proposal and enforcement powers and decentralized agenda implementation have advantages over those that don't use this type of organization. This chapter establishes the importance of this organizational structure in shaping the outcomes of individual NGO campaigns, the primary vehicle by which many nonstate actors advance their advocacy efforts. A campaign involves concentration on a given issue, and often NGOs employ multiple tactics to push for a certain cause. For instance, as outlined below, abolitionists' efforts in the nineteenth century involved petitioning public officials as well as grassroots strategies to stir up public support via town hall meetings and the purchase of commemorative items to mark the savagery of slavery.

A campaigns-oriented approach highlights the two aspects of political salience discussed in this book. First, it allows us to understand how certain human rights norms become politically salient internationally through the efforts of NGOs. By demonstrating that the distribution of agenda-setting and agenda-implementation powers is similar across successful cases, it gives us a sense of how transnational advocacy campaigns need to be run in order to advance new ideas. Second, successful campaigns reveal the importance of organizational structure for even prominent NGOs. Thus politically salient NGOs can still fail to get their issues on the international agenda because they choose to decentralize agenda-setting power, or do not take advantage of decentralized implementation techniques. Building on previous chapters, this chapter synthesizes the multiple meanings of political salience to demonstrate how the salience of organizations can be delinked from the salience of ideas.

For the most part, the campaigns discussed in this chapter have been successful in creating focal points for states and, in some cases, have compelled corporations to change their practices as well. All of the cases in this chapter are snapshots in the advancement of human rights, whether that means protections against wartime abuse, access to affordable medicines, or the right to earn a fair wage. Most of the examples, however, are campaign specific or short lived, or they may have yet to be realized as a modus operandi of a given organization.

Some of the examples are surprising. HRW, as described in the last chapter and in other accounts, has always centralized its implementation approach in the sense that it relied on its own staff to advocate change. There was not an effort to engage others beyond its own efforts. Its campaigns against the use of landmines and cluster munitions in warfare have marked a significant departure from its other campaigns. HRW led a network of NGOs in pursuit of an explicitly international strategy to get states to commit to the elimination of such weapons. In a sense, the Landmines and Cluster Munitions campaigns marked a departure from standard "human rights" fare, straying into territory more commonly associated with the ICRC's work on the conduct of war and the rights of civilians and belligerents.[1] In so doing, it brought some common strands between humanitarian and human rights discourse together in the resulting Ottawa Convention.

Other campaigns discussed here form the mainstay of our understanding of transnational advocacy, such as the ICRC's pursuit of humanitarian principles. Though there are efforts to distinguish between humanitarian and human rights law, the ICRC can be thought of as a human rights advocate in its pursuit to protect individuals' treatment in wartime (Forsythe 1990). Without its agitation to get states to commit to the first Geneva Convention in 1864 and its subsequent efforts to encourage Red Cross societies in every country, humanitarian principles would not have been institutionalized as a safeguard to the conduct of war. While the principles that the ICRC has always touted as imperative—impartiality, neutrality, and independence—have come under intense scrutiny in recent years (Polman 2010; Rieff 2003), in the end, its success has come from the establishment of organizations (national Red Crosses) and standards for humanitarianism. For at least humanitarian principles, the ICRC largely sets the agenda, passing along such notions to other parts of the Red Cross movement—the national sections and the International Federation of the Red Cross/Red Crescent. Another familiar case is Anti-Slavery International's (ASI) campaign against chattel slavery in the eighteenth and nineteenth centuries. Citizen protests, spearheaded by ASI (then known as the Society),[2] and supported by political leaders, brought the practices of slave trading and slave holding to an abrupt halt. ASI's antichattel slavery movement represents the epitome of centralized agenda setting and decentralized agenda implementation.

Finally, the other two successful campaigns discussed here are MSF's Access to Essential Medicines Campaign and Oxfam International's ongoing Fair Trade efforts, on behalf of right to medicines (health) and right to fair wage. The comparison between these two is worthwhile in the sense that MSF's Access campaign has a very particular, insulated structure that distinguishes it from much of the NGO's other témoignage work. It openly acknowledges its aspirations to affect policy, and while based on medical principles, the Access campaign is an advocacy-only activity that has implications for MSF as a whole. Access, therefore, represents MSF's advocacy position regarding prices for HIV/AIDS medications, in addition to proposing alternative patterns of pharmaceutical investments for research and development on diseases that disproportionately affect the developing world. By and large, the Access campaign has enjoyed international support and gotten states and corporations to act in accordance with some of its demands. The Access campaign centralizes both proposal and enforcement power, but utilizes a certain level of decentralization in implementation, relying on national-level MSF efforts to get its message the widest possible audience. In contrast to the relative novelty of the

Access campaign for MSF, Oxfam International has, since the mid-1990s, made efforts to solidify international linkages between sister organizations in order to mount much more advocacy-centric tasks. Centralizing agenda setting has therefore been a major goal of the International Secretariat and the sister NGOs. The Fair Trade movement marked the first of a series of now prominent projects that utilize more centralized proposal and enforcement powers, while at the same time capitalizing on the reach that having thirteen national locations gives Oxfam.

The chapter concludes with an examination of the International Action Network on Small Arms (IANSA), which has, since the 1990s, advocated for international regulation and limitation of the trade of small arms and light weapons. In this section, I demonstrate how the structure of this campaign, despite the participation of salient NGOs such as HRW, Amnesty, and Oxfam, has limited the ability of its supporters to make gains in policy. Furthermore, despite widespread support among NGOs, it has not formulated a coherent agenda about small arms and thus cannot capitalize on the vast reach of its members. This case serves to illustrate the importance of focusing on organizational structure as an explanatory variable rather than alternative explanations that focus on the political salience of campaign issues.

HRW and the Landmines Ban

The nature of HRW's work makes parsing out its effect particularly challenging. Because the bulk of its advocacy comes in the form of pressuring officials through face-to-face meetings and making sure they receive copies of HRW's reports, the actual mechanism of the NGO's influence convincing an official to reckon with his country's human rights-violating behaviors is immeasurable; it is, at the very least, not likely to be part of public record. Assessing the power of HRW in human rights politics, therefore hinges on evaluating the few cases where its work has been publicly directed. HRW does make exceptions to its usual policy and pursues a number of projects that deviate from its modal style of advocacy. This is a strategic choice that is informed by the goal of advocacy. Increasingly the goal of achieving new international legal standards inclines HRW to pursue both more public and more collaborative projects.[3] Put differently, if it seeks to establish principles, rather than monitor compliance with extant ones, HRW pursues the public option. Thus, though the modal form of advocacy for HRW is not in persuading publics through grassroots mobilization, it has certainly become more inclined to pursue more broad-based techniques over time. Moreover, it has come to the realization that partnerships with local NGOs contributes to the quality of its reporting and the sustainability of their impact. This perspective has changed markedly since the early 1990s, when follow-ups and on-the-ground engagement was not seen as crucial.[4] I explore two separate but related campaigns: the antipersonnel landmines campaign and the more recent move against cluster munitions. Both of these campaigns were framed as "humanitarian crises" that disproportionately affect civilians after hostilities have subsided.

One of the most notable instances of HRW's departure from its normal advocacy techniques is its leadership in the International Campaign to Ban Landmines (ICBL). The ICBL won recognition for its efforts both with the 1997 Ottawa Convention, which banned the manufacture, use, and stockpiling of all antipersonnel landmines, and its receipt of the Nobel Peace Prize in 1997, which it shared with its founding coordinator, Jody Williams. The success of the ICBL also suggested a template for future NGO work: forming partnerships with small and medium-sized states against large, powerful states such as the United States (Roth 1998). Both HRW's decision to form the ICBL and the ICBL itself provide helpful illustrations of the theory presented in this book: centralized agenda setting combined with decentralized implementation creates political salience, in this case through the creation of law.

The work of HRW and Physicians for Human Rights in the field in Cambodia led to the decision to collaborate to stop the use of antipersonnel landmines (Williams and Goose 1998). Initial efforts in support of a ban against landmines met some resistance until HRW made the decision to lead a coalition of NGOs on the issue (Carpenter 2011). In 1992, six NGOs collaborated to found the ICBL: Handicap International (France), HRW (USA), Medico International (Germany), Mines Advisory Group (UK), Physicians for Human Rights (USA), and the Vietnam Veterans of America Foundation (USA). These founding six NGOs became the original Steering Committee. The ICBL helped create salience for an issue on which the ICRC had lobbied since 1973 but had failed to generate movement in policy (Cottrell 2009). From the beginning, the ICBL was established as a movement without a formal center: it neither had formal registration in any country (as NGOs must in order to receive the tax and other benefits in states) nor shared financial agreements (Bernstein 2008, 32). The ICBL, as such, existed as a mechanism to transfer information, expertise, and resources without existing as a recognizable entity with offices and people at desks. The ICBL had no secretariat at the time it was awarded the Nobel Prize (Williams and Goose 2008, 184, fn 6).[5] This quickly changed after the Nobel recognition but only with reluctance among the organizers. Participants and analysts alike attribute the success of the ICBL in securing the Ottawa Convention to its flexible campaign style.

Despite its lack of formal infrastructure and rules, the ICBL had a core that held proposal power and controlled information: its founding member NGOs, of which HRW was a leading force. Its contribution, consistent with its other advocacy, was to provide the ICBL with accurate research on the production, use, and destructiveness of the antipersonnel landmines that the coalition sought to eradicate. Following up on the ICRC's earlier efforts, HRW partnered with Physicians for Human Rights on a number of reports on the use of landmines in 1992 and 1993 (Wexler 2003, 569–570; Williams and Goose 1998). HRW also supplied the ICBL with its legal expertise and previous experience in linking human rights law with humanitarian law by reframing the issue of antipersonnel landmines as one that wrongly injured or killed unwitting civilians in two senses: noncombatants and rights bearers (Rutherford 2000, 96). Very early on in 1993 (and again the following year), the campaign organized a conference of NGOs to discuss the issue of landmines to draw in like-minded participants, but also to bring attention to the issue of landmines (Rutherford 2000, 87). The ICBL itself recognized the need for publicity about its cause, anticipating that different audiences would interpret the idea of banning antipersonnel landmines from many perspectives (Anderson 2000; Wexler 2003; Williams and Goose 2008). Within its grand coalition of over twelve hundred NGOs (Williams and Goose 1998, 22), moreover, participants approached the problem of antipersonnel mines with a variety of motivations: from legal to medical or public health issues, to one about dealing with the aftermath of war as a social concern (Anderson 2000, 105).

Although analysts and participants in the ICBL have hailed the diversity in approaches to the problem as the ultimate factor for the campaign's success, this is not an entirely accurate statement. In fact, one could argue that despite the diversity of perspectives of members in the ICBL—especially on the Steering Committee—and despite its lack of formal agenda-setting powers, the network was able to unify advocacy around a core message: "a complete and total ban on the use, production, stockpiling, and transfer of [antipersonnel landmines]" (Cottrell 2009). First, the founding six NGOs and campaign coordinator Williams played a critical role in guiding the agenda of the movement through the exercise of proposal power. Information was produced by the coordinator of the campaign and disseminated widely among ICBL members. Regular meetings to discuss the advocacy agenda, as well as constant communication between members of the ICBL via faxes, newsletters, and eventually e-mails (Williams and Goose 2008), facilitated the ability for all of the NGOs involved in the campaign to co-ordinate their messages, in spite of the diversity of motivations and approaches. The Landmine Update, for example, was circulated quarterly by the coordinator of the campaign (Williams and Goose 1998, 23–24) to inform NGOs of country-level improvements, as well as bolstering a sense of momentum for the ICBL's efforts. In spite of the effort to preserve local flavors in campaigning, activists were made aware of the overall goals that informed their efforts: committed leadership and key workers, and a clear and simple advocacy agenda (Williams and Goose 2008, 184–187). Perhaps most tellingly, only two delegates represented the perspective of the ICBL during treaty negotiations (Short 1999, 494).

Second, Williams and the Steering Committee exercised proposal power over how the ICBL approached advocacy. Their efforts to unite the members of the ICBL under a common cause, however, were made a lot less complex by the fact that the campaign defined a clear and straight-forward task: secure law banning the use of antipersonnel landmines. This was really an extension of the work already begun by the ICRC in the 1974, when it convened the Conference of Governmental Experts on Weapons that May Cause Unnecessary Suffering or Have Indiscriminate Effects (Hubert and MacFarlane 2000, 4–6). ICRC work regulated the use of antipersonnel landmines, but this was clearly insufficient to curb their worst consequences. The ICBL sought to get rid of any legal ambiguity by prohibiting their creation, use, and stockpiling altogether. Setting the agenda, even among such a disparate coalition, was simplified by the fact that the goal of the campaign was clear, even if motivations among NGOs varied. The ICBL benefitted from having a clear agenda that came from the ability of the leadership to use proposal power and from knowing that efforts to regulate the use of landmines were not going to work. It went about doing its work by using the strengths of a diverse coalition—decentralized implementation—to achieve its goal of law banning antipersonnel landmines entirely.

Finally, while all of the NGOs in the original Steering Committee contributed to the ICBL's efforts, the work of Stephen Goose, who currently heads HRW's Arms Division, has motivated many of the actions of the coalition. Goose was one of the few nonstate representatives present in the negotiations in Ottawa for the eventual convention in 1997.[6] He was also active in representing the interests of the ICBL in thinking about legal strategies to achieve a ban against landmines (Price 1998, 630). Much of value added to the ICBL by HRW was the continuance of its normal line of work: fact-finding and reporting. It has played an important part by giving effective rejoinders to counterarguments offered by opponents of an antipersonnel landmine ban, for example, overcoming claims about the usefulness of mines by citing US Army reports that revealed uncertainty about the effectiveness of such weapons (Price 1998, 632).

The role of coalition NGOs was most important in implementation of the agenda. Rather like a singular international NGO in this analysis, the ICBL provided its twelve-hundred-member coalition with a simple, clear agenda—get a convention against landmines—while allowing them to advocate for that end in whatever way they saw fit for their respective contexts (Short 1999). Thus the larger international NGOs could continue doing what they did best, and smaller, domestically oriented NGOs could work on the campaign in a way consistent with their domestic constituencies. In this sense, the ICBL's diversity did not help shape the agenda and lead to the creation of the Ottawa Convention so much as the leadership's shaping of that agenda kept all of the NGO soldiers informed and in-line.

Since the Ottawa Convention, the role of HRW in pushing the ICBL's agenda actually expanded through the founding of Landmine Monitor. To ward off the sense that the landmines issue (somewhat akin to slavery) was dead with the ratification of the international law banning antipersonnel mines (Bernstein 2008), ICBL has moved into the business of monitoring compliance with the Ottawa Convention. Two figures have been credited for the Landmine Monitor—Goose and Bob Lawson in the Canadian Foreign Affairs department. Goose's—and HRW's—efforts on expanding the scope of the ICBL's activities did not go over without controversy (Wareham 2008, 49–51). However, along with establishing a permanent office, the Landmine Monitor was a way for the ICBL to continue its work, simultaneously giving the coalition a "new direction, focus, and unity" (Wareham 2008, 51).

Within the ICBL coalition, HRW has exerted continued influence over the nature of the agenda. Prior to the Nobel Prize, this role was probably slightly less important. The ICBL, after all, was founded with the goal of eradicating the manufacture, use, and presence of antipersonnel landmines in the ground. The Ottawa Convention effectively granted the movement a starting point to push states to achieve a zero-landmine world.[7] After getting states to sign on to the Ottawa Convention, however, the ICBL needed a new raison d'être. Moving into monitoring has changed the nature of the ICBL's work—from advocacy pushing policy adoption to one about ensuring compliance to that policy. Landmine Monitor has been credited with changing states' conceptions about the continuing problem with antipersonnel landmines by providing them with detailed reports about existing stockpiles and the destruction process (Wareham 2008). Though nonstate actors monitoring treaties is not a new thing—the ICRC monitors compliance with the Geneva Conventions—the self-appointment of the ICBL's Landmine Monitor as the guardian of the Ottawa Convention is. The creation of Landmine Monitor also ensures that, at least for now, a temporary coalition whose original goal has been fulfilled, endures.

A further development for which HRW can receive credit is the shift from antipersonnel landmines to cluster munitions, a related but separate issue. Cluster munitions are air-dropped or ground-launched bombs that release smaller bomblets. In the same way that antipersonnel landmines have been argued to violated human rights and humanitarian law because they are indiscriminate in their targets, HRW has made similar claims about the effects of cluster munitions. HRW released a series of reports documenting the use of such weapons by both Israel and Hezbollah in their battles in 2006, and both sides' use of cluster munitions in the 2008 Russia-Georgia battle over South Ossetia.[8] It sought to change international law around the use of cluster munitions after observing its effects on civilians in many other contexts. Applying the lessons from the ICBL, HRW turned to NGO partners to help foment a campaign to ban the use of such weapons,[9] securing the Convention on Cluster Munitions, which opened for signature in 2008. The convention prohibits the use, production, and stockpiling of cluster munitions. Notably, the same countries that are missing from the Ottawa Convention, such as the United States, China, and Russia, are missing from the signatory list. Since the convention, HRW has worked hard to sustain relationships with states and the UN to help achieve the goals of the treaty and has cooperated with other like-minded NGOs to report on the status of cluster munitions in 150 states.[10]

HRW's work over the past thirty-plus years has shifted with the changing nature of human rights violations. While its claim to fame revolved around shaming governments, namely the United States, to act consistently in its condemnation of abhorrent human rights practices, it has since moved from simple "naming and shaming" to include other types of techniques. HRW consistently targets a host of states with its reports, including perpetrators and allies beyond the United States to include IOs such as the UN and EU, and regionally powerful states such as Japan. These choices, however, are unremarkable in the grand scheme of things, reflecting tactical, rather than strategic changes: fundamentally, reporting and adding more targets to those reports and policy recommendations still aims for state compliance to existing law.

More remarkably for this project, HRW's efforts in the recent decade or so to cultivate networks of NGOs united behind a single cause is a shift in strategy, from holding states accountable to existing law to making new law to which states are accountable. Grassroots and coalition efforts are a movement away from simply producing well-informed reports and placing them on the right desks. HRW continues to specialize in information, but it also has come to an understanding that building links, whether in local contexts with domestic NGOs or among other international NGOs, helps it achieve its own goals of changing human rights-violating behavior better. Its leading role in the ICBL, as well as its spin-off into cluster munitions, demonstrates HRW's recognition that moving to advocate the creation of new international law requires more than just one NGO's efforts.[11] Furthermore, working with midlevel and smaller states to gain a minimum number of ratifications of treaties is also a technique that has generated both the Ottawa and Cluster Munitions conventions, though not without controversy (Anderson 2000; Roth 1998; Williams and Goose 2008). HRW has also openly exported the model to other issues, such as child soldiers and pushing for the Rome statute that established the International Criminal Court.

ASI and the End of Slavery

The opposition to slavery is one of the most intractable international norms. To speak about the legitimacy of slavery, and specifically chattel slavery today, one needs to be ready to encounter very stiff resistance, and moreover, a logic that has been established in national and international law since the turn of the twentieth century. ASI played a crucial role in defining the wrongness of slavery and politicizing the moral argument to encourage states to abandon the "peculiar institution" that arose out of market relations between the Americas, Europe, and African territories.

Although ASI still exists today, it has not been able to sustain its past successes. ASI in the twentieth and twenty-first centuries has not seen the same triumphs in broadening the definition of slavery beyond chattel slavery as it achieved in the eighteenth and nineteenth centuries in making slavery a politically salient (and prohibited) practice (Wong 2011). It has also lost its luster as a politically salient NGO: at the height of its influence, it was able to encourage the formation of like organizations in Brazil, the United States, France, and the Netherlands (Nadelmann 1990, 495). ASI has not been able to expand a global prohibitive regime against "new" slavery. This is largely explained by the radical shift in organizational structure between the first wave of success in prohibiting chattel slavery and subsequent efforts to mobilize support behind its extensions of the definition of slavery. ASI, to date, has moved away from engaging a decentralized form of agenda implementation to one of specific targeting of British legislators and advocacy at international organizations. Although this forms part of the reason for the Society's early antislavery victories, it is not a complete answer: individuals' demands were the motor of change, not high-level negotiations without popular support.

We can apply the lenses of proposal, enforcement, and implementation powers to view ASI's early successes. The Society's nineteenth-century ability to gain the British government's support of abolition employed a two-prong strategy that was directed by both charismatic leaders and a General Committee. Thomas Clarkson was the spiritual leader of the Society in both the vigor with which he traveled the country on speaking engagements and his employment of the notion of Providence to motivate people to reject the practice of slavery as immoral (Temperley 1980). Decentralized implementation was a key feature of the movement. When the Society first came about and pursued abolition in Great Britain, its leaders realized the power of grassroots implementation. Unlike its contemporaries, the Society—under the leadership of Clarkson in particular—encouraged the formation of grassroots, local chapters that would be part of the overall movement (Temperley 1972). While earlier incarnations of the organization were fully aware of the international nature of the problem of the slave trade, and its leaders corresponded with their counterparts in France and the United States, it focused on forging a broad coalition of support at home, bringing the issue of abolition to a "regular" person's perspective.

The Society's efforts to engage the population worked quite well. It was aggressive in pursuing different types of methods, including hosting conferences and paying speakers who would circuit Great Britain, generating momentum for the cause. One meeting in a Freemason's Hall in 1830 drew three thousand participants, with several hundred unable to gain admittance waiting outside (Anstey 1981, 48). A "monster petition" from just female supporters of the movement arrived in Parliament bedecked with 187,000 signatures in 1832. This feat is truly remarkable considering that pamphlets and riding the mail circuit from town to town were the two ways to get the word out. In the early 1830s, there were thirteen hundred local chapters of the Society that generated 5,484 petitions directed at Parliament in six months (Bales 2005, 71).

The Society also leveraged electoral politics to support and as a goal of grassroots mobilization. Because Great Britain was a democracy, leveraging the power of voters helped pressure national-level legislative change. One of the most effective strategies pursued by the Society was to mobilize constituencies to pressure their MPs, or replace them altogether, which is what eventually happened as the composition of the House of Commons changed after amendment of electoral rules through the Reform Act (Kaufmann and Pape 1999). Another strategy commonly employed was to gain the support of sympathetic MPs who would raise embarrassing questions about slavery and propose legislation in Parliament based on the Society's agenda (Welch 2008). The Society would identify legislators who could propose law that echoed its principles against slavery. The headquarters of ASI, still located near Parliament in London, speaks to the primacy of its strategy of pressuring legislators, and to this day, the NGO knows it has MPs it can lean on to get its messages across to the rest of the body.

Whether the Society pursued elite or nonelite mobilization techniques, its method of encouraging participation in its cause, using its advocacy agenda as the prime motivator, was the reason why it was so successful in changing British policy on slavery. Without a high level of decentralized implementation, changing general feelings toward slavery in the nineteenth century would not have been possible. Using a technique that took advantage of numbers and well-placed powerful people, the Society was able to change British policy.

Furthermore, proposal and enforcement powers were not necessarily exercised. There were few debates over the general idea of abolition—leaders of the Society agreed that slavery was wrong and set about to do something about it. A split in the Society occurred in 1830, but the division focused mainly on implementation techniques, rather than the content of the abolitionist agenda (Temperley 1972, 14–16). The impetus to further decentralize implementation came from younger members, who wanted to engage communities in the abolitionist debate, creating a grassroots movement, while most of the original Society members favored using elite connections in Parliament to secure change. These approaches were complimentary, and as such, posed very little problem for agreement over the agenda of abolishing slavery in Great Britain. Proposals were not controversial.

The end of chattel slavery came with monumental legislation passed in Britain and elsewhere in Europe and the abolition of slavery in the United States and other Caribbean countries. The Society would further solidify its efforts by securing the Brussels Act of 1890, a multilateral agreement between European powers to end slavery. In more recent years, the Society has had further luck in changing international law, but it has had less ability to encourage state cooperation and compliance. Under the League of Nations, it convinced bureaucrats to adopt the 1926 Slavery Convention. The victory of the 1956 Supplementary Convention had the cross-cutting effect of defining slavery more broadly, but also giving "antislavery" as a principled position much less coherence. Its current scope of action is defined as "bonded and forced labour, descent based slavery, early and forced marriage, worst forms of child labour and trafficking of people into forced labour."[12] However, what counts in each of these categories is not always clear, as those familiar with current debates contend (Bales 2005; Bales and Robbins 2001). The modern-day antislavery project lacks a core around which to rally a grassroots audience (Quirk 2006, 593), and it is in part ASI's efforts that created this vacuum through the rearticulation of slavery. Recent campaigns against the use of child labor in rugmaking, for instance, have met with mixed results. ASI established the Rugmark label in 1994 as the equivalent of a "fair trade" label to protect children from laboring and as a guarantee that carpetmakers receive a fair wage. This effort has been mired in complexities with both educating consumers, convincing retailers that certified carpets sell, and the more important question of how not buying child-labor-produced rugs helps the people whose livelihoods depend on those products (McDonagh 2002; Nooruddin and Sokhey 2012).

Thus the monumental achievement of the end of slavery has, thus far, marked the pinnacle of the advocacy work done by ASI, and subsequently it could not sustain this political salience. Part of the explanation lies with the difficulties faced by modern antislavery activists in expanding the definition laid out by earlier Society efforts. That is, the Society's depiction of slavery and the widespread effect of its advocacy solidified the notion to such an extent that elaborations are not possible. Certainly, ASI created an enduring sense of what slavery is, and the success of its prohibition efforts entrenched those ideas as definitive of "slavery." Other NGOs, such as Amnesty, have also created durable images of suffering and human rights violence that stick with the public imagination, but have also been able to move beyond those initial powerful images of Prisoners of Conscience and torture victims to the death penalty, LGBT rights activists, and women. The most important difference between ASI of the twentieth century and today is the lack of decentralized implementation power. Proposal and enforcement powers have remained roughly defined, improving—through professionalization—in the late 1980s. However, the grassroots support it enjoyed to motivate influential members of British Parliament in the 1800s has simply not been cultivated. The tactic of leaning on British government, moreover, has become antiquated and somewhat at odds with the redistribution of international power since the early twentieth century. Although it remains to be seen whether subjects such as forced labor or human trafficking find traction under the guise of slavery, the organizational structure of ASI since the early twentieth century has not helped its cause.

The ICRC and Rules of War

The importance of the ICRC in creating and diffusing the Geneva Conventions has been a subject that has received extensive scholarly attention (Finnemore 1996; Forsythe 1996, among others: 1976), and some have argued that the ICRC must be recognized not just as a humanitarian actor, but a human rights actor in the areas of laws of war and political imprisonment (Forsythe 1990). Since the ICRC's role in creating humanitarian norms in the conduct of war has been well-trod, the discussion here presents an analysis of the ICRC's organizational structure to explain why it has been able to generate widespread support for humanitarian concerns, but also to highlight how the tensions between it and other aspects of the Red Cross (described below) contribute to and complicate the ICRC's influence in international politics.

The ubiquity of the red cross on white background in conflict and disaster situations today is a fact of contemporary humanitarianism and accepted almost without question. However, few know that the symbol of the Red Cross (as well as the Red Crescent and Red Crystal) is actually shared by three different entities within the greater Red Cross network: the International Committee of the Red Cross (ICRC); the Federation of Red Cross Societies,[13] formed in 1919; and the national societies, which work with both the federation and the ICRC, but are in many places, also tied to the governments of their respective countries.[14] On June 4, 1859, a young Swiss businessman named Henri Dunant happened upon the grisly aftermath of one of the decisive battles of the war for Italian unity. In a northern Italian village called Solferino, the French and Sardinian forces had clashed with the Austrian army, causing massive bloodshed unknown since Waterloo. Dunant returned to Geneva and published his memoirs of his experience in *A Memory of Solferino,* which he then distributed to individuals of influence across Europe, including heads of state. With the cooperation of four other prominent philanthropic Genevans and the approval of the Geneva Society of Public Utility, Dunant launched what would later be known as the ICRC in 1863.

The Geneva Conventions would come a year later, the brainchild of Dunant, Moynier, and other early Swiss activists. States felt more reluctance toward the documents, but nonetheless signed on to make war more humane for those engaged in battle. Three more versions of the conventions followed, with the last signed in 1949. Taken together, the Geneva Conventions have now become customary international law, "taken for granted and virtually never questioned" (Meron 2005, 819). The ICRC's role in making the Geneva Conventions normative have been twofold. First, its advocacy led directly to the signing of the first convention in 1864. Signed by twelve Western states (excluding the United States and United Kingdom), this was to be the beginning of the role of the ICRC as caretaker of international humanitarian law (Forsythe 2005b). The ICRC therefore served as an advocate of the war wounded and pushed for laws protecting such individuals, but also provided medical services in wartime. It is the only nonstate actor specifically named by an international agreement as its caretaker. Second, its continued vigilance in ensuring that the conditions stated in the Geneva Conventions are met by states contributes to them moral importance attached to the agreements. In doing so, the ICRC also established the norms of neutrality, or apoliticism, and impartiality for humanitarian aid (Chandler 2001). With its work on landmines, the ICRC has also moved itself beyond traditional humanitarian work (Meron 2000).

In terms of structure, the ICRC is fundamentally a private Swiss organization with a cosmopolitan focus (Forsythe 2005b). The ICRC is a complex formal structure that can be divided into the leadership of the professional staff (Directorate) and the Assembly (also called the Committee). Historically, like the ILHR and the Society, the ICRC prized voluntary labor and nonprofessionalized leadership, and granted the proposal and enforcement powers to the Assembly and president, who comes from the Assembly. Formally, the ICRC strives to balance between voluntary and professional influences. Consistent with Swiss stereotypes, the ICRC functions in an arcane manner. The Assembly is composed of no more than twenty-five Swiss citizens at any one time, and new members may only join after being invited by standing members. In other words, these leaders of the ICRC, who can serve, practically speaking, three terms of four years each, are not accountable to anyone but themselves—not the Directorate or states. Renewal of one's term is subject to vote by Assembly members, though rules are built in so that the odds of staying on decrease over time. Similar to the other two NGOs studied in this chapter, the voluntary leadership of the ICRC has been cautious, conservative, and upper class; the ICRC has been reluctant to change much about the composition and proceedings of the Assembly.

The Assembly has quite considerable agenda-setting power in formal terms, particularly in terms of proposal and enforcement powers, although the Directorate these days takes on an increasingly larger role in making those types of decisions. It functions much as a board does: meeting five times a year, deciding the rules of the policymaking process, approving policy changes, such as the budget, and selecting top officials, including the president, who ranks as the leader of the ICRC.

Since the 1970s, the role of the professional staff under the aegis of the director-general has expanded as it takes on more active proposal power. Changes to the operations of the organization to accommodate a contemporary political climate that requires quicker responses and less caution led to the elevation of its paid Geneva-based staff to be able to propose solutions. The shift from largely volunteers in the field to paid staff has also taken place since the 1960s. Growing multinationalism in the staff since the 2000s, which used to be largely Swiss or European, has greatly inflated the ICRC's ranks as well. The ICRC employs approximately eleven thousand field workers at any given time, the majority of whom are locals (Forsythe and Rieffer-Flanagan 2007, 32). Formal enforcement power lies with the president and Directorate: they are the only two actors that can make decisions that are binding to the rest of the ICRC.[15] The Directorate's composition over time has varied, but is usually a mix of leaders from the professionalized staff and the president to balance political considerations in the Assembly as well as on-the-ground logistics.

Within the Red Cross, the ICRC serves an important and established agenda-setting role in terms of proposal and enforcement power. The ICRC alone carries the burden of inspecting and reporting on compliance with the Geneva Conventions and coordinates medical efforts in wartime. Work is implemented by ICRC staff, and in that sense, implementation power is quite centralized—there is not delegation beyond one's volunteers/staff. In the broader Red Cross, by contrast, the ICRC has very little implementation power at all. The national sections all control their own agendas; this posed problems for the ICRC early on in the twentieth century. The history of the establishment of the Red Cross is one that relied on nationalistic efforts—drumming up domestic support to create national sections through jingoism was not uncommon, and Red Cross societies frequently have had rivalries. The relationship between domestic militaries and their national Red Cross societies was, at least in the early days of the organization, essential, as the armed forces had to cooperate with civilian interference with treating wartime wounded (Hutchinson 1997, 175–182). Moreover, the ICRC saw itself as largely independent from national sections and the federation until the 1970s (Forsythe 2005b).

Taking into account the rest of the Red Cross yields a very interesting picture. When the federation was established, it was designed as a challenge to the way the ICRC conducted the business of humanitarianism. Founder Henry P. Davison wanted to capitalize on the support that national societies had received during World War I to advance common understanding across people and advance humanitarian principles (Hutchinson 1997, 285–286). Davison's "real" Red Cross posed an alternative to associating with the ICRC by involving itself not just in wartime activities, but also other emergency situations. In the past, the federation posed a serious challenge to the ICRC in redefining the bounds of humanitarian relief and in competing on humanitarian turf. Tense interactions in Biafra and Vietnam in the 1960s pointed to a need to figure out who was in charge. A boiling point came in Ethiopia in 1986 when the federation and ICRC adopted orthogonal positions. The Ethiopian government demanded that relief organizations help them relocate civilians in order to expose rebel forces, who were hiding among the people. The ICRC had rejected these demands on neutrality grounds, but the federation did not. It swooped in, accepting the terms in order to gain access to relief provision in the area. Distribution of tasks between the ICRC and federation are much more clearly delineated since the 1990s, having been ironed in a series of formal agreements in 1969, 1973, and 1997.

In terms of proposal and enforcement power within the ICRC, the centralization of those aspects of agenda setting is clear: although the Assembly has a critical formal role, the growing informal importance of the Directorate has generally guided the actions of the organization in the modern era. Among other parts of the Red Cross, the ICRC has struggled in the past with the federation and national sections. Relations were normalized between the two in the 1997 Seville Agreement: the ICRC coordinates the activities of national societies in times of war and those related to international humanitarian law; for disaster relief, national society efforts are coordinated by the federation.[16] One trump card the ICRC does hold is that it alone has the power to recognize new national societies. That power alone gives the ICRC tremendous enforcement power.

One thing the ICRC should be recognized for in terms of agenda setting is its role in creating what is known as the Red Cross' seven official principles, first used by the ICRC in 1901 and adopted by the rest of the Red Cross in 1965 (Barnett and Weiss 2008, 3; Forsythe 2005b, 29). These principles are infused throughout the Red Cross movement: humanity, impartiality, neutrality, independence, unity, universalism, and volunteerism. Of these, neutrality, impartiality, and independence are key components in creating the norms of humanitarian work, and to which the Red Cross has steadfastly kept, at times in the face of large human losses. The ICRC has come to define the Dunantist tradition, along with MSF, albeit they have orthogonal positions on the role of public advocacy (Stoddard 2003; Tong 2004). In that sense, the ICRC has been successful in diffusing its humanitarian principles beyond the Red Cross to other groups.

Since the 1990s (Lischer 2007), and especially since 9/11 (Rieffer-Flanagan 2009), it has gotten increasingly difficult for the ICRC to maintain a separation from state actions.[17] It finds itself increasingly in need of defining and reiterating the neutrality, independence, and impartiality of the humanitarian project, responding to challenges from states that declare humanitarianism NGOs a "force multiplier"[18] but also to other humanitarian actors, who see the role of humanitarians as expanding beyond simply the symptoms of suffering to the causes of suffering (Barnett and Weiss 2008). In answering critics, the ICRC needs to recognize the political nature of the notion of neutrality, bringing its views more in line with external audiences, who very much see humanitarianism as political (Barnett 2001; Forsythe 2005a; Rieffer-Flanagan 2009).

Oxfam's Fair Trade Coffee Campaign

Oxfam International's first campaign as a formalized network in the early 2000s was the issue of fair trade coffee, which would eventually form one of the pillars of the Make Trade Fair campaign that links advocacy to changing trade more broadly at the Doha round of negotiations of the World Trade Organization (WTO) that began in 2001.[19] Fair trade coffee has taken off as a moral and market phenomenon. It is one of the most recent efforts to link consumer purchasing power to ethical business practices (Levi and Linton 2003). In Canada, for instance, consumers purchased 21,500 kilograms of fair trade coffee in 1998. In 2004, the figure had jumped to 940,000 kilograms. Sales figures are similarly drastic, from $649,000 to $28.2 million.[20] Worldwide, fair trade coffee sales amounted to approximately 2.9 billion in 2008.[21] As a legally exported commodity, coffee's value internationally is second only to oil (Brown 2003; Levi and Linton 2003). Cafédirect was the first fair trade brand, launched in 1989. It was created by a joint effort between Oxfam Trading, Equal Exchange, Tradicraft, and Twin Trading, and has enjoyed commercial success as a high-quality instant coffee, finding its way onto supermarket shelves in the United Kingdom, with sales over £6 million in 1998/1999, becoming the sixth-largest coffee brand in the United Kingdom by 2002 (Low and Davenport 2005, 498; McDonagh 2002, 652–654).

Two major species of coffee are traded on global markets: Arabica beans, which are higher quality and require hand harvesting and precise growing conditions, and canephora (robusta) beans, which can be machine harvested and thus grown on large plantations. Arabica coffee finds its way to specialty retailers, such as Starbucks, while robusta tends to populate freeze dried instant coffees and lower-end products. The popularity of instant coffees and canned coffees has ensured a market for robusta beans. The purpose of fair trade coffee is to shield coffee producers from wild fluctuations in trading prices for coffee, which, for a number of reasons, had fallen dramatically by the 1990s and early 2000s. The breakdown of the International Coffee Agreement in 1989, which had previously regulated prices for producers and buyers, encouraged new entrants to the coffee production process. Vietnam became a major producer of robusta beans. Thus, markets were flooded with product, and on top of that, product of inferior quality but much cheaper (Levi and Linton 2003).

Low worldwide prices for coffee spells disaster for the workers who help grow and harvest the product, whose wages suffered the most when spot prices hit 46.2 cents (USD) per pound in December 2001 (Gresser and Tickell 2002). At its nadir, the cost of the actual beans in the final market price for consumers constitutes a mere 18 percent of the value (Gresser and Tickell 2002, 20), approximately 24 cents per pound (Brown 2003, 265). Producers of coffee rarely see the massive profits of end retailers. Fair trade advocates seek to rectify the imbalance in profit between coffee growers and coffee retailers in Western markets. Coffee is by and large produced by small and medium farms, rather than large-scale production—most of the coffee traded in the world is grown on farms of less than ten hectares, and many of these plots are family owned (Gresser and Tickell 2002, 7). As Levi and Linton (2003, 412–413) find, farmers can earn less than six hundred dollars yearly, pushing them into the economically unfavorable position of selling to intermediaries for a below-market price. Many rely on credit for future harvests to pay for costs of production. Coffee is also picked by itinerant laborers, whose plight is even worse than farmers'.

The success of Jubilee 2000—a coalition that only Oxfam GB and Ireland joined[22]—served as the impetus for Oxfam International to begin integrating the power of grassroots activism into gaining global, systemic policy change.[23] Jubilee 2000 brought together multisectoral alliances and actively recruited grassroots support, notably forming a human chain in Birmingham, United Kingdom, to protest the G-8 meeting held there in 1998. For the fair trade coffee campaign, Oxfam sought help from different types of partners, not just development or human rights groups, but trade unions, churches, and coffee producer unions. Oxfam's campaign on fair trade coffee marked a significant departure from its bread-and-butter style of advocacy: funding local projects. Although Oxfam did support local cooperatives, such as giving funding to El Salvador's only fair trade group, APECAFÉ (Linton 2008, 241–242), the main focus in the fair trade coffee campaign (and Make Trade Fair more broadly) was to apply lessons from sister Oxfams about global campaigning and plug into what it perceived as trends in advocacy at the global level.

To control the message while reaching the broadest possible audience, Oxfam employed a system of centralized agenda setting with decentralized implementation mechanisms. The overall policy direction for the fair trade coffee campaign was agreed to by the sister Oxfams, consistent with the efforts to achieve consensus from all of the national sections for international efforts. From the beginning, Oxfam's plan was to centralize the campaign around a core global team, selected from various sister Oxfams, that would be interdisciplinary in nature. The fair trade coffee campaign sought to build a team that could analyze, advertise, and mobilize its internal network of Oxfams, local partners, domestic NGOs, and potential supporters worldwide. The global group would coordinate the actions of the campaign as it trickled out to the different Oxfams and their many partner organizations—other domestic NGOs, farmer cooperatives, and other NGOs invested in changing the system that dictated the global exchange of coffee.[24] Key functions included creating a uniform international media presence and lining up grassroots campaigns to meet overall Oxfam goals. The global team followed all of the international negotiations on coffee serving as the focal point for the organization for updates on how policymakers were changing coffee markets. In other words, the global team controlled information on the fair trade coffee campaign for the rest of Oxfam. It also managed the campaign to be consistent with the overall vision produced by leaders at the Oxfam International, exercising proposal power when necessary to shift strategies and tactics as policy situations changed.

When it came to distributing advocacy tasks to the broader network of partners that Oxfam had created and also more specific roles to designated Oxfam sections, the global group's agenda setting created a broad guide for others to apply to their specific contexts. National, non-Oxfam partners were given plenty of leeway to decide how to best implement Oxfam's goals, and how best to drum up grassroots support. Partners were also expected to give back to Oxfam in kind, whether in terms of supplying research, representing Oxfam's coalition when necessary, and helping secure Oxfam's goals, as well as their own, domestically. In return, Oxfam offered recognition of the partner, support, and information regarding fair trade. Oxfams within the international network also contributed their comparative advantages. Oxfam GB took a large advocacy role, given its long history of campaigning; it was able to move funds in support of the fair trade coffee campaign rather quickly.[25] Various Oxfams that shared country headquarters with corporate roasting strongholds also took leads. Oxfam GB targeted instant coffee giant Nestle, Oxfam America focused on American conglomerate Kraft, makers of Maxwell House, among others, and Oxfam Novib worked on Dutch giant Douwe Egberts, which also has ties to US company Sara Lee. The logic behind distributing the tasks of lobbying the corporate giants was that getting each of the three to change corporate practices required different strategies, given their varying legal structures.

A case study of Oxfam America's work on fair trade coffee in Ethiopia demonstrates a multipronged approach that involved Ethiopian government-targeted advocacy to change the law so that small farmers would sell directly to international markets, rather than going through intermediaries. Oxfam America's efforts also emphasized partnering with local unions to work with coffee farmers and linking the Ethiopian case to the broader goals of Make Trade Fair and the rights-based advocacy Oxfam International was pushing (Rand and Watson 2007, section 6). On the ground starting in 2001, Oxfam America built partnerships with unions, coffee cooperatives, and the Ethiopian government, holding a conference in September 2002 to address the coffee crisis in Ethiopia. Following the model already laid out by Cafédirect in linking NGO advocacy with local partners ("participatory development") (Tallontire 2000), Oxfam's and its partner's efforts have increased profits for farmers by offering more competitive pricing for coffee beans, and strengthened the capacity of cooperatives and unions on the ground. Domestic policy in Ethiopia also shifted to be more favorable toward farmers and cooperatives. Campaigners fitted the case of Ethiopia into a broader agenda at the international level of mobilizing consumers to buy fair trade coffee, as well as encouraging corporations such as Starbucks and mass-producing roasters to change their purchasing practices. As of 2003, Proctor and Gamble agreed to offer fair trade coffee through its Millstone brand of specialty coffee, after pressure from Oxfam America, Global Exchange, Co-op America, and the Interfaith Fair Trade Initiative.[26]

Fair trade is not without its critics. Fair Trade certification does not guarantee coffee quality (Linton 2005; Linton, Liou, and Shaw 2004) or necessarily preach environmentally sustainable practices (Brown 2003). In fact, the profusion of labels and qualifications obscures the overall goal of the sustainable coffee solution, which is to find equitable wages for farmers for producing a superior product for consumers that also does not destroy the environment. In a more recent document entitled "Grounds for Change: Creating a Voice for Small Coffee Farmers and Farmworkers with the Next International Coffee Agreement,"[27] Oxfam International, along with its local partners, advocate for a socially just and environmentally friendly way of approaching sustainable coffee in the negotiations for the new International Coffee Agreement that was negotiated in 2007. Sustainability, as well as fair pricing mechanisms, are part of the new provisions of the agreement, which explicitly takes into account the UN's Millennium Development Goals.[28]

While the work of Oxfam International and its sister organizations is undoubtedly part of a much larger set of movements that take place with other NGOs and in the corridors of trade ministers and international meetings over trade policies, Oxfam's fair trade coffee movement demonstrates how the newly unified Oxfams went about implementing a very specific set of agenda goals via a widely dispersed—geographically, ideologically, and in terms of capacity—set of partnerships. Through control over the agenda in terms of proposal power and control of information, Oxfam was able to capitalize on the strengths of its own internal network and its broader coalition to create political salience around the issue of fair trade.

MSF's Access Campaign

For all of its claims of apoliticalness and the vagaries of témoignage, MSF has a much more difficult time denying the advocacy success of its Access campaign, set up in 1999. Access put MSF directly in a political argument about the right for patients to have the means to medicine.[29] For diseases with known treatments or cures, denying access to the poor constitutes a major injustice, the remedy for which can provide for the basic human right of entitlement to healthcare, but also links to claims about human dignity and the iniquities of poverty. MSF placed itself in the middle of an intense international debate over the cost of essential medicines for the treatment of chronic and acute diseases and the role of intellectual property under the World Trade Organization's TRIPS (Trade-Related Aspects of Intellectual Property Rights) agreement, which in inflating prices, effectively denies access to treatments in poor and mid-range developing countries. It joined the push against US pharmaceutical giants in 1998, after initial efforts by Health Action International and American activists Ralph Nader and James Love created political salience for the issue among US politicians (Sell 2001). One of the most prominent and dramatic examples from this debate is the argument in favor of cheap antiretroviral drugs (ARVs) for treating HIV/AIDS in the developing states, but other diseases have been in want as well. Diseases such as sleeping sickness and Chagas disease, which do not afflict the developed world, do not interest big pharmaceuticals that have the research capacity to develop treatments: those who would benefit from the work would not be able to pay, or pay much, for getting the drug. The Access campaign links economics to medical rights: income should not be a barrier to receive essential medicines.[30] Thus advocates in Access face a double challenge of lobbying pharmaceuticals to allow for generics to be produced and imported by poor countries (or at the very least to lower their prices for developing countries on the drugs they have created) and pushing them to overcome market disincentives to produce drugs for low-income but disease-stricken populations. Access and other advocates have lobbied the WTO to soften intellectual property rules over medicines and negotiated with large pharmaceuticals in the pursuit of accessible medicines. It also pursues updates to medical protocols issued by the World Health Organization (WHO), for example, which sets the standard for how health ministries shape their medical policies.

Access is just one small part of MSF's operations, but it is also among the more high-profile projects (Barnett and Weiss 2008, 37) that affect its overall network. When it won the Nobel Peace Prize in 1999, MSF put the entire monetary award toward the Access program (Sell 2001, 507), raising not just the profile of the project to the external world, but also signaling its importance for the NGO internally. The Access campaign took up many of the concerns of mid-income countries—India, Brazil, Thailand—about the premium they paid for patented, life-saving ARVs when generics could be made cheaply and thus much more accessible. Access claims that before the Doha round, a year's worth of ARVs would cost US $10,000 per patient. Since the 2001 Doha Declaration paved the way for the treatment of HIV/AIDS to become a focal point for criticizing high drug prices, costs have come down to about $100 per patient, per year.[31] This outcome is not all from MSF's efforts of course. In some ways Access and other NGOs amplified the positions of developing countries and gave it a new frame: protect health, not patents. Access's efforts in helping developing countries gain concessions at the Doha round of negotiations for the WTO can directly be credited to pushing public health to the forefront of economic concerns (Drahos 2007, 7–8). The Doha Declaration has been viewed as a major victory by anti-TRIPS activists, as it reinforces the right of WTO member countries to "protect public health and 'to promote access to medicines for all'" (Sell 2001, 517). Moreover, MSF's awareness-raising conferences in 1999 before the Seattle WTO ministerial meeting ("the Amsterdam Statement") helped promote and reinforce some of the policy options available to countries that wanted to lower pricing on ARVs: namely, compulsory licensing, which forces corporations to allow states to distribute licenses for generic drugs, even for drugs still under patent. A UN General Assembly Declaration a few months before the Doha Declaration emphasized access to essential medicines as not just a health concern, but one with political, economic, and human rights consequences (Sell 2001, 513).

Access has contributed to the debate around the cost of medicines to treat diseases in developing countries in other ways. After Doha, the struggle was to get ARVs to be listed as "essential medicines" by the WHO. In 2002, ARVs were included with the WHO's list, but the application of the essential medicines list to domestic contexts remains the responsibility of the government. Putting ARVs on the WHO's essential medicines list helps shape the health policies for many countries, confirming the prevalence of HIV/AIDS as a public health problem worldwide and government responsibility to help stem the tide of the disease. The affirmation by the WHO of the importance of the HIV/AIDS epidemic, along with the Doha Declaration and the August 30 decision in 2003 allowing countries to export generic versions of patented drugs to countries without the capacity to manufacture them, fundamentally shifted the relationship between states, public health, and the protection of intellectual property around pharmaceuticals.

On a different note, MSF was a key player in the founding of the Drugs for Neglected Diseases Initiative (DNDi).[32] This independent nonprofit researches cures for diseases that big pharmaceutical firms have little monetary incentive to work on. Creating DNDi also meant that NGOs such as MSF were not beholden to the whims of pharmaceuticals or dependent on ad hoc pressure to get corporations to resume the production of drugs that aid the developing world, as they were in the 1990s for treating sleeping sickness (Hamel 2004, 343). DNDi's founding was one of first waves of nongovernment funding for the development of drugs in poor countries. Charitable donations from private individuals, foundations, and even cooperative efforts by corporations make up an increasing percentage of funds to support the research and development of drugs for use in developing societies.[33] Work in this area has led to the development of new malaria therapies—combination ones—rather than the outdated chloroquine, a drug to which many parasites have grown resistant. While treatment of malaria has ridden the "coattails" of work on HIV/AIDS, treatment alternatives for other ailments, such as tuberculosis, have been less successful.[34]

All of these advancements created political salience for access to essential medicines, as states such as Brazil, India, Kenya, Malaysia, South Africa, and Thailand responded by applying Doha and the August 30 principles to their policies ('t Hoen 2009, 44–59). More interestingly, even non-WTO countries (which are then not legally subject to regulations created by the IGO) have taken advantage of the patent law flexibilities created by the WTO to strengthen their hands against pharmaceutical companies ('t Hoen 2009). Access is one part of a range of actors advocating for changing norms around access to essential medicines, but it served as an important bridge for middle-income states, who have led the breakthroughs in the way that drugs are distributed, created, and paid for in HIV/AIDS treatments, and Thailand has attempted to push the envelope more by adding medicines for cancer and heart disease to its list of essential medicines.

Access's success points to the ability of MSF to marry its advocacy aspirations with its medical delivery obligations through the creation of a streamlined organizational structure. The Access campaign is based out of MSF's International Office, but representatives occupy desks in the OCs and strategic national sections. It is funded by all nineteen national sections and is the largest collaboration at the international level. The campaign was created after MSF sections recognized that there were many similar problems that missions encountered in treating their populations. The main function of the campaign is to generate the research and create the ability for other MSFs to disseminate the information it provides. It maintains links to field missions that might encounter neglected diseases, or need to overcome the price of drugs. Access therefore exercises proposal power in this particular aspect of MSF's work. Access also sets the agenda for MSF's advocacy on providing essential medicines through proposal power by issuing position statements, letting the rest of the network implement that agenda through the distribution of materials and posting updates on Access activities. These statements do not necessarily go over easily with the more technically oriented platforms, such as the medical advisory board, whose tendency is to be more conservative with its recommendations by waiting for WHO policies.[35] However, there is not a real check on Access's work because it operates on different rules than the other MSF work described above, and other parts of the international NGO do not have enforcement power over the Access campaign.

Although all nineteen sections pay for the campaign, it is governed by a Steering Committee that represents the OCs, MSF-USA and MSF-Germany, and medical and administrative leaders. Unlike the MSF procedures described above, the Steering Committee does not operate based on consensus but instead relies on a "critical mass of support."[36] As such, decisions flow through with relative ease. Access statements do not require all relevant parties' approval, although staffers do consult as much as they can with those intimately involved with a particular disease or treatment. Access is able to exercise proposal and enforcement power over its statements because these do not go through the same channels as other MSF advocacy efforts. It should be no surprise that Access has become one of the most salient parts of MSF—the topic, its early successes at the Doha negotiations of the WTO, and the nature of its advocacy all speak to why it captures international attention. Unlike other parts of MSF's advocacy, Access focuses on general conditions, rather than the specifics tied to on-the-ground experiences of staffers. In contrast to the deliberative and cautious statements made with the approval of all five OCs, Access statements can be seen as more cutting-edge for even the NGO itself.[37] This should not be read as a criticism. MSF's perceives témoignage as having real life or death consequences; Access fights at a political and not a humanitarian level.

Unlike other parts of MSF, Access statements are unified in the sense that they apply to all parts of the MSF network, creating political salience around the issues it advocates. The nature of the work allows it to move beyond technical details into commentary about more generalized conditions in the world. It is the one part of the NGO that speaks on behalf of the others. What Access shows us is the ability of an NGO, even as decentralized as it is with its multiple centers of power in the five OCs, to launch coordinated and successful advocacy campaigns that change the behavior of states quite dramatically by reframing the debate as one of the right of access for essential medicines, rather than of circumventing patents.

IANSA through an Organizational Lens

The global campaign targeting the distribution of small arms and light weapons has been seen as a nonstarter in terms of policy, in spite of the attention paid to the issue by so-called "gatekeeper" NGOs (Carpenter 2011;

Shawki 2011) and the number of NGO supporters, numbering in the hundreds, that have joined forces since the 1990s. Although not all groups involved in the small arms movement belong to the umbrella network IANSA,[38] it is by far the most central actor on the issue (Grillot, Stapley, and Hanna 2006). Analysts often contrast the success of the ICBL in securing a landmines ban versus the "complete and abject failure" (as quoted in Grillot, Stapley, and Hanna 2006, 62) of IANSA to find any coherent policy position, despite many commonalities between the two networks: diverse and widespread membership, linking security issues to human rights, and their similar founding dates. Scholars have pointed out differences in organizational structure (Shawki 2011) and issues (O'Dwyer 2006) as explanations for the differential level of success of the two movements.

Since the mid-1990s, groups of concerned NGOs had met in various fora around the world to discuss small arms–related issues. IANSA was formally launched in 1999 at the Hague Appeal for Peace, which also commemorated the entry into force of the Ottawa Convention (Brem and Rutherford 2001). It currently has more than seven hundred member NGOs (Bob 2010, 191). Unlike other transnational campaigns before it, IANSA self-consciously tried to avoid criticisms about Northern NGO domination by leaving the network leaderless. This decision was a nod in acknowledgement of the network's diversity of participants and the numerousness of IANSA's stated goals: eleven in all (Grillot, Stapley, and Hanna 2006, 71).[39] Thus, despite conscious modeling on the ICBL's successes (O'Dwyer 2006), the small arms movement neglected to create an agenda setter for the network. IANSA emerged without a natural, informal center. IANSA chose to include in its agenda both the reasons for the proliferation problem and the consequences of the prevalence of small arms: gender-related issues, increase in violence, civilian displacement, poverty and underdevelopment, child soldiers, and a whole host of other topics (Grillot, Stapley, and Hanna 2006; Karp 2006; Shawki 2011). The broad topical reach of the movement is a manifestation of a lack of centralized proposal and enforcement powers. To make matters worse, by decentralizing these two powers, members of IANSA could effectively pursue the issue as they wished. This contrasts with the ICBL's method, which centralized proposal and enforcement powers but decentralized implementation, allowing its members to pursue a common agenda using techniques they saw fit for their own national or local environments; IANSA members, on the other hand, choose from among a plethora of issues and used their own techniques.

For the most part, the network was seen not as a campaign vehicle, but a source for information transmission for member NGOs (Grillot, Stapley, and Hanna 2006). Member NGOs were expected to advocate according to their own domestic needs and norms without a centralized agenda setter. Because of the number of goals for which IANSA stood, and because there was no leadership proclaiming an IANSA position on small arms, the network was decentralized along all three agenda-setting powers: proposal, enforcement, and implementation. Even though IANSA linked its members and provided them with information, the diversity and sheer number of goals, coupled with a self-imposed muting of Northern voices and the encouragement of multiple viewpoints diffused proposal power. Research has made clear that the same disparities between Northern and Southern NGOs that permeate other networks also affected IANSA: poorer NGOs from developing countries simply cannot afford to participate in international meetings (Grillot, Stapley, and Hanna 2006). The dominance of Northern NGOs is replicated in spite of structural efforts to decentralize proposal and enforcement powers. Because Northern NGOs have greater access to resources, furthermore, the lack of a core agenda around which to rally has resulted in organizations rallying around small arms in the ways that they know how, both in terms of framing and implementing their agendas. For instance, HRW and Amnesty portray small arms as human rights issues, while Oxfam or the World Council of Churches have stressed the ill consequences of small arms on development (Shawki 2011, 111).

It should come as no shock, then, when considering the policy or normative achievements of IANSA and the small arms movement more generally, that there is no equivalent of the Ottawa Convention for small arms. This was not for lack of NGO effort. O'Dwyer attests that states, manufacturers, and important transnational NGOs, namely the National Rifle Association in the United States, have strongly opposed the regulation of small arms. Instead of making it easier for small arms advocates to follow in its footsteps, the success of the landmines campaign prepared states to resist NGO efforts to enact policy change (O'Dwyer 2006, 89). Furthermore, events such as 9/11 have derailed modest international efforts to regulate small arms. The UN conference on small arms, which resulted in the nonbinding Program of Action, occurred just two months prior to 9/11 (O'Dwyer 2006, 87). Not surprisingly, following the attacks of 9/11, the international agenda shifted toward preventing the proliferation of terrorism, rather than the small arms.

When evaluating the effect of IANSA, many studies have argued that the complexity of the issue hampers the effectiveness of the network (Brem and Rutherford 2001; O'Dwyer 2006). As such, some observers have encouraged a more forgiving view of the small arms movement by claiming that the nature of the issue explains why, especially when compared to the ICBL, relatively little has been achieved by IANSA. This perspective eliminates the role of NGOs and transnational networks in framing the terms of debate. The struggle for IANSA to control the boundaries of its claims come back down to structure. True, accessibility of small arms, their widespread use in post-Cold War conflicts, and the uneven regulation of such weapons across states adds to the difficulty of agenda setting. Nonetheless, blaming the nature of an issue for the comparative lack of international policymaking not only exonerates IANSA from a lack of agenda-setting capacity but also negates the fact that the network that anti–small arms activists constructed has built-in structural problems. We can liken the small arms issue to an issue such as fair trade or the access to essential medicines, both complex economic concerns that depend on action from multiples levels of governance, with vested corporate interests and, often, reluctant state participants. Clearly, the nature of the issue plays some role in defining how NGOs might act, but it does not determine to what extent campaigns will succeed in making their agendas salient.

NGOs, if they do anything, offer an alternative understanding of issues from what states promote. IANSA's alternative vision has simply been indecisive. This indecision stems from structural choices that, while based on an ethos of equality and nondomination, create agenda-setting problems. Without centralized agenda setting, transnational campaigns can rarely hope to succeed because of the diversity of their membership in terms of geography, issue focus, and the organizational structure of individual NGOs within a broad-based coalition. As Karp contends, "Above all, the movement has been inhibited by the inability of control advocates to frame the issue in terms of readily understood and easily shared goals. In lieu of a straightforward program, the issue has been defined largely by its activities. The justification becomes tautological; the goals of small arms activity are whatever it does" (Karp 2006, 17). Although regulating small arms might be complex, the angle from which IANSA members attack the issue does not have to reflect this complexity. One way that centralized proposal and enforcement power can be exercised is in delegating tasks among network members and determining how an issue as multilayered as small arms can be managed under a common advocacy agenda.

In the case of IANSA, leadership and staff do not play a major role by design. Since the network was created without an agenda-setting center, the quality of leadership and staff has been irrelevant. A telling set of interviews conducted by Grillot and her colleagues reveals how a lack of centralized agenda-setting power actually made it difficult to check some powerful egos who were involved in the project. They find that "many respondents stated that particular individuals within the movement prevent the emergence of an effective leader" (Grillot, Stapley, and Hanna 2006, 76). IANSA, which would be a natural place to look for leadership, has not emerged as a leader for the rest of the small arms movement. Whether this lack of leadership has now become pathological rather than deliberate remains to be seen, but it does leave the network without a body to direct advocacy. To contrast, MSF has also long had a tradition of fostering democratic relations between its various members. In the Access campaign, however, it created a separate leadership for the purpose of generating attention around the issue of essential medicines and to attain policy change.

In terms of geographically based explanations, IANSA does not differ, in the end, from other Northern NGO-dominated networks, such as the fair trade campaign by Oxfam. Despite its explicit efforts to include Southern NGO views, there are certain roadblocks to NGOs from the developing world that even a nondomination scheme cannot prevent. The inclusion of Southern NGOs does not drive IANSA's comparative lack of success in international politics. Rather, it is the way by which IANSA has elected to include Southern NGOs—decentralizing proposal and enforcement powers—that thwarts its advocacy efforts.

The case of IANSA illustrates the limitations posed on transnational campaigns when their organizational structure limits their abilities to create coherent advocacy agendas. Even though the movement was auspiciously timed after the landmines campaign, and even specifically used the ICBL as a model, early architects designed a network that decentralized all three aspects of agenda setting. Thus, while it tried to capitalize on the heterogeneity of its member through decentralizing implementation, it left NGOs without guidance regarding what to advocate. Although small arms are salient as an issue, what makes it important, or what needs to be done, is not clear, and thus the issue can be ignored. IANSA's declared agenda contains too many items to create a coherent and unified agenda with which the campaign can demand policy change. While these organizational choices were deliberate in response to other types of concerns, they have certainly hampered IANSA and the small arms movement's ability to be politically relevant.

Assessing Campaigns' Structures and Outcomes

The analysis offered in this chapter forces us to ask: What does political salience of ideas mean? Relatedly, how can the political salience of NGOs and organizations differ from the salience of ideas? Can we say that NGOs have succeeded organizationally without necessarily being able to effect political salience for their ideas?

One way to think about political salience is to look closely at some of the campaigns discussed in the chapter. HRW's campaigns against landmines and cluster munitions meet the stringent criteria set by legalization scholars. Using a networked model, in which it actively engages other organizations in the implementation of an agenda that it leads in setting, HRW has been able to achieve policy goals in the form of enforceable treaties. The same can be said of the ICRC with the Geneva Conventions and ASI's ban on the practice of slavery. All of these organizations managed to create law, and all them adopted similar organizational structures during these campaigns to achieve those ends: centralization of proposal and enforcement powers, and decentralization of implementation power. Although these might not be their permanent structures, their use in the campaigns discussed here created political salience around their issues.

The usefulness of the redefinition of political salience becomes more apparent in less clear-cut cases. The question that remains for both MSF and Oxfam in this chapter is: Did they succeed in creating political salience for essential medicines or fair trade? The answer is remarkably similar for both campaigns. If political salience goes beyond law and also incorporates the idea of generating international focal points to foster international cooperation (whether political, economic, or something else), then we can think of both MSF's and Oxfam's efforts as quite successful. Both Access and the Make Trade Fair campaigns targeted state and corporate actors as well as IGOs such as the WTO and G-8. The Access campaign has spearheaded a movement that has given poorer states, such as India, Thailand, and Kenya the ability to resist the economic clout of multinational pharmaceutical companies, and it has substantiated the South African government's attempts to shift to more affordable medicines for its population through the use of generics and making the pricing more transparent. However, these are not quite shared practices, particularly among the rich—and drug-producing—states in Europe and the United States. In fact, with Doha negotiations stalled on precisely some of the intellectual property issues the Access campaign has struggled against, and the reluctance of G-8 states to take into account the interests of developing countries, the shift in attitude about providing essential medicines has bypassed states somewhat. Foundations and charitable efforts have stepped in to pick up at least some of the slack left by rich countries. Nonprofits try to replicate the functions of for-profit pharmaceuticals. To date, Access has bolstered states that have pursued alternatives to extant international intellectual property law but has not done much to change the minds of states with keen pharmaceutical interests.

Fair trade coffee has also targeted states, IGOs, and corporations. In addition, Oxfam campaigners have aimed their efforts at farming cooperatives and unions. Some of its most visible successes have been with corporate actors, getting them to buy into a fair trade coffee model. The revived International Coffee Agreement has declared fair trade principles as part of its tenets. States have changed their policies in some cases, creating more favorable conditions for farmers. These are preliminary steps toward change. The big factor in all of this is again the stalling of talks at Doha, which holds promise for those who would like to shift the economic structures in favor of poorer and weaker states, but unfortunately, have run into resistance at the WTO and other IGOs.

Similar to HRW's efforts in cluster munitions and landmines, Oxfam and MSF have experienced successes in linking their advocacy agendas to proposed overall change in principles at the international level. However, with less success than the Landmines and Cluster Munitions treaties, Oxfam's and MSF's efforts have not resulted in much substantive change at the international institutional level or in the behavior of powerful states.

They have changed some business' ways of thinking about profit, but they have not created massive systemic change or even gotten states to accede to widely held principles.

Until negotiations at IGOs become more favorable to the principles advocated by MSF and Oxfam, we should expect to see very little international norm change as well. It is unfair to say on the one hand that these efforts have been for naught. After all, both Oxfam and MSF's campaigns have gotten transnational corporate actors to at least begin to consider the backlash of ignoring populations in developing countries. Some have teamed with NGOs to equalize access or development. At that level, advocacy by actors like Oxfam or MSF played very important and direct roles in facilitating corporate change.

The case of IANSA reveals the advantages of examining organizational structure when explaining political salience of rights-related issues. Because of how its founders decentralized proposal and enforcement powers, the network was unable to frame the issue of small arms exclusively as one about legal injustice or bodily harm—even though some NGO members have done so. Because it lacks the formal and informal rules to funnel members toward a singular advocacy message, IANSA struggles in its efforts to make issues salient. Its conscious dealings with the power disparities between North and South have probably contributed to its agenda-setting disabilities, but are not necessarily causal for IANSA's inability to focus international policy regarding small arms. Finally, the lack of leadership and staff points directly to the structure underpinning the network. No leaders can emerge from IANSA because of the way proposal, enforcement, and implementation powers are decentralized, and similarly, no staff competence can overcome structural handicaps. Because of its organizational structure, IANSA flounders when it comes to making small arms politically salient among states and international actors. Thus, while the issue of small arms clearly generates attention among very prominent NGOs, even politically salient groups cannot act collectively to bring about policy change. The issue of small arms can be seen as politically salient among NGOs, but it is not politically salient to states and most IGOs.

The political salience of ideas is affected by multiple forces. While powerful states certainly affect the degree to which some transnational campaigns are successful—such as the Access campaign—examining the extant power structures in the world does not tell us why the issue became politically salient in the first place. Nor does it tell us how in spite of resistance from both the US government and US firms, a very strong countervailing movement for lowering the pricing on an increasing array of drugs exists. The linking of medicine to rights is another step that, given the economic and political power of pharmaceuticals, would not be expected.

Another important aspect of change is the increased market for, and in fact, demand for NGOs to assist with features of global governance. With the UN's explicit stamp of approval and institutionalized acceptance of NGO participation through ECOSOC, it became clear that these kinds of actors would have a place in international politics. The growth in the number of IGOs more generally since the end of World War II has created an increasing number of venues for NGOs to pursue with their advocacy. The pressures on these kinds of organizations has intensified with the end of the Cold War, as the "traditional" centers of influence in the United States and USSR narrowed to just one center (the United States), and now, in the current century, more states have become important as regional actors. The multiplicity of access points and nonstate actors that want to access policymaking has multiplied greatly, and indeed, this contributes to a system where supply and demand are up for NGOs to try to make human rights, among other things, politically salient. The attractiveness of rights and individualism as a concept (Elliott 2007), moreover, makes rights language and human rights-related work much more tractable. Put differently, political opportunities for NGOs have changed greatly since the ICRC mounted its campaign for the Geneva Convention, and ASI achieved its first antislavery victories.

One of the questions that human rights scholarship has yet to come up with a satisfactory answer for is why human rights have "evolved" the way they have in international politics. Arguments about the need for some types of rights to come about in order to ensure other types of rights, whether one comes at it from the perspective that civil and political rights must precede economic, social, and cultural rights, seem to be dispelled by priority placed on the indivisibility of rights since the UDHR (DeLaet 2005; Osiatynski 2009). The notion of three generations of rights, for example, follows from this kind of reasoning, with each type of right increasingly becoming more dissociated from individuals qua individuals, linked more and more to broader social and structural conditions that lack justicability. The progression of the human rights project, however, is not inevitable. Various NGOs and other actors emerge to influence the agenda of human rights, and the degree to which they are successful is measured in part as a function of whether the rights they advocate become international focal points.

The real benefit of using organizational structure as the variable of interest is seeing the patterns of agenda setting that persist among successful campaigns. Campaigns can also show how the political salience of organizations can be decoupled from the political salience of individual human rights. As far as transnational advocacy by NGOs goes, those with centralized enforcement and proposal powers and decentralized implementation power succeed more often at creating political salience for their human rights issues. Getting policy results, changing market practices, and convincing states to take collective international action requires not only clear, unified messaging, but the capacity to spread that message across a variety of contexts. The cases presented here demonstrate the importance of organizational structure as an underlying condition of agents that successfully generate political salience around human rights.

CONCLUSION

Now, we have great belief, I think, in the force of documents which do
express ideals. We think that, in themselves, they carry weight. But they
carry no weight unless the people know them, unless the people understand
them, unless the people demand that they be lived.

—ELEANOR ROOSEVELT

This book opened with two anecdotes. One described the birth of international human rights law, and the other chronicled a domestic project to
commemorate human rights. Both epitomize the politics of human rights:
at once inclusive and indecisive, full of inspiration, but vague on the details. Both cases are examples of efforts to definitively classify rights. The
UDHR sought the input of various states, and the Canadian Museum for
Human Rights has sought the opinions of average Canadians to create a
list of human rights. A list of rights, as this book has made clear, can only
tell us the starting point of where human rights politics might go. Rights
become more politically salient as they become focal points in international
politics, through use by states, NGOs, and IGOs. The rights articulated
in the UDHR, ICCPR, and ICESCR, among other documents, are not
all equally salient, and have not always been equally salient, in large part
because NGOs have not always worked on all of the rights they enshrine.

Korey argues: "It was NGOs who would take on the challenge of
transforming the words of the Declaration from a standard into reality;

it was they who would assume the function of implementing demands of international morality" (Korey 1998, 2). NGOs have become the primary way in which most people experience human rights, whether through defending existing rights, advocating the creation of new ones, or helping reify those rights through the provision of services, goods, and tools. This "curious grapevine," as Eleanor Roosevelt labeled them, has played a preeminent role in translating, framing, and packaging rights for individuals. They also engage in naming and shaming state behavior, condemning states when they violate fundamental protections. Some NGOs have become particularly good at generating widespread support for their actions, which enables them to advertise their particular brand of human rights and reach wide audiences with their work. In effect, these NGOs have become politically salient as organizations, advocating for rights that become focal points in international relations.

Political Salience as a Concept

The story in this book contains two intimately related sets of ideas about political salience in IR. First, it is an extension of the work of international relations scholars studying the effect of nonstate actors, namely NGOs and transnational actors. Organizational structure provides a means to explain why some NGOs find remarkable success in tapping support for their causes. By evaluating organizational structure, we move away from a model of evaluating "worthy" causes as a function of the analyst's own biases, a bias that has been well-documented by others (Bob 2010), to one in which all causes can be examined for their success in world politics. Just as left-leaning causes have secured policy support, right-leaning causes have also utilized these same fora to seek policy gains. While this study does not necessarily address multiple ideological causes, one of the implications of taking into account the level of centralization in agenda-setting powers among international NGOs is that we can look at both side of the political spectrum using a common metric. By relying less on the quality of a particular issue and putting more emphasis on the organizational characteristics of the actors promoting policy change, we can better predict which human rights issues might become politically salient.

The second part of the story is one that is more limited to the twentieth century. It asks how some NGOs have come to dominate the landscape on human rights. As researchers, our interventions into a particular subject matter are often colored by the moment in which we approach it. Many IR scholars became interested in the importance of nonstate actors in the 1990s, at a time when the most dominant players in the human rights scene had already been, or were well on their ways to being, entrenched in their roles. Amnesty had been around for approximately thirty years and had helped shape the human rights field as a political space. MSF had been active for nearly two decades. It seemed obvious to document the actions of the NGOs that were important and to explain their effects on international politics without exploring why and how those NGOs got to be where they stood in the 1990s. Who else existed before they came along, and why did those other NGOs flounder? Why did HRW suddenly become so important as a human rights actor? Why did the ILHR stumble?

I argued in the first chapter that political salience circumvents some of the difficulty that has become associated with the notion of norms in IR. Because of the analytical weight attached to the term, because of the heavy lifting that constructivists and other scholars have come to expect when labeling something a "norm," that language has lost much of its explanatory power in telling us what and who matter in international human rights politics. Although political salience as a concept shares many things with norms, it also does not require that all actors agree to a certain set of terms for a given idea. Political salience instead reconceptualizes how ideas or actors might become very important, even without consensus. The landmines ban, for instance, became codified as an international treaty not because powerful states such as the United States or Russia acceded to it, but because a handful of NGOs made the issue prominent politically, and the idea of a ban received support from some states and a wide, transnational network of NGOs. The issue of landmines became politically salient and has become part of international law, but it is contested as a norm. In lieu of arguing about whether the Ottawa Convention represents a norm, political salience acknowledges that the prohibition on the use and stockpiling of landmines constitutes an important international issue without getting into whether a lack of compliance by certain states weakens this prohibition as a norm.

Furthermore, when discussing NGOs or other transnational organizations, it is irrelevant to discuss them as normative. They differ in their ability to create norms in the sense that they vary in their success at making issues politically salient. Beside looking at their promotion of individual issues through campaigns, it is also important to consider their salience as organizations. As it has become clear, politically salient, or central, NGOs can both make or break issues, creating opportunities for issue adoption or nonadoption (Carpenter 2007). Political salience is both an object of study—why are some actors more politically salient—and an explanatory variable—why are some transnational campaigns successful? As I showed in chapter 5, however, political salience as an organization can be divorced from the political salience of individual human rights campaigns. The transnational network against the distribution of small arms and light weapons, for example, illustrates how very prominent NGOs—including several studied in this book—can join forces to advocate for policy outcomes without necessarily creating political salience around the issue.

This book ties the political salience of NGOs and the political salience of certain human rights together into a single narrative to explain how human rights came to take a certain shape in the twentieth century, and how we can anticipate a changing landscape in the future. As NGOs continue their work, and as they continue to bring political salience to human rights concerns, we should see certain patterns emerging in how individual NGOs organize themselves, and how coalitions of NGOs distribute agenda-setting powers among their members.

Political salience in one aspect does not make political salience inevitable in the other. The political salience of ideas is often linked to politically salient NGOs, but this is not always the case. Most of the time, politically salient NGOs manage to make their advocacy agendas politically salient, but this book has also offered notable examples when both conditions do not hold. On one hand, politically salient NGOs, such as Amnesty, Oxfam, and HRW, have advocated for greater oversight over small arms and light weapons, to little response from states. On the other hand, slavery continues to be one of the few strong prohibitive norms that exist internationally, even as the modern incarnation of its strongest proponent, ASI, wallows in relative obscurity among human rights NGOs. The relationship between the two forms of political salience is imperfectly aligned. The times when political salience of organizations does not lead to political salience of ideas, and vice versa, are windows into understanding how the organizational structure of the NGOs matters.

Organizational structure is determined by the distribution of agenda-setting power. Agenda-setting power can be broken down into three distinct dynamics: proposal, enforcement, and implementation powers. The central thesis of this book posits that centralizing proposal and enforcement power creates coherent advocacy agendas for international NGOs, thereby circumventing some of the challenges posed by the transnational dilemma. Decentralizing implementation power enables NGOs to capitalize on local capacities and knowledge, thereby promoting a uniform agenda with sensitivity to national or community-level concerns. The emphasis on agenda-setting power highlights the structure of the agents (NGOs), and not the structure surrounding NGOs, to explain why NGOs have had differential effects on the politics of human rights. Variations between NGO structures, even NGOs working on very similar things, begs the question of what effect structure has on the ability of NGOs to get what they want.

Political salience as a concept overcomes some of the difficulties with defining and measuring international norms. Because it does not require a common identity or purpose in order to highlight the appropriateness of certain behaviors, political salience is a way to conceive of focal points in international politics without necessarily requiring that those influenced by the ideas or actors agree with them. NGOs create focal points through their advocacy, and over time, they themselves might become focal points. States and other actors may not agree with what NGOs say, and they may oppose the very existence of human rights NGOs. Nonetheless, human rights become politically salient through what NGOs report, whom they accuse, and against what or whom they campaign. Political salience, in a sense, widens the possibilities on thinking about why some ideas in international politics are more important than others. Rather than thinking about how common identities shape behaviors, when considering the effect of NGOs on human rights, we should think not just about what states do in response to NGO campaigns, but how NGOs create an environment that focuses states' attention on certain rights. While NGOs cannot compel states to act, their agency and their influence is in choosing the rights they advocate and framing those rights for a greater—and partially hostile—audience.

This book has introduced three different ways to evaluate political salience as a concept—international law, the contours and outcomes of transnational networks, and the content of justifications for economic sanctions. All three tools are imperfect as approaches for conceptualizing political salience, but they also point to the multiplicity of ways in which NGOs can shape international politics. Choosing the right measure of political salience in large part depends on the research question, but it also requires thinking about political salience in more than one dimension for any given issue. It would be foolhardy to dismiss access to essential medicines or fair trade as politically salient issues just because of a lack of concentrated state action. Furthermore, it would be exceedingly rare for states, locked in an antagonistic relationship with advocacy NGOs by definition, to recognize NGO efforts or openly acknowledge that NGOs have influenced their behavior. The analysis in this book demonstrates that thinking about political salience requires a multiplicity of tools to more fully assess the degree to which ideas and organizations are international focal points. The process of defining and finding political salience is not streamlined, neat, or linear, but it is critical nonetheless in explaining who matters in shaping human rights politics, and why they matter.

Building Political Salience through Structure

There are a number of assumptions that are built into the current literature on understanding NGOs. Primarily, our understanding of NGOs and their power has largely settled on their information-providing and political framing abilities; they have the ability to set the international agenda on human rights (Ahmed and Potter 2006; Bloodgood 2011; Joachim 2003; Lecy, Mitchell, and Schmitz 2010; Raustiala 1997; Rodio and Schmitz 2010). Similar to the power of the media, NGOs serve as alternative forms of information. In many situations, they report on cases that would otherwise be unknown to the rest of the world, were it not for their efforts. It is very tempting to argue that their revelatory qualities mean that NGOs are important as matter of definition. The mere presence of NGOs, in some cases, seems to create legitimacy for what is being reported. The other assumption, linked to the first, is that international NGOs are coherent and cohesive entities. This, in fact, turns out to be quite a big assumption.

Among the NGOs I study here, several are or were loose affiliates of national or other groupings, such as MSF and pre-1995 Oxfam, often sharing very little but a common name. The informality or ambiguity of the associations between various parts of an NGO of the same name belies the influence we assign to international NGOs as game changers in international politics (Betsill and Corell 2010; Clark 1995; Teegen, Doh, and Vachani 2004; Wapner 1995; Wapner and Ruiz 2000). Many NGOs simply do not navigate the transnational dilemma well: they run aground on intersectional squabbles over principles, policies, and political positions because their organizational structures do not allow for the creation of a coherent advocacy agenda and an implementation strategy that focuses on maximizing applicability of that agenda across a variety of contexts. A fundamental choice that all NGOs must make is the degree to which agenda-setting powers will be centralized (that is, held by one or a few actors) or decentralized (held by many actors). Centralization and decentralization are relative measures that must be evaluated in a comparative sense with other NGOs, but a general rule might emphasize the relative number, that is, the proportion of actors in the NGO that have access to the three mechanisms of agenda setting.

What I have shown in this book is that NGOs are not all politically equal, even if they are internationally oriented. Organizational structure exerts effects on both NGO prominence and the capacity to make their advocacy agendas politically salient. Because of the significance of agenda setters in global politics, it should follow that their own internal agenda-setting arrangements matter for their capacities to influence the salience of human rights. I argue that in order to maintain a coherent advocacy agenda across a variety of international contexts, NGOs need to have centralized proposal and enforcement powers. However, because of the inherently diverse number of political, social, economic, and cultural contexts they encounter in their work, international NGOs also need to be able to tailor their efforts to varying situations. They therefore need to decentralize the implementation of their centralized agenda, which allows for both a focused advocacy message and sensitivity to the targets of advocacy. NGOs that successfully harness both of these dynamics are much more likely to become politically salient as actors and create political salience for "their" rights.

This book breaks agenda-setting power along three dimensions: proposal power, enforcement power, and implementation power. Proposal power is the power of suggestion. Such "positive agenda-setting power" allows those actors that hold it to not only highlight the importance of their own positions, but also limit the importance of alternatives. Proposal power provides an opportunity for framing a position such that it gains support across all of the relevant sections of an NGO, increasing the likelihood that a certain position or argument will be accepted as representative of the organization as a whole. The fewer entities that hold proposal power, the more centralized this power is.

Depending on the whether the same actors that have proposal power have enforcement power, these two mechanisms can act in concert to push a certain agenda, or they can work orthogonally as actors different from the proposers can pose barriers to the enactment of decisions. Enforcement power encompasses both veto power and the ability to enforce that veto. This is especially important in NGOs whose ties between national sections is tenuous, as enforcement power is often weak. The wide distribution of veto power, along with an inability to stop deviation from decisions without undertaking drastic actions, such as pulling the organization's trademark, creates coordination problems for NGOs. Thus centralizing enforcement power, especially when enforcement and proposal powers are held by the same agent(s), creates conditions whereby agendas can be formulated and agreed on. Proposal and enforcement powers determine the topics of advocacy.

The last agenda-setting power is the implementation of that agenda, which determines advocacy tactics. Implementation can mean many things to NGOs. Some NGOs pursue a diverse array of tactics when it comes to implementation, choosing multiple types of targets (states, multinational corporations, IGOs, individuals) and multiple ways to target (publishing reports, issuing press releases, negotiating with states, using grassroots support, concerts). The more types of tactics used, the more likely that an NGO will need to decentralize implementation power, as different tactics require different types of specialization. Writing a report requires topical expertise, negotiating with leaders necessitates lobbying savvy, and promoting rights at the grassroots level entails a fundamental understanding of the various audiences to generate support for and NGO's agenda. The more decentralized implementation power, the more likely an NGO will be able to affect the political salience of their rights.

Although initial choices about organizational structure might be sticky, several cases in this book demonstrate that structure can shift over time, depending on the composition of the NGO, changes in priorities, and the ability to overcome collective action problems for change. NGOs might elect to pursue a decentralized agenda-setting strategy because of sensitivity to representativeness, or because of the desire to institutionalize equality of certain actors. This is certainly the case of MSF, which wanted to grant equality to the first five national sections. The decision to do so has since created collective action problems for five OCs, as well as a lack of agenda control, as national sections are free to decide what they use to represent MSF in their respective countries.

Using the structural lens enables a deeper analysis of NGOs as organizations first, and dedicated norm-changers second. NGOs have to survive as political entities, and the way they think about and publicize human rights reflects an awareness of what works in advocacy, the presence of competition, and the constraints posed by the distribution of agenda-setting power. Organizational structure explains why certain rights emerge on the NGO's internal agenda and the prominence of the NGO in international politics. In turn, this perspective also tells us why certain rights are politically salient in the discourse of human rights.

Fitting into the Literature on Norm Entrepreneurs

The notion of norm entrepreneurs helps us understand the sources of ideational change in international relations and offers a basis with which to ground the analysis of norm change. Norm entrepreneurs encourage states to act "morally" (Nadelmann 1990; Busby 2010) through political activity and coalition building. Garnering enough support among a critical mass of states leads to a "norms cascade" at the international level (Finnemore and Sikkink 1998; Sunstein 1996). Norm entrepreneurs have been defined as those "who invent or deploy ideas and information to produce significant structural change" (Goddard 2009, 251). Thus norm entrepreneurs have been individuals, such as Bono (Busby 2007), or collectivities, which includes NGOs such as Amnesty, networks (Keck and Sikkink 1998), or like-minded groups of individuals, as in epistemic communities (Haas 1989, 1992). Determining the relative power of entrepreneurs, however, is a more difficult task. Some have offered systemic structural explanations that rely on insights from social network analysis that emphasize the relative positioning of actors within social and political relationships. Norm entrepreneurs need to be structurally central in order to act as agenda setters (Lake and Wong 2009), gatekeepers (Carpenter 2011), or brokers (Diani 2003; Goddard 2009).

There is something to be said about the qualitative differences between various nodes within a network, however, even if structural position helps to determine the influence of those agents.[1] For instance, what explains the centrality of certain actors, and are all actors equally likely to become central? The argument that positioning matters certainly fits into the theory in this book. NGOs, in order to be successful at influencing the political salience of human rights, must have one foot grounded at the international level in forming coherent advocacy agendas, and many feet in the implementation of that agenda. Thus this argument echoes those made by others who have found that a certain level of in-betweenness matters for moving between international and domestic levels, in terms of the compatibility of new norms with existing domestic ones.

By stressing the differences in organizational structure between NGOs, the theory here extends analyses of norm entrepreneurship. The likelihood of becoming a norm entrepreneur, at least at the international level, and having the ability to shape the political salience of human rights, is not equally distributed. There are organizational attributes that contribute to the salience of NGOs and their advocacy agendas, and there are only a select few NGOs in human rights that command attention from policymakers in multiple states and in intergovernmental fora. These NGOs are probably more likely to be centrally located in network terms. These qualities make an NGO likely to become prominent and successful in promoting its agenda work in conjunction with structural conditions that further contribute to an NGO's accomplishments. Structural centrality attracts other like-minded actors, as in scale-free networks. Hence, once NGOs reach a level of salience at the international level, and persuade states to change their human rights behavior or adopt new standards, it is much more likely they will be able to continue doing so. Their structures are set up to perpetuate their influence, and their salience in international politics creates more opportunities to serve as norm entrepreneur. We can see how this evinces itself in a very unlikely way, through economic sanctions and their use in regulating human rights behavior.

Internal Affairs: Beyond Human Rights?

Another benefit of using organizational structure as the primary explanatory variable is its translatability to other issue areas in transnational advocacy, or even to other actors beyond NGOs. Typically, the study of international nonstate actors has been siloed into various categories—development, environmental, global justice, human rights, humanitarian, religious, women's rights—and different languages according to discipline. What sociologists call a social movement organization, for instance, political scientists label NGOs. By parsing out agenda-setting and implementation processes within NGOs, the theory presented here aims toward transportability in other transnational issue areas. Two politically salient organizations, reviewed here, reflect the importance of proposal and enforcement powers and decentralizing implementation power, so critical to the success of human rights NGOs and campaigns.

Environmentalism at the Point of a Harpoon: Greenpeace International

Although a number of books about Greenpeace have been written by its founders and former members, academic analysis of the biggest and most controversial environmental NGO remain scant. Since its founding in 1970 as the Don't Make a Wave Committee in Vancouver, Canada, the NGO has courted notoriety and fame through splashy statements in the name of environmentalism. As one analysis observes, "One of Greenpeace's core competencies has been staging events that the media find irresistible" (Mintzberg and Westley 2000, 90), but this tendency has also sprouted charges that the NGO is irresponsible (Shaiko 1993). It began as a protest of US nuclear testing at Amchitka Island in the Aleutians, but quickly took on the French for their nuclear tests, and began an antiwhaling campaign that persists to this day. This NGO has become famous through the pluck of its actions, but also its phenomenal growth in members and budget. All of this has not come without cost and resistance from many enemies, but Greenpeace is the most visible of the transnational environmental NGOs (Mintzberg and Westley 2000), even if its positions may not meet the exacting standards of science (Moore 2010).

In 1971, the founders of Don't Make a Wave decided on a change in moniker to Greenpeace Foundation. As the organization gained attention for its daring sails into nuclear test sites and chasing off whaling boats, and as state and IGO policies shifted in favor of Greenpeace's positions, copycat groups arose, openly operating in similar fashion, sometimes working in the name of Greenpeace, some without authorization. Greenpeace groups were scattered in Canada, the United States, England, France, Germany, Australia, and New Zealand, and factions were forming between them. Groups were amassing serious funding—$12 million in 1979—and it became clear that the groups would need to consolidate.[2] The decision to become one Greenpeace International, however, was not easy. The group from San Francisco walked out of the second meeting of two held in 1978 and 1979. Finally, in October 1979, Greenpeace International was established with a headquarters in Amsterdam, with representatives from Australia, Canada, Denmark, France, Germany, the Netherlands, New Zealand, the United Kingdom, and the United States. To date, there are offices in forty countries.

Many of the things about Greenpeace's organizational structure should sound familiar. Greenpeace International's headquarters in Amsterdam houses the executive director, as well as the various program offices. By its own description, the International office "coordinates global Greenpeace policy and strategy,"[3] and its roles are portrayed as largely facilitative, rather than leading. There is an international Board that monitors the activities and operations of the wider organization, approves new campaigns and offices, controls the trademark, and decides on the voting status of national sections. The Board also appoints the international executive director (IED). An Annual General Meeting (Council) decides strategic, as well as operational issues, such as budget, Board composition, and the opening of new Greenpeace offices, but most of these decisions are subject to Board approval. There are also meetings of the IED with national executive directors, and international program officers meet with their national counterparts regularly as well.

The function of the International office seems at first one of support, but Greenpeace's Rules of Procedure outline a much larger formal enforcement role for Amsterdam. There are two types of national sections, voting and nonvoting, and voting sections must meet certain financial and performance standards to keep their voting status. For example, all national sections must demonstrate to the International that it has established a "nucleus of a supporter base."[4] National sections must create a development plan, which is approved by the IED. All national-level campaigns must be selected from among those defined by the International (with exceptions). Any voting office that is determined by the IED to be nonfunctioning will be recommended to the Board to have its voting rights stripped.

The IED also holds a great deal of proposal power. While there are at least two yearly mandated meetings with national-level executive directors in which major strategic and organizational issues are discussed, the IED may also make her own proposals to the Board without first consulting other executive directors.[5] Although the international Council and the Board share "political authority" (i.e., proposal and enforcement powers) for Greenpeace formally at the international level, it seems that there are ways in which the IED and the International office can manage Greenpeace affairs. Because of the coordinative role of the Amsterdam office, and because national sections must seek approval from either the IED or one of her lieutenants for financial, campaign, and strategic choices, the International office exercises a great deal of proposal and enforcement power. I expect that further research will yield that, like Amnesty International, Greenpeace's international movements are largely determined by the IED and her staff, despite the fact that formal rules identify the Board and Council as the political authorities. Critics of Greenpeace have already alleged that the Amsterdam office is the most powerful player for Greenpeace, collecting the money from its most prosperous national offices to pay for its activities (see Spencer 1991).

In terms of implementation power, national sections drive the engine of politics at the local level. This means there is a disconnect between the global politics of Greenpeace International and the actual running of campaigns on the ground. Organizationally, Greenpeace relies on national sections to carry out the campaigns decided on at the international level, but these national-level projects require approval from Amsterdam. Thus the implementation of Greenpeace's global campaigns seems to be much less open to lower-level interpretations than Amnesty's, Oxfam's, or some of the campaigns in this book, such as Access or the ICBL. Using organizational structure as the lens, it would appear that Greenpeace has highly centralized proposal and enforcement powers, and moderately decentralized implementation power because of the oversight national offices are subjected to in the way they carry out campaigns.

Churches like Starbucks: Redeemed
Christian Church of God

In the West, we have a history of sending religious missionaries abroad to convert the unholy. The reverse trend was far less plausible until very recently. Church movements from Nigeria in particular have made inroads into other countries. One prominent Pentecostal movement is the Redeemed Christian Church of God (RCCG), which is the largest born-again church in Nigeria, and boasts of "church plantings" the world over, spreading into one hundred nations in Africa, the Americas, Asia, and Europe (Marshall 2009).[6] The spread of this sect of Pentecostalism has to do, I argue, with not just the adaptability of the RCCG message, but also its organizational structure, which taps local energies, but centralizes many of the main aspects of the church: tithing, growth strategies, and the production of the overall message.

More than other types of Christian denominations, Pentecostalism lends itself to attracting adherents because of its comparative lack of structure. There is no official Pentecostal doctrine, no special ordination that all Pentecostals must endure. As one recent *New York Times* article states: "Pentecostalism is not so much an organized religion—it has no central authority—as a set of beliefs and practices that can be adapted by local entrepreneurs. It is perfectly suited to harness the modern forces of global crosspollination."[7] Thus, the various strands of Pentecostalism might coalesce freely around their own interpretations of God's word, relying on preachers who had had holy visions to lead them to salvation. Each Pentecostal movement, however, structures itself differently, and some, particularly those aggressively seeking converts globally, have familiar forms of organization: centralized proposal and enforcement powers, and decentralized implementation power. The RCCG is a shining example of a relatively new church that has not only taken its native country by storm but has advanced its goal of saving every soul in the world.[8] As one of its pastors attests: "We want to start churches, if possible, like Starbucks."[9]

RCCG was founded in 1952 by an illiterate pastor, Josiah Akindayomi. In the beginning, the church was an exclusively Yoruba affair, with service conducted only in Yoruba and drawing on urban Yoruba from the lower middle class (Marshall 2009). In the 1970s, a lecturer in mathematics the University of Lagos, Enoch A. Adeboye, was plucked by Akindayomi to join the church and eventually become his successor. Adeboye became the general overseer (GO) of the church in 1981, and immediately set his sights on expanding the reach of the RCCG. Under Akindayomi, he had begun translating services from Yoruba into English. Adeboye also sought to enlarge the appeal of the church, and take advantage of the youthful zeal that characterized the revivalist movement that had seized Nigeria in the 1960s and 1970s. The changes were drastic. Under his watch, the RCCG has expanded exponentially in Nigeria and beyond. Holy Ghost Camp, located outside of Lagos, attracted tens of thousands of worshippers for all-night monthly services in the late 1990s, and the yearly Holy Ghost Congress draws millions (Marshall 2009). RCCG has a university (Redeemer's University for Nations) and runs schools (Ukah 2008, 132).

On the one hand, Adeboye's leadership and personal attributes have made RCCG the Pentecostal force it is today. Without a doubt, his staff of RCCG officers respond to his demands, and much of Adeboye's power comes from informal sources. On the other hand, Adeboye has built RCCG on the basis of a very complicated set of formal rules. The formal rules devolve power to the GO and a limited number of lieutenants, who make decisions for the RCCG. These decisions affect the overall expansion strategy of the church, the rules of ordination for pastor, and new programs and affiliates—including ties to business and political leaders—that transmit the message of RCCG to the world.

Although religious organizations are very different from human rights NGOs, the same principles of agenda setting and implementation follow. The agenda of the RCCG is deceptively simple—restore Christianity and morality to the world—but the means to do so have changed since its founding, "Whereas [Akindayomi] idea of restitution involved putting oneself right with God by making amends for one's sins, Adeboye preaches that giving to God is an investment which will bring rich blessings in return" (Ukah 2008, xx). Poverty is seen as an impediment to spreading God's word (Ukah 2008, 123). Adeboye shifted from the emphasis on ascetic values of the original RCCG followers by setting up new parishes called "model parishes" that targeted the young and upwardly mobile in urban Nigeria. The Christ the Redeemer's Ministry plays an important role for mission work and the spread of the RCCG, but also makes money for the church and finds employment for churchgoers. It runs countless programs for the church, including such varied activities as publishing, creating video, campus outreach, and hosting a computer training school (Ukah 2008, 121).

While Adeboye certainly has many personal attributes that lend him great informal powers, the formal distribution of agenda-setting and implementation powers bolster his decisions. As GO, he controls the strategic agenda of the church, and the public projection of its message. Unlike NGO leaders, however, Adeboye's powers extend beyond formal powers of office, as the GO is not only an organizational leader, but links his followers to God (Ukah 2008, 96). As such, because of the role of faith within the organization, the centralization of agenda-setting power in the RCCG is even more apparent than in its secular counterparts.

As the RCCG has gained more adherents, more structures have been added to the church. Here I discuss the most up-to-date information, available from Ukah (2008). The supreme office of the organization is the GO, which spans both the national Nigerian operation and the international. The post is filled by nomination and proclamation, as the incumbent GO names his successor before death (Ukah 2008, 96). The GO is in office for life and guides the spiritual and strategic directions of the mission, provides discipline for officers of the church and followers, and ordains pastors. The GO is advised by a Governing Council, made up of seven of the most senior pastors in the church. In addition, each of these pastors oversees a portfolio of duties concerning the administration and church life (e.g., planning and education) as assistant GOs, and serves as the coordinator of a region of the church in Nigeria. Although the exact distribution of proposal and enforcement power is murky, it is clear that the Governing Council is the highest decision-making body in the church, and the GO wields power that is not really checked, except by God (Ukah 2008, 96–97). Including the wife of the GO (Mother-in-Israel), there are a total of nine individuals who have the formal power to propose and enforce the agenda in the RCCG. Ukah remarks: "There seems to be no reason why such duties are heaped on single individuals…other than the concentration of power on a few trusted male allies, a veritable strategy of controlling charisma and authority" (Ukah 2008, 103–104). Below the Governing Council, indeed, most of the work is about spreading the word to the people, and not creating or shaping the word.

To contrast, implementation power is highly decentralized. As with any other church, implementation of the RCCG's message is done through its congregation and conversion. The RCCG has spread, in Nigeria and beyond, through the initial "planting" of small parishes (Marshall 1991), often with modest attendance, that gradually swell. These church plantings are vigorous, with high goals set by the RCCG leadership—usually the GO himself. A *New York Times* story recounts a meeting in which North American leaders were scolded for not planting quickly enough: "'Last year in October, we had 297 parishes in North America,' he said. 'As of September of this year, we have 374. Praise the Lord!'...Fadele's voice turned stern. 'To Daddy G.O., that's a failure,' he snapped. The number of parishes had increased by 25 percent in just a year, but Adeboye had asked for twice that."[10]

Once planted, however, parishes seem to have plenty of leeway. Oversight for individual pastors, once ordained, is not incredibly tight, and pastors use different approaches to attract the faithful. Many pastors have not had formal training at seminaries, attending more informal bible study programs that ranged from one to six months (Marshall 2009, 133). Furthermore, their respective flocks are fluid, and many congregants shop around from one born-again church to another. Because the standard by which church plantings are measured is by the number of parishes and the collection of tithes, the movement of followers matters. The RCCG, in the same vein as other Pentecostal churches, lures members with its distinctive style of emotional preaching, "healings," and speaking in tongues, but also draws members based on their concern with lifestyle and worldly matters, such as personal prosperity. One congregant in Maryland remarked: "'I'm really making money because of what the pastor is always telling us. You know, even if you have your job that you're doing, you need to have something by the side.'"[11] The exemplar of the RCCG spread beyond Nigeria is Jesus House, a congregation led by a female pastor, based in London, that has planted subsequent Jesus Houses in North America, including large cities such as Washington, DC; Chicago; and Toronto, as well as less densely populated areas, such as Moncton, Halifax, and New Jersey. Jesus House in London boasts of an auditorium that can seat a thousand, a bookstore, catering, offices, and other facilities (Hunt and Lightly 2001).

Implementation is thus decentralized, but not without direction. The leadership sets goals and delegates to lower-level officials, who go about planting churches. Once planted, each parish largely functions on its own.

Of course, they are encouraged to meet targets, and some, like Jesus House, become their own sources of new church plantings. The overall message of the church spreads through the efforts of both RCCG-appointed individuals and the fervor of its believers, but the growth is carefully calculated by the GO and Council. Thus, similar to the human rights NGOs studied in this book, the RCCG holds tightly centralized control over proposal and enforcement powers, but allows for local implementation techniques to populate its parishes and generate interest in new ones. Using this method, the RCCG has grown from a small Nigerian church concentrated in its Christian south to a worldwide flock that was estimated to be close to 1 million worldwide in 2001 (Hunt and Lightly 2001, 109).

More than Morals

Many actors have morals, even if this is not their founding credo. Politicians can act morally, but are rarely conceived as moral leaders, whereas religious leaders are. Religious leaders of terrorist groups, however, are not valorized, at least by their targets. Thus the morality of an actor, and more important, the morality of his/her actions is both relative to the audience and is not the reason for success. For every Hamas, there are several other similarly motivated groups that claim the same moral stance and desire corresponding political goals. Hamas, however, is Hamas because of its organizational structure: its reach into the community, its use of violence, and its provision of social services (Iannaccone and Berman 2006). The lesson about Hamas can be transposed to that of human rights NGOs: it is both the appeal of their ideas and the power of the organizational structure behind those ideas. Organizational structure gives conviction the means with which to succeed. Through contemporary and historical cases, I have demonstrated the explanatory power of organizational structure in the creation and spread of human rights norms, and have contributed to the debate on how norm entrepreneurs set the political agenda, the ways in which they deal with structural constraints in their efforts to make their agendas salient, and how states are forced to react to the demands of nonstate actors.

The insights provided here have policy and theoretical implications. From a policy perspective, NGOs that wish to influence international norms through advocacy need to consider the distribution of internal agenda-setting power. To become politically salient and create political salience for their rights of interest, NGOs must centralize proposal and enforcement powers to create a coherent agenda. Simultaneously, decentralized implementation power helps to ground their universal human rights stances in local contexts. NGOs have followed various models, as can be seen here, and perhaps at one point in history, different structures seemed to have efficacy. However, in the post–Cold War world in particular, balancing the tension between centralized agenda setting and decentralized agenda implementation positions NGOs to best navigate the transnational dilemma. As increasing numbers of "non–human rights NGOs" decide that advocacy has a legitimate place in their organizational goals, we should see movement toward the structure discussed in these pages.

From a theoretical view, the theory and cases in this book represent an effort to seriously engage the question of what affects the efficacy of NGOs in their pursuit of changing international norms around human rights. How do they recast various rights as important and make them important for other actors, such as states and IGOs? Why is it that even after sixty-plus years of universal human rights in the post–World War II world, only a few NGOs have risen to the top (not for others' lack of trying)? Organizational structure gives us a tool by which to observe and assess various NGOs that does not rely on a subjective moral claim or an evaluation of the qualities of an idea or set of ideas. The argument of this book bridges the structure-agent divide that characterizes some of the larger, paradigmatic debates in international relations (Wendt 1987, 1992) by focusing on the structure of the agents involved in human rights politics. These agents, in turn, are sensitive to the ramifications of the distribution of power in the international system, but their success is not necessarily predicated on which states are great powers at any given point in time. Distinguishing between the relative political salience of NGOs and their advocacy efforts requires a closer look at the agents themselves. I have highlighted how they distribute agenda-setting power as a central criterion of analysis. These insights from the study of human rights norms can be transported to an investigation of advocacy in other transnational sectors, many of which have crept into human rights politics by adopting a language of rights: development, environmentalism, economic inequality.[12] As more NGOs seek change in the political salience of ideas in the international arena, they will need to navigate the transnational dilemma through structural choices.

Notes

Introduction

1. Scholars have produced very good reads on the topic (Burgers 1992; Glendon 2002; Morsink 2002).

2. Notably, the USSR and its allies abstained, as well as Saudi Arabia and South Africa.

3. Chile has a museum dedicated to its own human rights struggles in the 1970s that just opened in 2010 (http://www.globalpost.com/dispatch/chile/100216/memory-human-rights-museum) (accessed March 15, 2010). Japan's Osaka Human Rights Museum mainly looks at the history of discrimination in the country against ethnic, gendered, sexual, and disabled populations. In the United States, the National Civil Rights Museum in Memphis chronicles the systematic discrimination against African-Americans and the political struggle against such abuses.

4. http://www.cbc.ca/arts/story/2009/05/22/museum-discussion.html (accessed March 15, 2010).

5. http://www.winnipegfreepress.com/local/human-rights-museums-ideals-may-be-tough-to-attain-59978402.html (accessed March 15, 2010), as well as extensive speculation in the blogosphere.

6. http://www.simcoereformer.ca/ArticleDisplay.aspx?archive=true&e=1528299 (accessed March 15, 2010). Victims of the Rwandan genocide of 2004, for example, as an underrepresented group in Canada, run the risk of being left on the cutting table.

7. The first was the case of *Lawless v. Ireland,* which addressed the detention of violent political dissidents without trial.

8. State of the Union Address, January 11, 1944.

9. When I consulted the US section's collection in 2005, it was housed at the University of Colorado, Boulder.

1. Salience in Human Rights

1. The actual achievement of legislation may not be as important as the process of getting there (see Finnemore and Toope 2001).

2. This idea of a tipping point is not new to the study of norms (Finnemore and Sikkink 1998; Schelling 2006).

3. There are three categories of organizations with consultative status before the UN. Originally, Category A organizations have "a basic interest in most of the activities of the Council." Category B organizations have a "special competence" in limited fields. Category C (or Register) organizations focus on "the development of public opinion and with the dissemination of information." Since 1968, NGOs with consultative status have been recategorized as Category I, Category II, and the Roster, but the same rules essentially apply to the new names (see Willetts 1996).

4. Article 5: "All human rights are universal, indivisible and interdependent and interrelated. The international community must treat human rights globally in a fair and equal manner, on the same footing, and with the same emphasis." http://www.unhchr.ch/huridocda/huridoca.nsf/%28symbol%29/a.conf.157.23.en (accessed September 10, 2010).

5. University of Minnesota, "The Administration of Justice during States of Emergency," in *Human Rights in the Administration of Justice* http://www1.umn.edu/humanrts//monitoring/adminchap16.html (accessed September 10, 2010).

6. From Article 4: these are Articles 6, 7, 8 (paragraphs 1 and 2), 11, 15, 16, 18. These articles include discrimination/genocide; torture; slavery; imprisonment based on contract; post-hoc convictions; recognition before the law; and freedom of thought, conscience, and religion.

7. The boomerang pattern emphasized the role of third-party states or intergovernmental organizations on changing the behavior of human rights–violating states. The spiral model explains how the process of socializing states to human rights regimes works through advocacy.

8. http://www.amnesty.org/ (accessed July 7, 2011).

9. This logic is similar to those investigating whether IGO membership has consequences on human rights norms diffusion (Greenhill 2010).

10. If norms are standards of behavior for a given identity, a lack of economic sanctions over, for example, cannibalism, does not mean that anticannibalism is not a norm. It is safe to say that states are opposed cannibalism without resorting to sanctioning because that is a taboo practice. Most norms, however, are contested among different identities, for instance, "Western" versus "non-Western" states, and sanctioning demonstrates the rights that states want to protect abroad through costly behavior.

11. Sanctions, like war, are "sticks," while other ways of eliciting behavioral change, such as offering new aid packages or using persuasion are "carrots." Though carrots may also be indicators of normative investment, economic sanctions impose both an economic and reputational cost on the sender state, which carrots may not.

12. Nooruddin argues that the lack of success indicates more about selection bias (only in cases where sanctions happen), which excludes from consideration cases where sanctions were threatened, and targets backed down (success without sanction) (Nooruddin 2002).

13. There is, therefore, an inherent irony to the use of economic sanctions to measure state commitment to human rights norms. This has not seemed to stop states from using them in the name of human rights.

14. In Hufbauer et al. (1990) and Drury (1998), some of the episodes that seem to be clearly human rights-related were not labeled as such. Some have since been revised in the 2007 edition, but South African Apartheid continues to lack a "human rights" label. Including the democracy-based sanctions biases my analysis but also covers possible divergences in opinion between the authors and myself about what constitutes a "human rights"-based sanction.

15. For example, prominent databases used in international relations to analyze regime type, such as POLITY and Freedom House, both employ various human rights and freedoms as measures of "democracy" and "autocracy."

16. By contrast, the Inter-American Court of Human Rights does not allow for individual standing.

17. This follows along its earlier behavior regarding human rights, when it and its allies abstained from signing the UDHR.

18. Notably, economic sanctions against Chile were implemented by the United States in 1975 and supported by the USSR in 1977 (Ropp and Sikkink 1999).

2. The Importance of Organizational Structure

1. The insistence on the distinction between "for" and "non" profit enterprises is similar to the discussion in Sell and Prakash (2004) regarding "materially" versus "value" motivated networks (see pages 147–49). I agree with their assessment that what is important is assessing whose ideas become predominant and why, assuming that both nonprofit and for-profit agents seek recognition for their agendas.

2. See for example, "Report I from the Administration Committee," May 1, 1967, AI Index ORG 06//67 and "Amnesty International: Growth" and "Growth and Development of Amnesty International—Part Two (Paper by Irmgard Hutter)," AI Index NS 271//76.

3. Save the Children Sweden has been most active in promoting the rights-based approach.

4. For interesting counters to this position, see Cooley and Ron 2002, Reimann 2006, Polman 2010.

5. Several good reviews of the literature are out there, see: (Borgatti and Foster 2003; Kahler 2009; M. E. J. Newman 2002; Podolny and Page 1998).

6. Other specifications of centrality include eigenvector centrality, information centrality, and flow betweenness (see Hafner-Burton, Kahler, and Montgomery 2009).

7. Mathematically, something is technically scale-free only if the population of consideration is unbounded (Watts 2004: 111–14). As a theoretical guide, the insights derived from marking differences between scale-free and other types of networks does not require that phenomena extent out infinitely. Such a requirement would exclude the study of nearly all social and political phenomena, and yet there are clear (even visual) differences between various types of man-made networks (see Barabási 2003).

8. For an extensive review, see Eilstrup-Sangiovanni and Jones 2008, 7–11.

9. This is also where the oft-cited "strength of weak ties" fits in (Granovetter 1973). Casual acquaintants are more likely to be of help in job searches, because they are the link outside of your cluster and therefore know many that you do not necessarily know. See also "structural holes" (Burt 1995).

10. This vulnerability is probably most important for security or technology network, where knowing who the central node is can assist in breaking down networks. The networks and organizations discussed in this book are (to date at least) not the subject of such sabotage.

11. http://www.nytimes.com/2010/09/07/business/07gift.html (accessed October 1, 2010).

12. This is similar to claims made by human rights theorists who make "soft" universalist arguments (see Donnelly 2007; Osiatynski 2009).

13. Chandler's ideas have been applied in thinking about hierarchy in international relations (Cooley 2008).

3. Amnesty International

1. Hopgood's *Keepers of the Flame,* of course, is a notable exception, covering the 1980s into the 2000s. This book's focus is on the earlier period, to explain what made Amnesty the human rights juggernaut it was by the 1980s.

2. http://www.amnesty.org/en/who-we-are (accessed October 29, 2009).

3. Following a desire to maintain impartiality in the Cold War era, adoption groups were initially given three cases at a time: one from each of the First, Second, and Third worlds. As the NGO grew in membership, however, this model increasingly became untenable and groups were given cases in a much less rigid fashion.

4. Originally, the appeal only specified articles 18 and 19 (expression, religion, conscience). Nonetheless, its mandate quickly expanded, though it is hard to pinpoint the precise moment at which it moved from these two original rights to the more inclusive 5, 9, 18, and 19. The statute of Amnesty International adopted by the Sixth International Assembly, Stockholm, Sweden, in August 1968 officially states that the four articles are the objects of the organization. The Swedish section formally proposed adoption of article 5 in the 1966 International Assembly meeting in Copenhagen, Denmark, but it was not adopted until 1968. Under the influence of Secretary General Thomas Hammarberg, the death penalty would become part of the mandate in the early 1970s.

5. After 1966, the Library became one of the three major components of the IS. It was also known as the Registry or Investigation Department, and later became known as the Research Department, before disappearing altogether as an independent department under the restructuring completed by Secretary General Pierre Sané in the 1990s (see Hopgood 2006, 125–128).

6. Oral History Pilot Project, "Peter Benenson," November 12, 1983.

7. "Minutes of the Second Meeting of the Amnesty International Committee," October 8, 1961, London.

8. Interview AI-007.

9. "Statute of Amnesty International," Adopted by the Sixth International Assembly, Stockholm, August 25, 1968.

10. Ibid.

11. Ibid.

12. See Buchanan (2004), as well as the report generated for 1967 internal Amnesty investigation, written by Peter Calvocoressi, entitled "Report on Certain Matters Affecting Amnesty, presented to Sean MacBride." The report was presented at the March 11–12 meeting of the IEC in Elsinore, Denmark.

13. A very early version of the statute was written after the July 22–23, 1961, meeting in Luxembourg. This document, however, like subsequent governing documents, concerns itself mostly with establishing the philosophical bases of POCs and advocacy on their behalf, as well as tactical and strategic considerations. Not until 1968 does the statute focus extensively on the structure of the organization.

14. The 1968 ICM officially voted in favor of opposing the use of the death penalty in all cases. See "Amnesty International Review," November 25, 1968. Amnesty officially adopted opposition to the death penalty as part of the mandate in 1973 (Thompson 2008).

15. Interviews AI-005, AI-012, AI-013.

16. Interview AI-008.

17. Interview AI-017.

18. See 1985 ICM Helsinki.

19. The most recent is posted online: http://www.amnesty.org/en/who-we-are/accountability/statute-of-amnesty-international (accessed October 29, 2009); it is consistent with historical versions in this regard.

20. Interview AI-008.

21. Interview AI-007.

22. Interviews AI-010, AI-011.

23. Decision 33 of 1979 ICM. Until From 1968–1989, a Borderline Committee of three independent evaluators would advise the IS on how to proceed on a case on the margin. By the

mid-1980s, however, it became increasingly clear that the Borderline Committee's work had been taken over by the IS.

24. Amnesty document: POL 21/IEC/02/82.

25. POL 21/IEC/O3/82.

26. Amnesty International Report and Decisions of the Second International Council Meeting, Geneva, Switzerland, September 13–14, 1969.

27. Adoption groups still exist, but the Threes model no longer works.

28. Interview AI-013.

29. Report of IEC meetings in St. Gallen, Switzerland, September 10–14, 1975 (NW 211).

30. Money remained an issue throughout the 1970s. See for example, "Report I from the Administration Committee," May 1, 1967, AI Index ORG 06//67. The idea of having members simply be financial contributors (and not letter-writers or campaigners) was floated in "Amnesty International—Five Years Hence, Report and Recommendations," May 31, 1972.

31. See "Amnesty International: Growth" and "Growth and Development of Amnesty International—Part Two (Paper by Irmgard Hutter)," AI Index NS 271//76.

32. See "The Role of C.A.T. in Amnesty International," AI Index NS 44//76.

33. Ibid.

34. See *Amnesty International Annual Report, 1972–1973* and *Amnesty International Annual Report, 1973–1974.*

35. Interview AI-012.

36. "Archives Amnesty International, International Secretariat," IISG, Amsterdam, The Netherlands, accessed October 9–20, 2006.

37. Interview AI-012.

38. Famously, Amnesty refused to grant ANC leader Nelson Mandela POC status because of the charges of sabotage that accompanied his imprisonment.

39. Interview AI-007. Other national sections also were able to break WOOC on the death penalty as well, but the US section was the first.

40. Interview AI-013.

41. The latter two practices being perhaps direct reactions to the extensive documentation by international actors of Chilean human rights abuses a few years earlier. Thus the Argentine junta hoped to hide the evidence through different, less overt techniques (Sikkink 1993, 423).

4. Other Models of Advocating Change

1. Originally known as the International League for the Rights of Man.

2. The ICRC was widely criticized for its failures to speak about what they observed in Nazi concentration camps in World War II. Its attempts to do so in the 1994 Rwandan genocide are also widely cited as heroic challenges to the rest of the world's apathy toward the situation (Dallaire and Power 2004).

3. In some ways, HRW had to model itself against Amnesty. Under Neier, it deemphasized the individual and focused on understanding the broader context of human rights abuses. It also openly lobbied the US government to change its policies.

4. http://www.hrw.org/en/node/75138 (accessed August 2, 2009).

5. http://www.hrw.org/en/node/75136 (accessed October 29, 2009).

6. "George Soros to Give $100 million to Human Rights Watch," Human Rights Watch, September 7, 2010.

7. Interview HRW-010.

8. Not to be confused with the French-based FIDH.

9. Baldwin also helped found the American Civil Liberties Union in 1920.

10. A declaration announcing the organization was released in 1941, but it was incorporated in New York the next year.

11. http://www.ilhr.org/ (accessed January 20, 2010).

12. Human Rights First was originally founded in 1978 as the Lawyer's Committee on International Human Rights, which was a spin-off from the ILHR. It became completely independent from the ILHR in 1980.

13. In 1977, there were thirty-five national affiliates (Ray and Taylor 1977). A survey of the current ILHR webpage http://www.ilhr.org/ (accessed January 17, 2010) reveals little information about the state of the network or the size of the organization.

14. See Black (1992) for a comprehensive account of the NGO pre-1990s.

15. The Canadian branch was the first outpost established around 1943, but was only formally incorporated in 1966.

16. Interview OX-001.

17. At the time, Oxfam New Zealand was part of Community Aid Abroad.

18. Interview OX-003.

19. Ibid.

20. Ibid.

21. Interview OX-002.

22. http://www.msf.org/msfinternational/invoke.cfm?objectid=130CB2BA-E018–0C72–097046C7C42A8573&component=toolkit.indexArticle&method=full_html (accessed November 4, 2009).

23. http://nobelprize.org/nobel_prizes/peace/laureates/1999/ (accessed December 10, 2010).

24. Luxembourg is now officially part of OC-Brussels.

25. Currently, MSF-Canada, MSF-Germany, MSF-UK (including Ireland), and MSF-Holland.

26. http://www.doctorswithoutborders.org/press/release.cfm?id=5412 (accessed November 22, 2011).

27. Ibid.

28. The first thematic program was Women's Rights, established in 1990. More currently, there are six regional directors (the United States was given its own) and eleven thematic program directors (http://www.hrw.org/en/node/75139#exec, accessed October 28, 2009).

29. Interviews HRW-005, HRW-009.

30. Interview HRW-004.

31. Interview HRW-007.

32. Interviews HRW-006, HRW-009.

33. Interview HRW-011.

34. Interview HRW-017.

35. Interview MSF-004.

36. Interview MSF-014.

37. Multiple desks report to an operations director.

38. Interview MSF-003.

39. OC-Brussels coordinates the mission, which has funding and personnel from multiple OCs.

40. See Oxfam constitution http://www.oxfam.org/en/about/accountability (accessed November 1, 2009).

41. Interviews OX-001, OX-003.

42. Oxfam-New Zealand was the last Oxfam to be sponsored by a single Oxfam (Oxfam-Australia).

43. http://www.oxfam.org/en/about/history (accessed November 10, 2010).

44. Interviews OX-001, OX-003.

45. Interview HRW-017.

46. Interview HRW-002.

47. Among others interviews: MSF-001, MSF-002, MSF-004, MSF-016, MSF-018.

48. Interview MSF-009.

49. Interview MSF-016.

50. Stephan Smith, "On its Own, MSF France Leaves the Rwandan Camps," *Libération* (in French), November 15, 1994 (Binet 2003).

51. Interview MSF-014.

52. MSF-France Board meeting, November 25, 1994 (Binet 2003).

53. MSF-Greece was reinstated in 2003.

54. Interview OX-001.

55. Ibid.

56. Interview OX-002.

57. Interview OX-002.

58. As of 2009, this was 1 percent to the International Secretariat, 0.2 percent to a shared growth fund, Interview MX-003.

59. Michael Posner, Human Rights First's former president, serves in the Obama administration as US Assistant Secretary of State for Democracy, Human Rights, and Labor.

60. http://www.hrw.org/en/node/75138 (accessed December 14, 2009).

61. Interview HRW-011.

62. Interview HRW-012.

63. Personal correspondence with Roger Clark.

64. "The U.N. Chief Makes a Plea for Captives," *New York Times,* August 17, 1985.

65. Interview MSF-018.

66. Interview OX-004.

67. Interview OX-006.

68. Interview OX-004.

69. Interview OX-003.

70. Interview OX-001.

71. Interview OX-003.

72. http://www.ilhr.org/ilhr/who/index.html (accessed July 25, 2011).

73. Aid Watch is an organization set up to collect information about NGOs working on human rights and humanitarianism. It lists ILHR as one of the groups for which there is very little information (see http://www.observatoire-humanitaire.org/fusion.php?l=GB&id=57, accessed July 25, 2011), although there is some analysis of its spin-off, Human Rights First.

74. "MSF Activity Report 2009," available at http://www.msf.org/msf/articles/2010/07/msf-international-activity-report-2009.cfm (accessed July 25, 2011).

75. Amnesty Charity Limited report, 2010, available at http://www.amnesty.org/en/who-we-are/accountability/financial-reports (accessed June 29, 2011).

76. Human Rights Watch, Inc. Financial Statements, 2010, available at http://www.hrw.org/en/about/financials (accessed June 29, 2011).

77. "Oxfam Annual Report, 2009–10" available at http://www.oxfam.org/en/about/annual-reports (accessed July 25, 2011). Oxfam International's office maintains a separate financial report, see "Stichting Oxfam International Annual Report and Non-Statutory Financial Statements, 2009–10," available at http://www.oxfam.org/en/about/accountability (accessed July 25, 2011).

5. Using Campaigns to Examine Organizational and Ideational Salience

1. In fact, the ICRC originated the campaign against landmines in 1974.

2. An organization with such longevity has gone through many name changes, as documented below. From 1839 to 1995, the organization was known as the Anti-Slavery Society (and an appendage that reflected the focus of its work at the time). From 1947 to 1956, the NGO

was known simply as Anti-Slavery Society. Since 1995, it has called itself Anti-Slavery International. Throughout, I refer to ASI when speaking to the movement en toto to the present day. Otherwise, for historical, pre-1995 references, I will use the term "the Society."

3. Interview HRW-013.

4. Ibid.

5. Initially, ICBL had no means to cash in on its winnings.

6. Interview HRW-018.

7. This will be a difficult goal to reach. Notably missing from the list of signatories are the United States, Russia, and China.

8. "Human Rights Watch's Recent Work on Cluster Munitions," Human Rights Watch, August 2009.

9. Human Rights Watch's Recent Work on Cluster Munitions," Human Rights Watch, November 2008.

10. Ibid.

11. Interview HRW-013.

12. http://www.antislavery.org/english/what_we_do/antislavery_international_today/frequently_asked_questions.aspx (accessed January 6, 2010).

13. Originally known as the "League"—the name was changed in 1991.

14. When I use "Red Cross" in this chapter, it is to denote all three of these parts of the greater Red Cross movement.

15. See Article 13.1 of ICRC Statute http://www.icrc.org/web/eng/siteeng0.nsf/html/icrc-statutes-080503 (accessed January 30, 2010).

16. http://www.ifrc.org/what/ (accessed February 1, 2010).

17. See also speech by Jakob Kellenberger, president of ICRC, December 3, 2003 (http://icrc.org/Web/eng/siteeng0.nsf/htmlall/5WNJHD?OpenDocument&style=custo_print) (accessed February 3, 2010).

18. Colin L. Powell, "Remarks to the National Foreign Policy Conference for Leaders of Nongovernmental Organizations," October 26, 2001 (http://avalon.law.yale.edu/sept11/powell_brief31.asp) (accessed February 3, 2010).

19. Interview OX-005.

20. Figures from http://www.cbc.ca/news/background/fair-trade/ (accessed March 17, 2010).

21. http://www.fairtrade.net/facts_and_figures.html (accessed March 17, 2010).

22. http://www.jubileeresearch.org/jubilee2000/uk.html (accessed March 17, 2010).

23. Interview OX-005.

24. Ibid.

25. Ibid.

26. For the press release, see http://www.globalexchange.org/update/press/1043.html (accessed March 17, 2010).

27. Document available at http://www.oxfam.org/en/policy/bn0604-coffee-groundsforchange (accessed January 12, 2010).

28. http://www.ico.org/history.asp (accessed March 17, 2010).

29. Oxfam was also very active in early essential medicines campaigns.

30. "Essential medicines are those that satisfy the priority health care needs of the population. They are selected with due regard to public health relevance, evidence on efficacy and safety, and comparative cost-effectiveness. Essential medicines are intended to be available within the context of functioning health systems at all times in adequate amounts, in the appropriate dosage forms, with assured quality and adequate information, and at a price the individual and the community can afford." http://www.who.int/topics/essential_medicines/en/ (accessed March 11, 2010).

31. http://www.msfaccess.org/about-us/ (accessed March 10, 2010).

32. DNDi was opposed notably by MSF-Germany (Siméant 2005).

33. "A Spoonful of Ingenuity," *The Economist,* January 7, 2010.

34. Interview MSF-008.

35. Interview MSF-011.

36. Ibid.

37. Ibid.

38. International Action Network on Small Arms.

39. At the time of writing, IANSA lists fourteen different issue areas in which it seeks redress; see http://www.iansa.org/workareas (accessed July 27, 2011).

Conclusion

1. For example, why Scandinavian states are seen as good norm entrepreneurs (Ingebritsen 2002).

2. Rex Weyler, "Waves of Compassion," *Utne Reader.* http://www.utne.com/print-article.aspx?id=8984 (Accessed August 6, 2011). This piece gives a brief rundown of the activities between 1970 and 1979.

3. http://www.greenpeace.org/international/en/about/how-is-greenpeace-structured/governance-structure/ (accessed August 3, 2011).

4. "Stichting Greenpeace Council Rules of Procedure" http://www.greenpeace.org/international/PageFiles/24182/Rules%20of%20Procedure.pdf (accessed August 3, 2011).

5. Ibid., page 8.

6. Andrew Rice, "Mission from Africa," *New York Times,* April 12, 2009.

7. Ibid.

8. From "Reverse Missionaries," *Religion & Ethics Newsweekly,* PBS Radio, January 8, 2010. Transcript.

9. Ibid.

10. "Mission from Africa."

11. "Reverse Missionaries."

12. This reflects the move by development NGOs to use human rights as a tool for making demands on states and as a credible justification for their demands, some of which we touched on in the discussion of Oxfam's structural transition (Uvin 2004). Since the 1990s, the emergence of "environmental rights" as a combination of human rights and environmentalism has also occurred (Anton and Shelton 2011; Hiskes 2009; Shelton 1991).

REFERENCES

Abbott, Kenneth W., and Duncan Snidal. 2000. "Hard and Soft Law in International Governance." *International Organization* 54(3): 421–456. http://dx.doi.org/10.1162/002081800551280.

Acharya, Amitav. 2004. "How Ideas Spread: Whose Norms Matter? Norm Localization and Institutional Change in Asian Regionalism." *International Organization* 58(2): 239–275. http://dx.doi.org/10.1017/S0020818304582024.

Achvarina, Vera, and Simon Reich. 2006. "No Place to Hide: Refugees, Displaced Persons, and the Recruitment of Child Soldiers." *International Security* 31(1): 127–164. http://muse.jhu.edu/journals/international_security/v031/31.1achvarina.html.

Adler, Emanuel. 1992. "The Emergence of Cooperation: National Epistemic Communities and the International Evolution of the Idea of Nuclear Arms Control." *International Organization* 46(01): 101–145. http://dx.doi.org/10.1017/S0020818300001466.

Aghion, Philippe, and Jean Tirole. 1997. "Formal and Real Authority in Organizations." *Journal of Political Economy* 105(1): 1–29. http://www.jstor.org.myaccess.library.utoronto.ca/stable/2138869.

Ahmed, Shamima, and David Potter. 2006. *NGOs in International Politics*. Illustrated ed. Bloomfield, CT: Kumarian Press.

Aldrich, Howard E. 1979. *Organizations and Environments*. Englewood Cliffs, NJ: Prentice-Hall.

Alston, Philip. 1990. "The Fortieth Anniversary of the Universal Declaration of Human Rights: A Time More for Reflection than for Celebration." In *Human Rights in a Pluralist World: Individuals and Collectivities,* ed. Jan Berting, Peter R. Baehr, J. Herman Burgers, Cees Flinterman, Barbara de Klerk, Rob Kroes, Cornelius A. van Minnen, and Koo VanderWal, Westport, CT: Meckler Corporation, 1–14.

———. 1998. "Making Space for New Human Rights: The Case of the Right to Development." *Harvard Human Rights Yearbook* 1(1): 3–40. http://heinonline.org.myaccess.library.utoronto.ca/HOL/Page?handle=hein.journals/hhrj1&id=9&div=&collection=journals.

Anderson, Kenneth. 2000. "The Ottawa Convention Banning Landmines, the Role of International Non-governmental Organizations and the Idea of International Civil Society." *European Journal of International Law* 11(1): 91–120. http://ejil.oxfordjournals.org.myaccess.library.utoronto.ca/cgi/content/abstract/11/1/91.

Anstey, Roger T. 1981. "Religion and British Slave Emancipation." In *The Abolition of the Atlantic Slave Trade: Origins and Effects in Europe, Africa, and the Americas,* ed. David Eltis and James Walvin, Madison: University of Wisconsin Press, 37–61.

Anton, Donald K., and Dinah Shelton. 2011. *Environmental Protection and Human Rights.* Melbourne: Cambridge University Press.

Asal, Victor, and R. Karl Rethemeyer. 2008. "The Nature of the Beast: Organizational Structures and the Lethality of Terrorist Attacks." *Journal of Politics* 70(2): 437–449. http://dx.doi.org/10.1017/S0022381608080419.

Avant, Deborah D., Martha Finnemore, and Susan K. Sell. 2010. *Who Governs the Globe?* New York: Cambridge University Press.

Bachrach, Peter, and Morton S. Baratz. 1970. *Power and Poverty: Theory and Practice.* New York: Oxford University Press.

Baehr, Peter R. 1994. "AI and its Self-Imposed Limited Mandate." *Netherlands Quarterly of Human Rights* (1): 5–21.

Bales, Kevin. 2005. *Understanding Global Slavery: A Reader.* 1st ed. Berkeley: University of California Press.

Bales, Kevin, and Peter Robbins. 2001. "'No one shall be held in slavery or servitude': A Critical Analysis of International Slavery Agreements and Concepts of Slavery." *Human Rights Review* 2(2): 18–45. http://dx.doi.org/10.1007/s12142-001-1022-6.

Bandy, Joe, and Jackie Smith. 2005. *Coalitions across Borders: Transnational Protest and the Neoliberal Order.* Lanham, MD: Rowman and Littlefield.

Barabási, Albert-László. 2003. *Linked: How Everything Is Connected to Everything Else and What It Means.* New York: Plume.

Barnett, Michael. 2001. "Humanitarianism with a Sovereign Face: UNHCR in the Global Undertow." *International Migration Review* 35(1): 244–277. http://www.jstor.org.myaccess.library.utoronto.ca/stable/2676060.

———. 2005. "Humanitarianism Transformed." *Perspectives on Politics* 3(4): 723–740. http://dx.doi.org/10.1017/S1537592705050401.

———. 2009. "Evolution without Progress? Humanitarianism in a World of Hurt." *International Organization* 63(4): 621–663. http://resolver.scholarsportal.info/resolve/00208183/v63i0004/621_ewphiawoh.xml.

Barnett, Michael, and Martha Finnemore. 1999. "The Politics, Power, and Pathologies of International Organizations." *International Organization* 53(4): 699–732. http://www.jstor.org.myaccess.library.utoronto.ca/stable/2601307.

Barnett, Michael, and Thomas G. Weiss. 2008. "Humanitarianism: A Brief History of the Present." In *Humanitarianism in Question,* ed. Michael Barnett and Thomas G. Weiss, Ithaca: Cornell University Press, 1–48.

Bartlett, Christopher A., and Sumantra Ghoshal. 1991. *Managing across Borders: The Transnational Solution.* Boston: Harvard Business School Press.

Baumgartner, Frank R., Suzanna De Boef, and Amber E. Boydstun. 2008. *The Decline of the Death Penalty and the Discovery of Innocence.* New York: Cambridge University Press.

Baxi, Upendra. 1998. "Voices of Suffering and the Future of Human Rights." *Transnational Law and Contemporary Problems* 8: 125–170.

Bedau, Hugo Adam. 2004. "Abolishing the Death Penalty in the United States: An Analysis of Institutional Obstacles and Future Prospects." In *Capital Punishment: Strategies for Abolition,* ed. Peter Hodgkinson and William A. Schabas, Cambridge: Cambridge University Press, 186–207.

Benford, Robert D., and David A. Snow. 2000. "Framing Processes and Social Movements: An Overview and Assessment." *Annual Review of Sociology* 26(1): 611–639. http://dx.doi.org/10.1146/annurev.soc.26.1.611.

Berger, Peter L., and Thomas Luckmann. 1967. *The Social Construction of Reality: A Treatise in the Sociology of Knowledge.* New York: Anchor.

Bernstein, Elizabeth. 2008. "Still Alive and Kicking: The International Campaign to Ban Landmines." In *Banning landmines: Disarmament, Citizen Diplomacy, and Human Security,* ed. Jody Williams, Stephen D. Goose, and Mary Wareham, Lanham, MD: Rowman and Littlefield, 31–48.

Betsill, Michele M., and Elisabeth Corell. 2010. "NGO Influence in International Environmental Negotiations: A Framework for Analysis." *Global Environmental Politics* 1(4): 65–85. http://dx.doi.org/10.1162/152638001317146372.

Binet, Laurence. 2003. *Rwandan Refugee Camps in Zaire and Tanzania 1994–1995.* Paris: Médecins sans Frontières.

Bite, Vita. 1981. *Human Rights in US Foreign Relations: Six Key Questions in the Continuing Policy Debate.* Washington, DC: Library of Congress.

Black, Maggie. 1992. *A Cause for Our Times: Oxfam—The First Fifty Years.* New ed. London: Oxfam Professional.

Bloodgood, Elizabeth A. 2011. "The Interest Group Analogy: International Non-Governmental Advocacy Organisations in International Politics." *Review of International Studies* 37(1): 1–28.

Bob, Clifford. 2005. *The Marketing of Rebellion: Insurgents, Media, and International Activism.* New York: Cambridge University Press.

———. 2010. "Packing Heat: Pro-gun Groups and the Governance of Small Arms." In *Who Governs the Globe?* Cambridge: Cambridge University Press, 183–201.

Boli, John, and George Thomas. 1999. *Constructing World Culture: International Nongovernmental Organizations since 1875.* 1st ed. Palo Alto, CA: Stanford University Press.

Boltanski, Luc. 1999. *Distant Suffering: Morality, Media, and Politics.* New York: Cambridge University Press.

Bolton, John R. 2000. "Should We Take Global Governance Seriously." *Chicago Journal of International Law* 1: 205–221. http://heinonline.org/HOL/Page?handle=hein. journals/cjil1&id=213&div=&collection=journals.

Borgatti, Stephen P, and Pacey C. Foster. 2003. "The Network Paradigm in Organizational Research: A Review and Typology." *Journal of Management* 29(6): 991–1013. http://resolver.scholarsportal.info/resolve/01492063/v29i0006/991_tnpiorarat.xml.

Bortolotti, Dan. 2006. *Hope in Hell: Inside the World of Doctors without Borders.* Richmond Hill, ON: Firefly Books.

Brafman, Ori, and Rod A. Beckstrom. 2006. *The Starfish and the Spider: The Unstoppable Power of Leaderless Organizations.* New York: Portfolio.

Brem, Stefan, and Ken Rutherford. 2001. "Walking Together or Divided Agenda? Comparing Landmines and Small-Arms Campaigns." *Security Dialogue* 32(2): 169–186. http://resolver.scholarsportal.info/resolve/09670106/v32i0002/169_wtoda. xml.

Brown, David S., J. Christopher Brown, and Scott W. Desposato. 2008. "Who Gives, Who Receives, and Who Wins? Transforming Capital into Political Change through Nongovernmental Organizations." *Comparative Political Studies* 41(1): 24–47. http:// dx.doi.org/10.1177/0010414007309205.

Brown, Grace H. 2003. "Making Coffee Good to the Last Drop: Laying the Foundation for Sustainabililty in the International Coffee Trade." *Georgetown International Environmental Law Review* 16: 247–280. http://heinonline.org/HOL/Page?handle=hein. journals/gintenlr16&id=257&div=&collection=journals.

Brown, L. David. 2007. "Oxfam America and Oxfam International: Expanding Leverage in a Globalizing World." Cambridge, MA. Working paper.

Brown, Widney. 2001. "Human Rights Watch: An Overview." In *NGOs and Human Rights: Promise and Performance,* ed. Claude E. Welch, Philadelphia: University of Pennsylvania Press, 72–84.

Brunnée, Jutta, and Stephen J. Toope. 2000. "International Law and Constructivism: Elements of an Interactional Theory of International Law." *Columbia Journal of Transnational Law* 39: 19–74. http://heinonline.org/HOL/Page?handle=hein. journals/cjtl39&id=27&div=&collection=journals.

———. 2010. *Legitimacy and Legality in International Law: An Interactional Account.* Cambridge: Cambridge University Press.

Brysk, Alison. 1993. "From Above and Below: Social Movements, the International System, and Human Rights in Argentina." *Comparative Political Studies* 26(3): 259–285.

———. 2002. *Globalization and Human Rights.* 1st ed. Berkeley, CA: University of California Press.

Buchanan, Tom. 2002. "'The Truth Will Set You Free': The Making of Amnesty International." *Journal of Contemporary History* 37(4): 575–597. http://www.jstor.org/ stable/3180761.

———. 2004. "Amnesty International in Crisis, 1966–7." *Twentieth Century British History* 15(3): 267–289. http://resolver.scholarsportal.info/resolve/09552359/v15i0003/267_ aiic1.xml.

————. 2009. "Human Rights Campaigns in Modern Britain." In *NGOs in Contemporary Britain: Non-state Actors in Society and Politics since 1945,* ed. Nick Crowson, Matthew Hilton, and James McKay, New York: Palgrave Macmillan, 113–128.

Bull, Hedley. 1977. *An Anarchical Society: A Study of Order in World Politics.* New York: Columbia University Press.

Burgerman, Susan. 2001. *Moral Victories: How Activists Provoke Multilateral Action.* Ithaca: Cornell University Press.

Burgers, Jan Herman. 1992. "The Road to San Francisco: The Revival of the Human Rights Idea in the Twentieth Century." *Human Rights Quarterly* 14(4): 447–477. http://www.jstor.org.myaccess.library.utoronto.ca/stable/762313.

Burt, Ronald. 1995. *Structural Holes: The Social Structure of Competition.* New ed. Cambridge, MA: Harvard University Press.

Busby, Joshua W. 2007. "Bono Made Jesse Helms Cry: Jubilee 2000, Debt Relief, and Moral Action in International Politics." *International Studies Quarterly* 51(2): 247–275. http://dx.doi.org/10.1111/j.1468-2478.2007.00451.x.

————. 2010. *Moral Movements and Foreign Policy.* New York: Cambridge University Press.

Cameron, Charles Metz. 2000. *Veto Bargaining: Presidents and the Politics of Negative Power.* New York: Cambridge University Press.

Carpenter, R. Charli. 2003. "'Women and Children First': Gender, Norms, and Humanitarian Evacuation in the Balkans 1991–95." *International Organization* 57(4): 661–694.

————. 2007a. "Setting the Advocacy Agenda: Theorizing Issue Emergence and Nonemergence in Transnational Advocacy Networks." *International Studies Quarterly* 51(1): 99–120.

————. 2007b. "Studying Issue (Non)-Adoption in Transnational Advocacy Networks." *International Organization* 61(3): 643–667.

————. 2010. *Forgetting Children Born of War: Setting the Human Rights Agenda in Bosnia and Beyond.* New York: Columbia University Press.

————. 2011. "Vetting the Advocacy Agenda: Network Centrality and the Paradox of Weapons Norms." *International Organization* 65(1): 69–102.

Carrington, Peter J., John Scott, and Stanley Wasserman. 2005. *Models and Methods in Social Network Analysis.* New York: Cambridge University Press.

Castells, Manuel. 2000. *The Rise of the Network Society: The Information Age, Economy, Society and Culture, Volume I.* 2nd ed. Malden, MA: Wiley-Blackwell.

Chandler, Alfred D. 1969. *Strategy and Structure: Chapters in the History of the American Industrial Enterprise.* Cambridge: The MIT Press.

Chandler, David. 2001. "The Road to Military Humanitarianism: How the Human Rights NGOs Shaped A New Humanitarian Agenda." *Human Rights Quarterly* 23(3): 678–700.

Charnovitz, Steve. 1996. "Two Centuries of Participation: NGOs and International Governance." *Michigan Journal of International Law* 18: 183–286.

Chayes, Abram, and Antonia Handler Chayes. 1993. "On Compliance." *International Organization* 47(2): 175–205.

Checkel, Jeffrey T. 1997. "International Norms and Domestic Politics." *European Journal of International Relations* 3(4): 473 -495.

——. 2001. "Why Comply? Social Learning and European Identity Change." *International Organization* 55(3): 553–588.

Chong, Daniel P.L. 2010. *Freedom from Poverty: NGOs and Human Rights Praxis.* Philadelphia: University of Pennsylvania Press.

Christakis, Nicholas A., and James H. Fowler. 2009. *Connected: The Surprising Power of Our Social Networks and How They Shape Our Lives.* New York: Little, Brown.

Cingranelli, David L., and Thomas E. Pasquarello. 1985. "Human Rights Practices and the Distribution of U.S. Foreign Aid to Latin American Countries." *American Journal of Political Science* 29(3): 539–563.

Cingranelli, David L., and David L. Richards. 2001. "Measuring the Impact of Human Rights Organizations." In *NGOs and Human Rights: Promise and Performance,* ed. Claude E. Welch, Philadelphia: University of Pennsylvania Press, 225–237.

Clark, Ann Marie. 1995. "Non-Governmental Organizations and Their Influence on International Society." *Journal of International Affairs* 48(2): 507–526.

——. 2001. *Diplomacy of Conscience: Amnesty International and Changing Human Rights Norms.* Princeton, NJ: Princeton University Press.

Clark, Ann Marie, Elisabeth J. Friedman, and Kathryn Hochstetler. 1998. "The Sovereign Limits of Global Civil Society: A Comparison of NGO Participation in UN World Conferences on the Environment, Human Rights, and Women." *World Politics* 51(1): 1–35.

Clark, Roger S. 1981. "The International League for Human Rights and South West Africa 1947–1957: The Human Rights NGO as Catalyst in the International Legal Process." *Human Rights Quarterly* 3(4): 101–136.

——. 1999. "Human Rights Strategies of the 1960s within the United Nations: A Tribute to the Late Kamleshwar Das." *Human Rights Quarterly* 21(2): 308–341.

Coase, R. H. 1937. "The Nature of the Firm." *Economica* 4(16): 386–405.

Collier, Ruth Berins, and David Collier. 1991. *Shaping the Political Arena: Critical Junctures, the Labor Movement, and Regime Dynamics in Latin America.* Princeton, NJ: Princeton University Press.

Cook, Helena. 1996. "Amnesty International at the United Nations." In *"The Conscience of the World": The Influence of Non-Governmental Organisations in the UN System,* ed. Peter Willetts, Washington, DC: Brookings Institution, 181–213.

Cooley, Alexander. 2008. *Logics of Hierarchy: The Organization of Empires, States, and Military Occupations.* Ithaca: Cornell University Press.

Cooley, Alexander, and James Ron. 2002. "The NGO Scramble: Organizational Insecurity and the Political Economy of Transnational Action." *International Security* 27(1): 5–39.

Cortell, Andrew P., and James W. Davis. 1996. "How Do International Institutions Matter? The Domestic Impact of International Rules and Norms." *International Studies Quarterly* 40(4): 451–478.

Cortright, David, and George A. Lopez. 2000. *The Sanctions Decade: Assessing UN Strategies in the 1990s.* Boulder, CO: Lynne Rienner.

Cottrell, M. Patrick. 2009. "Legitimacy and Institutional Replacement: The Convention on Certain Conventional Weapons and the Emergence of the Mine Ban Treaty." *International Organization* 63(2): 217–248.

Cox, Gary W., and Mathew D. McCubbins. 1993. *Legislative Leviathan: Party Government in the House.* Berkeley: University of California Press.

———. 2005. *Setting the Agenda: Responsible Party Government in the U.S. House of Representatives.* Illustrated ed. New York: Cambridge University Press.

Crawford, Neta C. 2002. *Argument and Change in World Politics: Ethics, Decolonization, and Humanitarian Intervention.* New York: Cambridge University Press.

Dallaire, Roméo, and Samantha Power. 2004. *Shake Hands with the Devil: The Failure of Humanity in Rwanda.* New York: Carroll and Graf.

Davies, Thomas Richard. 2008. "The Rise and Fall of Transnational Civil Society: The Evolution of International Non-Governmental Organizations since 1839." London. Working paper.

Dechaine, D. Robert. 2006. *Global Humanitarianism: Ngos and the Crafting of Community.* Annotated ed. Lanham, MD: Lexington Books.

DeLaet, Debra L. 2005. *The Global Struggle for Human Rights: Universal Principles in World Politics.* 1st ed. Stamford, CT: Wadsworth.

Diani, Mario. 2003. "'Leaders' or Brokers? Positions and Influence in Social Movement Networks." In *Social Movements and Networks: Relational Approaches to Collective Action,* ed. Mario Diani and Doug McAdam, New York: Oxford University Press, 105–122.

Dicken, Peter, Philip F. Kelly, Kris Olds, and Henry Wai-Chung Yueng. 2001. "Chains and Networks, Territories and Scales: Towards a Relational Framework for Analysing the Global Economy." *Global Networks* 1(2): 89–112.

DiMaggio, Paul J., and Helmut K. Anheier. 1990. "The Sociology of Nonprofit Organizations and Sectors." *Annual Review of Sociology* 16: 137–159.

DiMaggio, Paul J., and Walter W. Powell. 1983. "The Iron Cage Revisited: Institutional Isomorphism and Collective Rationality in Organizational Fields." *American Sociological Review* 48(2): 147–160.

Dobrev, Stanislav D., Tai-Young Kim, and Glenn R. Carroll. 2002. "The Evolution of Organizational Niches: U.S. Automobile Manufacturers, 1885–1981." *Administrative Science Quarterly* 47(2): 233–264.

Donaldson, Lex. 2001. *The Contingency Theory of Organizations.* Thousand Oaks: Sage.

Donnelly, Jack. 1986. "International Human Rights: A Regime Analysis." *International Organization* 40(3): 599–642.

———. 2006. *International Human Rights.* 3d ed. Cambridge, MA: Westview Press.

———. 2007. "The Relative Universality of Human Rights." *Human Rights Quarterly* 29(2): 281–306.

Dorussen, Han, and Jongryn Mo. 2001. "Ending Economic Sanctions: Audience Costs and Rent Seeking as Commitment Strategies." *Journal of Conflict Resolution* 45(4): 395–426.

Drahos, Peter. 2007. "Four Lessons for Developing Countries from the Trade Negotiations over Access to Medicines." *Liverpool Law Review* 28(1): 11–39.

Drezner, Daniel W. 1999. *The Sanctions Paradox? Economic Statecraft and International Relations.* New York: Cambridge University Press.

———. 2003. "The Hidden Hand of Economic Coercion." *International Organization* 57(3): 643–659.

Druckman, James N. 2001. "On the Limits of Framing Effects: Who Can Frame?" *Journal of Politics* 63(4): 1041–1066.

Drury, A. Cooper. 1998. "Revisiting Economic Sanctions Reconsidered." *Journal of Peace Research* 35(4): 497 -509.

Dudziak, Mary L. 2002. *Cold War Civil Rights: Race and the Image of American Democracy.* Princeton, NJ: Princeton University Press.

Eaton, Jonathan, and Maxim Engers. 1999. "Sanctions: Some Simple Analytics." *American Economic Review* 89(2): 409–414.

Eilstrup-Sangiovanni, Mette, and Calvert Jones. 2008. "Assessing the Dangers of Illicit Networks: Why al-Qaida May Be Less Threatening Than Many Think." *International Security* 33(2): 7–44.

Elliott, Michael A. 2007. "Human Rights and the Triumph of the Individual in World Culture." *Cultural Sociology* 1(3): 343–363.

Emirbayer, Mustafa, and Jeff Goodwin. 1994. "Network Analysis, Culture, and the Problem of Agency." *American Journal of Sociology* 99(6): 1411–1454.

Evans, Tony. 1996. *US Hegemony and the Project of Universal Human Rights.* Basingstoke: Palgrave Macmillan.

———. 1998. "Introduction: Power, Hegemony, and the Universalization of Human Rights." In *Human Rights Fifty Years On: A Reappraisal,* ed. Tony Evans. Manchester: Manchester University Press, 2–23.

Everett, Martin, and Stephen P. Borgatti. 2006. "Extending Centrality." In *Models and Methods in Social Network Analysis,* ed. Peter J. Carrington, John Scott, and Stanley Wasserman, New York: Cambridge University Press, 57–76.

Finnemore, Martha. 1996. *National Interests in International Society.* Ithaca: Cornell University Press.

Finnemore, Martha, and Kathryn Sikkink. 1998. "International Norm Dynamics and Political Change." *International Organization* 52(4): 887–917.

Finnemore, Martha, and Stephen J. Toope. 2001. "Alternatives to 'Legalization': Richer Views of Law and Politics." *International Organization* 55(3): 743–758.

Fitzpatrick, Sheila. 2008. *The Russian Revolution.* 3rd ed. New York: Oxford University Press.

Florini, Ann, ed. 2000. *The Third Force: The Rise of Transnational Civil Society.* Washington, DC: Carnegie Endowment for International Peace.

Forsythe, David P. 1976. "The Red Cross as Transnational Movement: Conserving and Changing the Nation-State System." *International Organization* 30(4): 607–630.

———. 1990. "Human Rights and the International Committee of the Red Cross." *Human Rights Quarterly* 12(2): 265–289.

———. 1996. "International Humanitarian Assistance: The Role of the Red Cross." *Buffalo Journal of International Law* 3: 235–260.

———. 2005a. "Naming and Shaming: The Ethics of ICRC Discretion." *Millennium—Journal of International Studies* 34(1): 461–474.

———. 2005b. *The Humanitarians: The International Committee of the Red Cross.* Cambridge University Press.

———. 2006. *Human Rights in International Relations (Themes in International Relations).* 2nd ed. New York: Cambridge University Press.

Forsythe, David P., and Barbara Ann J. Rieffer-Flanagan. 2007. *The International Committee of the Red Cross: A Neutral Humanitarian Actor.* Annotated ed. London: Routledge.

Franck, Thomas M. 2001. "Are Human Rights Universal." *Foreign Affairs* 80(1): 191–204.

Freeman, John, and Michael T. Hannan. 1983. "Niche Width and the Dynamics of Organizational Populations." *American Journal of Sociology* 88(6): 1116–1145.

———. 1989. "Setting the Record Straight on Organizational Ecology: Rebuttal to Young." *American Journal of Sociology* 95(2): 425–439.

Freeman, Linton C. 1978. "Centrality in Social Networks Conceptual Clarification." *Social Networks* 1(3): 239.

Gaer, Felice D. 1995. "Reality Check: Human Rights Nongovernmental Organisations Confront Governments at the United Nations." *Third World Quarterly* 16(3): 389–404.

Galtung, Johan. 1967. "On the Effects of International Economic Sanctions: With Examples from the Case of Rhodesia." *World Politics* 19(3): 378–416.

Gamson, William A., and David S. Meyer. 1996. "Framing Political Opportunity." In *Comparative Perspectives on Social Movements,* ed. Doug McAdam, John D. McCarthy, and Mayer N. Zald, New York: Cambridge University Press, 275–290.

Gibbons, Elizabeth D. 1999. *Sanctions in Haiti: Human Rights and Democracy under Assault.* Westport, CT: Praeger.

Gilbert, Xavier. 2007. "Globalizing Local Knowledge in Global Companies." In *Knowledge Creation and Management,* ed. Kazuo Ichijo and Ikujiro Nonaka, New York: Oxford University Press, 215–228.

Gilpin, Robert G. 1996. "No One Loves a Political Realist." *Security Studies* 5(3): 3–26.

Glendon, Mary Ann. 2002. *A World Made New: Eleanor Roosevelt and the Universal Declaration of Human Rights.* Reprint. New York: Random House.

Goddard, Stacie E. 2009. "Brokering Change: Networks and Entrepreneurs in International Politics." *International Theory* 1(2): 249–281.

Goldstein, Judith, and Robert O. Keohane. 1993. "Ideas and Foreign Policy: An Analytical Framework." In *Ideas and Foreign Policy,* ed. Judith Goldstein and Robert O. Keohane, Ithaca: Cornell University Press, 3–30.

Goodale, Mark, and Sally Engle Merry. 2007. *The Practice of Human Rights: Tracking Law between the Global and the Local.* New York: Cambridge University Press.

Goodman, Ryan, and Derek Jinks. 2003. "Measuring the Effects of Human Rights Treaties." *European Journal of International Law* 14(1): 171–183.

———. 2008. "Incomplete Internalization and Compliance with Human Rights Law." *European Journal of International Law* 19(4): 725 -748.

Granovetter, Mark S. 1973. "The Strength of Weak Ties." *American Journal of Sociology* 78(6): 1360.

Greenhill, Brian. 2010. "The Company You Keep: International Socialization and the Diffusion of Human Rights Norms." *International Studies Quarterly* 54(1): 127–145.

Gresser, Charis, and Sophia Tickell. 2002. *Mugged: Poverty in Your Coffee Cup.* Oxfam International.

Grillot, Suzette R., Craig S. Stapley, and Molly E. Hanna. 2006. "Assessing the Small Arms Movement: The Trials and Tribulations of a Transnational Network." *Contemporary Security Policy* 27(1): 60–84.

Haas, Peter M. 1989. "Do Regimes Matter? Epistemic Communities and Mediterranean Pollution Control." *International Organization* 43(3): 377–403.

———. 1992. "Introduction: Epistemic Communities and International Policy Coordination." *International Organization* 46(1): 1–35.

Hafner-Burton, Emilie M. 2008. "Sticks and Stones: Naming and Shaming the Human Rights Enforcement Problem." *International Organization* 62(04): 689–716.

———. 2009. *Forced to Be Good: Why Trade Agreements Boost Human Rights.* Cornell University Press.

Hafner-Burton, Emilie M., Miles Kahler, and Alexander H. Montgomery. 2009. "Network Analysis for International Relations." *International Organization* 63(3): 592.

Hafner-Burton, Emilie M., and Alexander H. Montgomery. 2006. "Power Positions: International Organizations, Social Networks, and Conflict." *Journal of Conflict Resolution* 50(1): 3.

Hafner-Burton, Emilie M., and Kiyoteru Tsutsui. 2005. "Human Rights in a Globalizing World: The Paradox of Empty Promises." *American Journal of Sociology* 110(5): 1373–1411.

Hamel, Annick. 2004. "Of Medicines and Men." In *In the Shadow of 'Just Wars': Violence, Politics, and Humanitarian Action,* ed. Fabrice Weissman, Ithaca: Cornell University Press, 341–356.

Hannan, Michael T., Glenn R. Carroll, and Laszlo Polos. 2003. "The Organizational Niche." *Sociological Theory* 21(4): 309–340.

Hannan, Michael T., and John Freeman. 1977. "The Population Ecology of Organizations." *American Journal of Sociology* 82(5): 929–964.

———. 1988. "The Ecology of Organizational Mortality: American Labor Unions, 1836–1985." *American Journal of Sociology* 94(1): 25–52.

Hannan, Michael T., László Pólos, and Glenn Carroll. 2007. *Logics of Organization Theory: Audiences, Codes, and Ecologies.* Princeton, NJ: Princeton University Press.

Hansmann, Henry B. 1980. "The Role of Nonprofit Enterprise." *Yale Law Journal* 89(5): 835–901.

Harris, Milton, and Artur Raviv. 2002. "Organization Design." *Management Science* 48(7): 852–865.

Hasanali, Farida. 2004. "Critical Success Factors of Knowledge Management." In *Knowledge Management Lessons Learned: What Works and What Doesn't,* ed. Michael E.D. Koenig and T. Kanti Srikantaiah, New Jersey: Information Today, 55–69.

Hathaway, Oona A. 2007. "Why Do Countries Commit to Human Rights Treaties?" *Journal of Conflict Resolution* 51(4): 588–621.

Hausmann, Ricardo, Dani Rodrik, and Andres Velasco. 2005. "Growth Diagnostics." In *The Washington Consensus Reconsidered: Towards a New Global Governance,* ed. Narcis Serra and Joseph E. Stiglitz, New York: Cambridge University Press, 324–255.

Haveman, Heather A. 2000. "The Future of Organizational Sociology: Forging Ties among Paradigms." *Contemporary Sociology* 29(3): 476–486.

Hawkins, Darren. 2004. "Explaining Costly International Institutions: Persuasion and Enforceable Human Rights Norms." *International Studies Quarterly* 48(4): 779–804.

Hertel, Shareen. 2006. *Unexpected Power: Conflict and Change among Transnational Activists.* 1st ed. Ithaca: Cornell University Press.

Hiskes, Richard P. 2009. *The Human Rights to a Green Future: Environmental Rights and Intergenerational Justice.* New York: Cambridge University Press.

Hòdgkinson, Peter. 2000. "Europe—A Death Penalty Free Zone: Commentary and Critique of Abolitionist Strategies." *Ohio Northern University Law Review* 26: 625–664.

Hopgood, Stephen. 2006. *Keepers of the Flame: Understanding Amnesty International.* Annotated ed. Ithaca: Cornell University Press.

———. 2010. "Amnesty International: The Politics of Morality." openDemocracy. http://www.opendemocracy.net/globalization-vision_reflections/amnesty_morality_3625.jsp.

Hubert, Don, and S. Neil MacFarlane. 2000. *The Landmine Ban: A Case Study in Humanitarian Advocacy.* Providence, RI: Thomas J. Watson Jr. Institute for International Studies.

Huckerby, Jayne, and Sir Nigel Rodley. 2009. "Outlawing Torture: The Story of Amnesty International's Efforts to Shape the U.N. Convention against Torture." In *Human Rights Advocacy Stories,* ed. Deena R. Hurwitz and Margaret L. Satterthwaite with Doug Ford, New York: New York Foundation Press/Thomson West, 15–41.

Hudson, Bryant A., and Wolfgang Bielefeld. 1997. "Structures of Multinational Nonprofit Organizations." *Nonprofit Management and Leadership* 8(1): 31–49.

Hufbauer, Gary Clyde, and Jeffrey J. Schott. 1985. *Economic Sanctions Reconsidered: History and Current Policy.* Washington, DC: Institute for International Economics.

Hufbauer, Gary Clyde, Jeffrey J. Schott, and Kimberly Ann Elliott. 1990. *Economic Sanctions Reconsidered: Supplemental Case Histories.* 2nd ed. Washington, DC: Institute for International Economics.

———. 2007. *Economic Sanctions Reconsidered.* 3rd ed. Washington, DC: Peterson Institute for International Economics.

Hunt, Stephen, and Nicola Lightly. 2001. "The British Black Pentecostal 'Revival': Identity and Belief in the 'New' Nigerian Churches." *Ethnic and Racial Studies* 24(1): 104–124.

Huntington, Samuel P. 1973. "Transnational Organizations in World Politics." *World Politics* 25(3): 333–368.

———. 1997. "The Erosion of American National Interests." *Foreign Affairs* 76(5): 28–49.

Hutchinson, John. 1997. *Champions of Charity: War and the Rise of the Red Cross.* Boulder, CO: Westview Press.

Hwang, Hokyu, and Walter W. Powell. 2009. "The Rationalization of Charity: The Influences of Professionalism in the Nonprofit Sector." *Administrative Science Quarterly* 54(2): 268–298.

Iannaccone, Laurence R., and Eli Berman. 2006. "Religious Extremism: The Good, the Bad, and the Deadly." *Public Choice* 128(1–2): 109–129.

Ingebritsen, Christine. 2002. "Norm Entrepreneurs: Scandinavia's Role in World Politics." *Cooperation and Conflict* 37(1): 11–23.

Jackson, Matthew O. 2008. *Social and Economic Networks.* Princeton, NJ: Princeton University Press.

James, Estelle, and Susan Rose-Ackerman. 1986. *The Nonprofit Enterprise in Market Economics.* Chur, Switzerland: Harwood Academic.

Jayawickrama, Sherine. 2010. "Médecins sans Frontières: Laying the Groundwork for Extensive Reform." In *Adaptation and Change in Six NGOs: Drivers, Tensions, and Lessons.* Hauser Center for Nonprofit Organizations at Harvard University, 15–18.

Joachim, Jutta. 2003. "Framing Issues and Seizing Opportunities: The UN, NGOs, and Women's Rights." *International Studies Quarterly* 47(2): 247–274.

Johnson, Erica, and Aseem Prakash. 2007. "NGO Research Program: A Collective Action Perspective." *Policy Sciences* 40(3): 221–240.

Kaempfer, William H., and Anton D. Lowenberg. 1988. "The Theory of International Economic Sanctions: A Public Choice Approach." *American Economic Review* 78(4): 786–793.

Kahler, Miles, ed. 2009. *Networked Politics: Agency, Power, and Governance.* Ithaca: Cornell University Press.

Karp, Aaron. 2006. "Escaping Reuterswärd's Shadow." *Contemporary Security Policy* 27(1): 12–28.

Katzenstein, Peter J., ed. 1996. *The Culture of National Security: Norms and Identity in World Politics.* New York: Columbia University Press.

Kaufman, Edy. 1991. "Prisoners of Conscience: The Shaping of a New Human Rights Concept." *Human Rights Quarterly* 13(3): 339–367.

Kaufmann, Chaim D., and Robert A. Pape. 1999. "Explaining Costly International Moral Action: Britain's Sixty-Year Campaign against the Atlantic Slave Trade." *International Organization* 53(4): 631–668.

Keck, Margaret E., and Kathryn Sikkink. 1998. *Activists beyond Borders: Advocacy Networks in International Politics.* Ithaca: Cornell University Press.

Keith, Linda Camp. 1999. "The United Nations International Covenant on Civil and Political Rights: Does It Make a Difference in Human Rights Behavior?" *Journal of Peace Research* 36(1): 95–118.

Khagram, Sanjeev, James V. Riker, and Kathryn Sikkink. 2002. *Restructuring World Politics.* Minneapolis: University of Minnesota Press.

Kingdon, John W. 2002. *Agendas, Alternatives, and Public Policies (Longman Classics Edition).* 2nd ed. New York: Longman.

Kirkup, Alex, and Tony Evans. 2009. "The Myth of Western Opposition to Economic, Social, and Cultural Rights? A Reply to Whelan and Donnelly." *Human Rights Quarterly* 31(1): 221–237.

Klotz, Audie. 2002. "Transnational Activism and Global Transformations: The Anti-Apartheid and Abolitionist Experiences." *European Journal of International Relations* 8(1): 49–76.

Knoke, David. 1994. *Political Networks: The Structural Perspective.* New York: Cambridge University Press.

Knoke, David, and Song Yang. 2007. *Social Network Analysis.* 2nd ed. Thousand Oaks: Sage.

Koch, Dirk-Jan, Axel Dreher, Peter Nunnenkamp, and Rainer Thiele. 2009. "Keeping a Low Profile: What Determines the Allocation of Aid by Non-Governmental Organizations?" *World Development* 37(5): 902–918.

Koh, Harold H. 2003. "On American Exceptionalism." *Stanford Law Review* 55(5): 1479–1527.

Koji, Teraya. 2001. "Emerging Hierarchy in International Human Rights and Beyond: From the Perspective of Non-derogable Rights." *European Journal of International Law* 12(5): 917–941.

Korey, William. 1968. *The Key to Human Rights Implementation.* New York: Carnegie Endowment for International Peace.

———. 1998. *NGO's and the Universal Declaration of Human Rights: A Curious Grapevine.* 1st ed. New York: Palgrave Macmillan.

Krasner, Stephen D. 1983. *International Regimes.* Ithaca: Cornell University Press.

———. 1993. "Sovereignty, Regimes, and Human Rights." In *Regime Theory and International Relations,* ed. Volker Rittberger, Oxford: Clarendon Press, 139–167.

Laber, Jeri. 2005. The Courage of Strangers: *Coming of Age with the Human Rights Movement.* New ed. New York: PublicAffairs.

Lake, David A. 1993. "Leadership, Hegemony, and the International Economy: Naked Emperor or Tattered Monarch with Potential?" *International Studies Quarterly* 37(4): 459–489.

Lake, David A., and Wendy H. Wong. 2009. "The Politics of Networks: Interests, Power, and Human Rights Norms." In *Networked Politics: Agency, Power, and Governance,* ed. Miles Kahler, Ithaca: Cornell University Press, 127–150.

Landman, Todd. 2005. *Protecting Human Rights: A Comparative Study.* Washington, DC: Georgetown University Press.

Larsen, Egon. 1979. A Flame in Barbed Wire: *The Story of Amnesty International.* New York: Norton.

Lawrence, Paul R., and Jay W. Lorsch. 1967. *Organization and Environment: Managing Differentiation and Integration.* Boston: Harvard Business School.

Lecy, Jesse D., George E. Mitchell, and Hans Peter Schmitz. 2010. "Advocacy Organizations, Networks, and the Firm Analogy." In *Advocacy Organizations and Collective Action,* ed. Aseem Prakash and Mary Kay Gugerty, Cambridge: Cambridge University Press, 229–251.

Legro, Jeffrey W., and Andrew Moravcsik. 1999. "Is Anybody Still a Realist?" *International Security* 24(2): 5–55.

Leonard-Barton, Dorothy. 1998. *Wellsprings of Knowledge: Building and Sustaining the Sources of Innovation.* Cambridge, MA: Harvard Business Press.

Levi, Margaret, and April Linton. 2003. "Fair Trade: A Cup at a Time?" *Politics Society* 31(3): 407–432.

Levitt, Peggy, and Sally Engle Merry. 2009. "Vernacularization on the Ground: Local Uses of Global Women's Rights in Peru, China, India and the United States." *Global Networks* 9(4): 441–461.

Lijphart, Arend. 1999. *Patterns of Democracy: Government Forms and Performance in Thirty-Six Countries.* New Haven: Yale University Press.

Lindenberg, Marc, and Coralie Bryant. 2001. *Going Global: Transforming Relief and Development NGOs.* West Hartford, CT: Kumarian Press.

Linton, April. 2005. "Partnering for Sustainability: Business-NGO Alliances in the Coffee Industry." *Development in Practice* 15(3/4): 600–614.

———. 2008. "A Niche for Sustainability? Fair Labor and Environmentally Sound Practices in the Specialty Coffee Industry." *Globalizations* 5(2): 231–245.

Linton, April, Cindy Chiayuan Liou, and Kelly Ann Shaw. 2004. "A Taste of Trade Justice: Marketing Global Social Responsibility via Fair Trade Coffee." *Globalizations* 1(2): 223–246.

Lipschutz, Ronnie D. 1992. "Reconstructing World Politics: The Emergence of Global Civil Society." *Millennium - Journal of International Studies* 21(3): 389–420.

———. 1996. *Global Civil Society and Global Environmental Governance: The Politics of Nature from Place to Planet*. Albany, NY: State University of New York Press.

Lischer, Sarah Kenyon. 2007. "Military Intervention and the Humanitarian Force Multiplier." *Global Governance* 13(1): 99–118.

Low, William, and Eileen Davenport. 2005. "Has the Medium (Roast) become the Message?" *International Marketing Review* 22(5): 494–511.

Lopez, George A., and David Cortright. 1997. "Economic Sanctions and Human Rights: Part of the Problem or Part of the Solution?" *International Journal of Human Rights* 1(2): 1–25.

Luban, David. 2007. "Liberalism, Torture, and the Ticking Bomb." In *Intervention, Terrorism, and Torture,* ed. Steven P. Lee. A.A. Dordrecht: Springer Netherlands, 249–262. http://www.springerlink.com.myaccess.library.utoronto.ca/content/u07517381648766l/ (accessed July 13, 2011).

Luong, Pauline Jones, and Erika Weinthal. 1999. "The NGO Paradox: Democratic Goals and Non-Democratic Outcomes in Kazakhstan." *Europe-Asia Studies* 51(7): 1267–1284.

Lutz, Ellen L., and Kathryn Sikkink. 2000. "International Human Rights Law and Practice in Latin America." *International Organization* 54(3): 633–659.

Mahoney, James and David Collier. 1996. "Research Note: Insights and Pitfalls: Selection Bias in Qualitative Research." *World Politics* 49(1): 56–91.

Malia, Martin. 1995. *Soviet Tragedy: A History of Socialism in Russia*. New York: Free Press.

Maoz, Zeev. 2006. "Network Polarization, Network Interdependence, and International Conflict, 1816–2002." *Journal of Peace Research* 43(4): 391–411.

Maoz, Zeev, Ranan D. Kuperman, Lesley G. Terris, and Ilan Talmud. "Structural Equivalence and International Conflict: A Social Networks Analysis." *Journal of Conflict Resolution* 50(5): 664–689.

Marsden, Peter V. 1990. "Network Data and Measurement." *Annual Review of Sociology* 16: 435–463.

Marshall, Ruth. 2009. *Political Spiritualities: The Pentecostal Revolution in Nigeria*. Chicago: University of Chicago Press.

Martin, Lisa L. 1992. *Coercive Cooperation*. Princeton, NJ: Princeton University Press.

McAdam, Doug, Sidney Tarrow, and Charles Tilly. 2001. *Dynamics of Contention*. New York: Cambridge University Press.

McDonagh, Pierre. 2002. "Communicative Campaigns to Effect Anti-Slavery and Fair Trade." *European Journal of Marketing* 36(5/6): 642–666.

McPherson, J. Miller and Thomas Rotolo. 1996. "Testing a Dynamic Model of Social Composition: Diversity and Change in Voluntary Groups." *American Sociological Review* 61(2): 179–202.

McPherson, J. Miller, Lynn Smith-Lovin, and James M. Cook. 2001. "Birds of a Feather: Homophily in Social Networks." *Annual Review of Sociology* 27: 415–444.

Mearsheimer, John J. 1994–95. "The False Promise of International Institutions." *International Security* 19(3): 5–49.

Médecins sans Frontières. 2005. *My Sweet La Mancha*. Paris: Médecins sans Frontières.

Meier, Benjamin Mason. 2010. "The World Health Organization, the Evolution of Human Rights, and the Failure to Achieve Health for All." In *Global Health and Human Rights: Legal and Philosophical Perspectives*, ed. John Harrington and Maria Stuttaford, New York: Routledge.

Meron, Theodor. 2000. "The Humanization of Humanitarian Law." *American Journal of International Law* 94(2): 239–278.

———. 2005. "Revival of Customary Humanitarian Law." *American Journal of International Law* 99(4): 817–834.

Mertus, Julie A. 2008. *Bait and Switch*. London: Routledge.

Meyer, John W., and Brian Rowan. 1977. "Institutionalized Organizations: Formal Structure as Myth and Ceremony." *American Journal of Sociology* 83(2): 340–363.

Milner, Helen V. 1998. "Globalizing Human Rights: The Work of Transnational Human Rights NGOs in the 1990s." *International Organization* 52(4): 759–786.

Mintzberg, Henry. 1981. "Organizational Design: Fashion or Fit?" *Harvard Business Review* 59(1): 103–116.

Mintzberg, Henry and Frances Westley. 2000. "Sustaining the Institutional Environment." *Organization Studies* 21(1): 71–94.

Moore, Patrick Albert. 2010. *Confessions of a Greenpeace Dropout: The Making of a Sensible Environmentalist*. Vancouver: Beatty Street Publishing, Inc.

Moravcsik, Andrew. 1997. "Taking Preferences Seriously: A Liberal Theory of International Politics." *International Organization* 51(4): 513–553.

———. 1999. "A New Statecraft? Supranational Entrepreneurs and International Cooperation." *International Organization* 53(2): 267–306.

Morgan, Gareth. 2006. *Images of Organization*. Beverly Hills, CA: Sage Publications, Inc.

Morgenthau, Hans. 1948. *Politics Among Nations: The Struggle for Power and Peace*. New York: Alfred A. Knopf.

Morsink, Johannes. 2002. *The Universal Declaration of Human Rights: Origins, Drafting, and Intent*. Toronto: Scholarly Book Services, Inc.

Moyn, Samuel. *The Last Utopia: Human Rights in History*. Cambridge, MA: Belknap Press.

Murdie, Amanda, David R. Davis, and David Brewington. 2009. "The Ties that Bind: A Network Analysis of Human Rights INGOs." Paper presented at International Studies Association annual meeting.

Mutua, Makau. 2001. "Savages, Victims, and Saviors: The Metaphor of Human Rights." *Harvard International Law Journal* 42: 201–246.

Nadelmann, Ethan A. 1990. "Global Prohibition Regimes: The Evolution of Norms in International Society." *International Organization* 44(04): 479–526.

Neier, Aryeh. 2005. *Taking Liberties: Four Decades in the Struggle for Rights*. New York: Public Affairs.

Nelson, Paul J., and Ellen Dorsey. 2003. "At the Nexus of Human Rights and Development: New Methods and Strategies of Global NGOs." *World Development* 31(12): 2013–2026.

——. 2007. "New Rights Advocacy in a Global Public Domain." *European Journal of International Relations* 13(2): 187–216.

——. 2008. *New Rights Advocacy: Changing Strategies of Development and Human Rights NGOs.* Washington, DC: Georgetown University Press.

Nelson, Thomas E., and Zoe M. Oxley. 1999. "Issue Framing Effects on Belief Importance and Opinion." *Journal of Politics* 61(4): 1040–1067.

Neumayer, Eric. 2005. "Do International Human Rights Treaties Improve Respect for Human Rights?" *Journal of Conflict Resolution* 49(6): 925–953.

Newman, M.E.J. 2002. "The Structure and Function of Networks." *Computer Physics Communications* 147: 40–45.

Newman, Mark. 2010. *Networks: An Introduction.* New York: Oxford University Press, USA.

Nonaka, Ikujiro. 1991. "The Knowledge-Creating Company." *Harvard Business Review* 69(6): 96–104.

Nonaka, Ikujiro, and Hirotaka Takeuchi. 1995. *The Knowledge-Creating Company: How Japanese Companies Create the Dynamics of Innovation.* New York: Oxford University Press.

Nonaka, Ikujiro, and Ryoko Toyama. 2007. "Why Do Firms Differ? The Theory of the Knowledge-Creating Firm." In *Knowledge Creation and Management,* ed. Kazuo Ichijo and Ikujiro Nonaka, New York: Oxford University Press, 13–31.

Nooruddin, Irfan. 2002. "Modeling Selection Bias in Studies of Sanctions Efficacy." *International Interactions: Empirical and Theoretical Research in International Relations* 28(1): 59.

Nooruddin, Irfan, and Sarah Wilson Sokhey. 2012. "Credible Certification of Child Labor Free Production." In *The Credibility of Transnational NGOs: When Virtue Is Not Enough,* ed. Peter Gourevitch, David A. Lake, and Janice Stein, Cambridge: Cambridge University Press.

Nossal, Kim Richard. 1989. "International Sanctions as International Punishment." *International Organization* 43(02): 301–322.

Nye, Joseph S., and Robert O. Keohane. 1971a. "Transnational Relations and World Politics: A Conclusion." *International Organization* 25(3): 721–748.

——. 1971b. "Transnational Relations and World Politics: An Introduction." *International Organization* 25(3): 329–349.

Oestreich, Joel E. 2007. *Power and Principle: Human Rights Programming in International Organizations.* Washington, DC: Georgetown University Press.

O'Dwyer, Diana. 2006. "First Landmines, Now Small Arms? The International Campaign to Ban Landmines as a Model for Small Arms Advocacy." *Irish Studies in International Affairs* 17: 77–97.

Osiatynski, Wiktor. 2009. *Human Rights and Their Limits.* 1st ed. New York: Cambridge University Press.

Pape, Robert A. 1997. "Why Economic Sanctions Do Not Work." *International Security* 22(2): 90–136.

Phelan, Kevin P. Q. 2008. "From Idea to Action: The Evolution of Médecins Sans Frontières." In *The New Humanitarians: Inspiration, Innovations, and Blueprints for Visionaries,* ed. Chris E. Stout, Westport, CT: Praeger, 1–29.

Pipes, Richard. 1991. *The Russian Revolution.* 1st ed. New York: Vintage.

Podolny, Joel M., and Karen L. Page. 1998. "Network Forms of Organization." *Annual Review of Sociology* 24: 57–76.

Poe, Steven C., Sabine C. Carey, and Tanya C. Vazquez. 2001. "How Are These Pictures Different? A Quantitative Comparison of the US State Department and Amnesty International Human Rights Reports, 1976–1995." *Human Rights Quarterly* 23(3): 650–677.

Poe, Steven C., and C. Neal Tate. 1994. "Repression of Human Rights to Personal Integrity in the 1980s: A Global Analysis." *American Political Science Review* 88(4): 853–872.

Polman, Linda. 2010. *The Crisis Caravan: What's Wrong with Humanitarian Aid?* New York: Metropolitan Books.

Popielarz, Pamela A., and J. Miller McPherson. 1995. "On the Edge or In Between: Niche Position, Niche Overlap, and the Duration of Voluntary Association Memberships." *American Journal of Sociology* 101(3): 698–720.

Powell, Walter W. 1990. "Neither Market nor Hierarchy: Network Forms of Organization." *Research in Organizational Behavior* 12: 295–336.

Powell, Walter W., and Paul J. DiMaggio. 1991. *The New Institutionalism in Organizational Analysis.* 1st ed. Chicago: University Of Chicago Press.

Powell, Walter W., Kenneth W. Koput, and Laurel Smith-Doerr. 1996. "Interorganizational Collaboration and the Locus of Innovation: Networks of Learning in Biotechnology." *Administrative Science Quarterly* 41(1): 116–145.

Powell, Walter W., Douglas R. White, Kenneth W. Koput, and Jason Owen-Smith. 2005. "Network Dynamics and Field Evolution: The Growth of Interorganizational Collaboration in the Life Sciences." *American Journal of Sociology* 110(4): 1132–1205.

Power, Jonathan. 1981. *Amnesty International: The Human Rights Story.* New York: Mcgraw-Hill.

———. 2002. *Like Water on Stone.* New ed. London: Penguin UK.

Price, Richard M. 1995. "A Genealogy of the Chemical Weapons Taboo." *International Organization* 49(1): 73–103.

———. 1998. "Reversing the Gun Sights: Transnational Civil Society Targets Land Mines." *International Organization* 52(3): 613–644.

Provan, Keith G. 1983. "The Federation as an Interorganizational Linkage Network." *Academy of Management Review* 8(1): 79–89.

Quirk, Joel. 2006. "The Anti-Slavery Project: Linking the Historical and Contemporary." *Human Rights Quarterly* 28(3): 565–598.

Rabben, Linda. 2002. *Fierce Legion of Friends: A History of Human Rights Campaigns and Campaigners.* Hyattsville, MD: Quixote Center.

Rand, Jude, and Gabrielle Watson. 2007. *Rights-based Approaches Learning Project.* Woburn, MA: Oxfam GB.

Raustiala, Kal. 1997. "States, NGOs, and International Environmental Institutions." *International Studies Quarterly* 41(4): 719–740.

Ray, Philip L. Jr, and J. Sherrod Taylor. 1977. "The Role of Nongovernmental Organizations in Implementing Human Rights in Latin America." *Georgia Journal of International and Comparative Law* 7: 477–506.

Reimann, Kim D. 2006. "A View From The Top: International Politics, Norms and the Worldwide Growth of NGOs." *International Studies Quarterly* 50(1): 45–68.

Rieff, David. 2003. *A Bed for the Night: Humanitarianism in Crisis.* Reprint. New York: Simon and Schuster.

Rieffer-Flanagan, Barbara A. 2009. "Is Neutral Humanitarianism Dead? Red Cross Neutrality: Walking the Tightrope of Neutral Humanitarianism." *Human Rights Quarterly* 31(4): 888–915.

Risse, Thomas. 2000a. "'Let's Argue!' Communicative Action in World Politics." *International Organization* 54(1): 1–39.

———. 2000b. "The Power of Norms versus the Norms of Power: Transnational Civil Society and Human Rights." In *The Third Force: The Rise of Transnational Civil Society,* ed. Ann Florini, Washington, DC: Carnegie Endowment for International Peace, 177–210.

Risse, Thomas, Stephen C. Ropp, and Kathryn Sikkink. 1999. *The Power of Human Rights: International Norms and Domestic Change.* New York: Cambridge University Press.

Risse-Kappen, Thomas. 1994. "Ideas Do Not Float Freely: Transnational Coalitions, Domestic Structures, and the End of the Cold War." *International Organization* 48(2): 185–214.

Rivkin, Jan W., and Nicolaj Siggelkow. 2003. "Balancing Search and Stability: Interdependencies among Elements Organizational Design." *Management Science* 49(3): 290–311.

Rodio, Emily B., and Hans Peter Schmitz. 2010. "Beyond Norms and Interests: Understanding the Evolution of Transnational Human Rights Activism." *International Journal of Human Rights* 14(3): 442–459.

Ron, James, Howard Ramos, and Kathleen Rodgers. 2005. "Transnational Information Politics: NGO Human Rights Reporting, 1986–2000." *International Studies Quarterly* 49(3): 557–588.

Ropp, Stephen C., and Kathryn Sikkink. 1999. "International Norms and Domestic Politics in Chile and Guatemala." In *The Power of Human Rights: International Norms and Domestic Change,* ed. Thomas Risse, Stephen C. Ropp, and Kathryn Sikkink, New York: Cambridge University Press, 172–204.

Roth, Kenneth. 1998. "New Minefields for NGOs: After the War on Landmines, These Organizations Started New Campaigns." *The Nation* 266(13): 22–24.

———. 2004. "Defending Economic, Social and Cultural Rights: Practical Issues Faced by an International Human Rights Organization." *Human Rights Quarterly* 26(1): 63–73.

Rothenberg, Laurence E. 2003. "International Law, U.S. Sovereignty, and the Death Penalty." *Georgetown Journal of International Law* 35: 547–596.

Rutherford, Kenneth R. 2000. "The Evolving Arms Control Agenda: Implications of the Role of NGOs in Banning Antipersonnel Landmines." *World Politics* 53(1): 74–114.

Salancik, Gerald R. 1995. "Review: WANTED: A Good Network Theory of Organization." *Administrative Science Quarterly* 40(2): 345–349.

Sano, Hans-Otto. 2000. "Development and Human Rights: The Necessary, but Partial Integration of Human Rights and Development." *Human Rights Quarterly* 22(3): 734–752.

Schabas, William A. 1993. The Abolition of the Death Penalty in International Law. Cambridge: Grotius.

——. 2004. "International Law and the Death Penalty: Reflecting or Promoting Change?" In *Capital Punishment: Strategies for Abolition,* Ed. Peter Hodgkinson and William A. Schabas, Cambridge: Cambridge University Press, p. 116–142.

Schattschneider, Elmer Eric. 1960. *The Semisovereign People.* New York: Holt, Rinehart and Winston.

Schelling, Thomas C. 2006. *Micromotives and Macrobehavior.* Revised ed. New York: W. W. Norton.

Schlesinger, Arthur. 1978. "Human Rights and the American Tradition." *Foreign Affairs* 57(3): 503–526.

Scott, John P. 2000. *Social Network Analysis: A Handbook.* 2nd ed. New York: Sage.

Scott, W. Richard. 1998. *Organizations: Rational, Natural, and Open Systems.* Upper Saddle River, NJ: Prentice Hall.

——. 2007. *Institutions and Organizations: Ideas and Interests.* 3rd ed. Thousand Oaks: Sage.

Sell, Susan K. 2001. "TRIPS and the Access to Medicines Campaign." *Wisconsin International Law Journal* 20(3): 481–522.

Sell, Susan K., and Aseem Prakash. 2004. "Using Ideas Strategically: The Contest between Business and NGO Networks in Intellectual Property Rights." *International Studies Quarterly* 48(1): 143–175.

Selznick, Philip. 1984. *Leadership in Administration: A Sociological Interpretation.* Reprint. Berkeley, CA: University of California Press.

——. 1996. "Institutionalism 'Old' and 'New.'" *Administrative Science Quarterly* 41(2): 270–277.

Sen, Amartya. 2000. *Development as Freedom.* Reprint. New York: Anchor.

Shaiko, Ronald G. 1993. "Greenpeace U.S.A.: Something Old, New, Borrowed." *Annals of the American Academy of Political and Social Science* 528: 88–100.

Shawki, Noha. 2011. "Organizational Structure and Strength and Transnational Campaign Outcomes: A Comparison of Two Transnational Advocacy Networks." *Global Networks* 11(1): 97–117.

Shelton, Dinah. 1991. "Human Rights, Environmental Rights, and the Right to Environment." *Stanford Journal of International Law* 28: 103–138.

Shestack, Jerome J. 1978. "Sisyphus Endures: The International Human Rights NGO." *New York Law School Law Review* 24: 89–123.

Short, Nicola. 1999. "The Role of NGOs in the Ottawa Process to Ban Landmines." *International Negotiation* 4(3): 483–502.

Short, Tom. 2004. "Knowledge Management in Action: Nine Lessons Learned." In *Knowledge Management Lessons Learned: What Works and What Doesn't,* ed. Michael E.D. Koenig and T. Kanti Srikantaiah, New Jersey: Information Today, 31–53.

Siggelkow, Nicolaj, and Jan W. Rivkin. 2005. "Speed and Search: Designing Organizations for Turbulence and Complexity." *Organization Science* 16(2): 101–122.

Sikkink, Kathryn. 1993. "Human Rights, Principled Issue-Networks, and Sovereignty in Latin America." *International Organization* 47(3): 411–441.

——. 2004. *Mixed Signals: U.S. Human Rights Policy and Latin America.* Century Foundation Books, Ithaca: Cornell University Press.

Siméant, Johanna. 2005. "What Is Going Global? The Internationalization of French NGOs 'Without Borders.'" *Review of International Political Economy* 12(5): 851–883.

Simmons, Beth A. 2009. *Mobilizing for Human Rights.* New York: Cambridge University Press.

Singh, Jitendra V., and Charles J. Lumsden. 1990. "Theory and Research in Organizational Ecology." *Annual Review of Sociology* 16: 161–195.

Sinno, Abdulkader H. 2008. *Organizations at War in Afghanistan and Beyond.* 2d ed. Ithaca: Cornell University Press.

Smith, Jackie, Ron Pagnucco, and Winnie Romeril. 1994. "Transnational Social Movement Organisations in the Global Political Arena." *Voluntas* 5(2): 121–154.

Smith, Jackie, Ron Pagnucco, and George A. Lopez. 1998. "Globalizing Human Rights: The Work of Transnational Human Rights NGOs in the 1990s." *Human Rights Quarterly* 20(2): 379–412.

Smith, Jackie and Dawn Wiest. 2005. "The Uneven Geography of Global Civil Society: National and Global Influences on Transnational Association." *Social Forces* 84(2): 621–652.

Snidal, Duncan. 1985. "The Limits of Hegemonic Stability Theory." *International Organization* 39(04): 579–614.

Snow, David A., E. Burke Rochford, Steven K. Worden, and Robert D. Benford. 1986. "Frame Alignment Processes, Micromobilization, and Movement Participation." *American Sociological Review* 51(4): 464–481.

Soussan, Judith. 2008. *MSF and Protection: Pending or Closed?* Paris: Médecins sans Frontières.

Spencer, Leslie. 1991. "The Not so Peaceful World of Greenpeace." *Forbes* 148(11): 174–180.

Spiro, Peter J. 2000. "The New Sovereigntists: American Exceptionalism and Its False Prophets." *Foreign Affairs* 79(6): 9–15.

Stoddard, Abby. 2003. *Humanitarian NGOs: Challenges and Trends.* London: Overseas Development Institute. HPG Report.

Stroup, Sarah. 2010. "Borders Among Activists." Middlebury College. Unpublished manuscript.

Sunstein, Cass. 1996. "Social Norms and Social Roles." *Columbia Law Review* 96(4): 903–968.

———. 2006. *The Second Bill of Rights: FDR's Unfinished Revolution—And Why We Need It More Than Ever.* New York: Basic Books.

Tallontire, Anne. 2000. "Partnerships in Fair Trade: Reflections from a Case Study of Cafédirect (Partenariats dans le cadre du commerce équitable: réflexions tirées d'une étude de cas de Cafédirect / Parceria no Comércio Justo: reflexões a partir de um estudo de caso da Cafédirect / Sociedades para un comercio justo: reflexiones del estudio de caso de Cafédirect)." *Development in Practice* 10(2): 166–177.

Tanguy, Joelle. 1999. "The Médecins sans Frontières Experience." In *A Framework for Survival: Health, Human Rights, and Humanitarian Assistance in Conflicts and Disasters,* ed. Kevin M. Cahill, New York: Routledge, 226–244.

Tarrow, Sidney. 1998. *Power in Movement: Social Movements and Contentious Politics.* 2d ed. New York: Cambridge University Press.

——. 2010. "Outsiders Inside and Insiders Outside: Linking Transnational and Domestic Public Action for Human Rights." *Human Rights Review* 11(2): 171–182.

Taylor, Frederick Winslow. 1911. *The Principles of Scientific Management.* New York: Harper.

Teegen, Hildy, Jonathan P. Doh, and Sushil Vachani. 2004. "The Importance of Nongovernmental Organizations (NGOs) in Global Governance and Value Creation: An International Business Research Agenda." *Journal of International Business Studies* 35(6): 463–483.

Temperley, Howard. 1972. *British Antislavery: 1833–1870.* London: Longman.

——. 1980. "Anti-Slavery as a Form of Cultural Imperialism." In *Anti-Slavery, Religion, and Reform,* ed. Christine Bolt and Seymour Drescher, Hamden, CT: Archon Books, 335–350.

Thakur, Ramesh. 1994. "Human Rights: Amnesty International and the United Nations." *Journal of Peace Research* 31(2): 143–160.

't Hoen, Ellen F.M. 2009. *The Global Politics of Pharmaceutical Monopoly Power.* Diemen, Netherlands: AMB.

Thompson, Andrew S. 2008. "Beyond Expression: Amnesty International's Decision to Oppose Capital Punishment, 1973." *Journal of Human Rights* 7(4): 327–340.

Thompson, Grahame F. 2003. *Between Hierarchies and Markets: The Logic and Limits of Network Forms of Organization.* New York: Oxford University Press.

Thompson, James. 2003. *Organizations in Action: Social Science Bases of Administrative Theory.* 1st ed. New Brunswick, NJ: Transaction.

Tilly, Charles, and Sidney Tarrow. 2007. *Contentious Politics.* Boulder, CO: Paradigm.

Tong, Jacqui. 2004. "Questionable Accountability: MSF and Sphere in 2003." *Disasters* 28(2): 176–189.

Tsebelis, George. 2002. *Veto Players: How Political Institutions Work.* Princeton, NJ: Princeton University Press.

Tushman, Michael L., William H. Newman, and Elaine Romanelli. 1986. "Convergence and Upheaval: Managing the Unsteady Pace of Organizational Evolution." *California Management Review* 29(1): 29–44.

Tushman, Micheal L., and Charles A. O'Reilly III. 1996. "Ambidextrous Organizations: Managing Evolutionary and Revolutionary Change." *California Management Review* 38(4): 8–30.

Ukah, Asonzeh. 2008. *A New Paradigm of Pentecostal Power: A Study of the Redeemed Christian Church of God in Nigeria.* Trenton, NJ: Africa World Press.

Uvin, Peter. 2004. *Human Rights and Development.* Bloomfield, CT: Kumarian Press.

Van Evera, Stephen. 1997. *Guide to Methods for Students of Political Science.* Ithaca: Cornell University Press.

Vertovec, Steven. 1999. "Conceiving and Researching Transnationalism." *Ethnic and Racial Studies* 22(2): 447–462.

Vreeland, James Raymond. 2008. "Political Institutions and Human Rights: Why Dictatorships Enter into the United Nations Convention Against Torture." *International Organization* 62(01): 65–101.

Waltz, Kenneth N. 1979. *Theory of International Politics.* New York: Longman Higher Education.

Waltz, Susan Eileen. 2001. "Universalizing Human Rights: The Role of Small States in the Construction of the Universal Declaration of Human Rights." *Human Rights Quarterly* 23(1): 44–72.

Wapner, Paul. 1995. "Politics beyond the State: Environmental Activism and World Civic Politics." *World Politics* 47(3): 311–340.

Wapner, Paul Kevin, and Lester Edwin J. Ruiz. 2000. *Principled World Politics: The Challenge of Normative International Relations.* Lanham, MD: Rowman and Littlefield.

Wareham, Mary. 2008. "Evidence-Based Advocacy: Civil Society Monitoring of the Mine Ban Treaty." In *Banning landmines: Disarmament, Citizen Diplomacy, and Human Security,* ed. Jody Williams, Stephen D. Goose, and Mary Wareham, Lanham, MD: Rowman and Littlefield, 49–67.

Wasserman, Stanley, and Katherine Faust. 1994. *Social Network Analysis: Methods and Applications.* 1st ed. New York: Cambridge University Press.

Watts, Duncan J. 2004. *Six Degrees: The Science of a Connected Age.* New York: W.W. Norton & Co.

Weber, Max. 1978. *Economy and Society: An Outline of Interpretive Sociology.* Berkeley: University of California Press.

Weinstein, Deena. 1989. "The Amnesty International Concert Tour: Transnationalism as Cultural Commodity." *Public Culture* 1(2): 60–65.

Weiss, Thomas G., David Cortright, George A. Lopez, and Larry Minear, eds. 1997. *Political Gain and Civilian Pain: Humanitarian Impacts of Economic Sanctions.* Lanham, MD: Rowman and Littlefield.

Welch, Claude E., ed. 2001. *NGOs and Human Rights: Promise and Performance.* Philadelphia: University of Pennsylvania Press.

———. 2008. "Defining Contemporary Forms of Slavery: Updating a Venerable NGO." Buffalo, NY: Buffalo Legal Studies Research Paper Series.

Wellman, Barry. 1983. "Network Analysis: Some Basic Principles." *Sociological Theory* 1: 155–200.

Wendt, Alexander E. 1987. "The Agent-Structure Problem in International Relations Theory." *International Organization* 41(3): 335–370.

———. 1992. "Anarchy Is What States Make of It: The Social Construction of Power Politics." *International Organization* 46(2): 391–425.

Werleigh, Claudette Antoine. 1995. "The Use of Sanctions in Haiti: Assessing the Economic Realities." In *Economic Sanctions: Panacea or Peacebuilding in a Post-Cold War World?* ed. David Cortright and George A. Lopez, Boulder, CO: Westview Press,161–172.

Wexler, Lesley. 2003. "International Deployment of Shame, Second-Best Responses, and Norm Entrepreneurship: The Campaign to Ban Landmines and the Landmine Ban Treaty." *Arizona Journal of International and Comparative Law* 20: 561–606.

Whelan, Daniel J., and Jack Donnelly. 2007. "The West, Economic and Social Rights, and the Global Human Rights Regime: Setting the Record Straight." *Human Rights Quarterly* 29(4): 908–949.

Wiener, Antje. 2009. "Enacting Meaning-in-Use: Qualitative Research on Norms and International Relations." *Review of International Studies* 35(1): 175–193.

Wiener, Antje, and Uwe Puetter. 2009. "Quality of Norms is What Actors Make of It Critical—Constructivist Research on Norms" *Journal of International Law and International Relations* 5: 1–16.

Willetts, Peter. 1996. "Consultative Status for NGOs at the United Nations." In *"The Conscience of the World": The Influence of Non-governmental Organisations in the UN System,* ed. Peter Willetts, ed. Peter Willetts. Washington, DC: Brookings Institution, 31–62.

Williams, Jody, and Stephen D. Goose. 1998. "The International Campaign to Ban Landmines." In *To Walk without Fear: The Global Movement to Ban Landmines,* ed. Maxwell A Cameron, Robert J. Lawson, and Brian W. Tomlin, Toronto: Oxford University Press, 20–47.

———. 2008. "Citizen Diplomacy and the Ottawa Process: A Lasting Model?" In *Banning landmines: Disarmament, Citizen Diplomacy, and Human Security,* ed. Jody Williams, Stephen D. Goose, and Mary Wareham, Lanham, MD: Rowman and Littlefield, 181–198.

Williamson, Oliver E. 1983. *Markets and Hierarchies? Analysis and Antitrust Implications.* Reprint. New York: Free Press.

Wilson, Richard A. 1997. "Human Rights, Culture and Context: An Introduction." In *Human Rights, Culture, and Context: Anthropological Perspectives,* ed. Richard A. Wilson, London: Pluto Press, 1–27.

Winston, Morton E. 2001. "Assessing the Effectiveness of International Human Rights NGOs: Amnesty International." In *NGOs and Human Rights: Promise and Performance,* ed. Claude E. Welch, Philadelphia: University of Pennsylvania Press, 25–54.

Wiseberg, Laurie S., and Harry M. Scoble. 1977. "The International League for Human Rights: The Strategy of a Human Rights NGO." *Georgia Journal of International and Comparative Law* 7: 289–313.

Wong, Wendy H. 2011. "Is Trafficking Slavery? Anti-Slavery International in the 21st Century." *Human Rights Review* 12(1): 315–328.

Wotipka, Christine Min, and Kiyoteru Tsutsui. 2008. "Global Human Rights and State Sovereignty: State Ratification of International Human Rights Treaties, 1965–2001." *Sociological Forum* 23(4): 724–754.

Yanacopulos, Helen. 2001. "The Dynamics of Governance: The Emergence of Development NGO Coalitions in World Politics." Ph.D. diss., Cambridge University, Cambridge UK.

Young, Dennis R. 1989. "Local Autonomy in a Franchise Age: Structural Change in National Voluntary Associations." *Nonprofit and Voluntary Sector Quarterly* 18(2): 101–117.

———. 1992. "Organising Principles for International Advocacy Associations." *Voluntas* 3(1): 1–28.

Zald, Mayer N., and Patricia Denton. 1963. "From Evangelism to General Service: The Transformation of the YMCA." *Administrative Science Quarterly* 8(2): 214–234.

Zimring, Franklin E. 2004. *The Contradictions of American Capital Punishment.* New York: Oxford University Press.

INDEX